GOOD WORKS, LOVE RULES

Facing Change, Resurrecting Community, Transforming Our Fractured World Together

Simona Perry

Luz y Sombra

Published in 2025 by Luz y Sombra.

ISBN 979-8-9924728-0-6 (Paperback)
ISBN 979-8-9924728-1-3 (Kindle)

Cover photography © CreativeNature_nl via Canva.com

Printed in the United States of America

Dedicated to the lives of Marvin, Joanna, Kathy, Mary, Terry, Ted, John, Rita, Aspen, and Don.

All persons who are concerned about social change understand very clearly that it is never enough merely to try to change the insides of people's hearts. This is important. It is crucial. It is necessitous. But it is not enough, because the thing that guarantees the sense of private and personal stability for the individual is a sense of being supported, sustained, maintained in community.

From Howard Thurman's April 16, 1961 sermon, "Community and the Self", delivered at Marsh Chapel, Boston University, Boston, MA. The Howard Thurman Digital Archive, https://thurman.pitts.emory.edu/items/show/1064.

CONTENTS

PREFACE

My mom was afraid of drowning. I forget the story of why exactly because like many aspects of my mom's young life the experiences she had were never fully revealed, but she and her family had experienced some traumatizing events around water and almost drowning and seeing others drown as a young girl that had made her petrified of getting her head wet. She loved the beach and would dip her toes in, but anything else and she thought she would be pulled under by some magnetic force. Even at a young age, I understood that it was not only water, there were other experiences she had faced – with horses, with hospitals, with giving birth, as just a few examples – that had left her fearful and that these were things I should also be wary of or avoid entirely. But, my dad, lover of water and eternal optimist, intervened on my behalf in at least one instance: her passing along to me her fear of drowning. He insisted, beyond resistance, that I learn to swim and not be frightened of the water or of drowning. As a young girl, I remember Dad's joy at the ocean and waves. Some of my earliest memories are of sitting in the sand at Tybee Island, watching the little fishes caught in the pools of water as the tide receded, chasing the tiny colorful clams burying themselves in sand with the in-out rhythm of the waves, riding on dad's back into the surf and holding onto his neck as he lowered his body as the next oncoming wave approached. I also remember the hotel pools, the city pool, and trusting my dad over my mom's protestations and fears to hold me up in the water as he swam. I loved those plastic arm floats that gave me the independence to paddle towards the deep end all on my own. To feel independence from my mom's fears and anxieties and to let the water support me. By the time I was six or seven, like my dad, the water had become my freedom, my escape, a source of joy. But I suppose the transference of fear from mom never quite left me.

I craved the joy and freedom I felt when I was in the water so much so that when I was about ten years old I asked dad if I could enroll in swim classes. I had decided I wanted to be an Olympic swimmer! I will never forget, as much as I've tried to forget, that hot muggy afternoon when I participated in some sort of swim assessment in Savannah's Daffin Park pool. It was a complete and total disaster. I was asthmatic and suffered from chronic bronchitis, and I just couldn't seem to get the right breathing rhythm on some of the strokes. I finished a full two laps behind the other kids, some of them much younger. I was humiliated, ashamed, and tearfully disappointed. The swim coach told my dad and mom that I was not a natural swimmer and would have to be put in a class with the younger kids to learn the basic skills of swimming. I remember feeling like a hot stake had been run through my heart. What I don't remember is if my parents made the decision for me to not take lessons, or if they let me make that decision for myself. Either way, I do remember quitting my swimming dreams right there and the feeling of loss and giving up on my hopes and dreams that lingered long after.

There are at least three important lessons I learned from all of this, that for anyone who will dare to listen are relevant to why I wrote this book. The first lesson is an awareness of the enormous power others can have in transferring or even perpetuating their own fears and traumas with and through us without our consent or knowledge, until those fears become our own. My mom did not succeed in transferring her fear of water and drowning because of my dad's interceding, but she certainly did instill in me a fear of horses, hospitals, and giving birth. And, in the end I can't help but think that her continuing fearful protestations around my swimming ambitions played some part in dissuading me from persisting in overcoming my limitations and acquiring the skills necessary to be the great swimmer I dreamed of being. At the very least, her fears and anxieties, even if I did not internalize them into my own fears, made it easier for me to give up and not pursue my dreams despite the loss and disappointment.

The second simple-sounding, but oh so difficult, lesson is that in order to achieve our hopes and dreams requires an awareness and consciousness to first recognize, then overcome our limitations and fears. The limitations we and others set for ourselves, as well as the fears we have acquired from others and through our own experiences, are the largest barriers to finding our true path and achieving freedom whether in a specific ambition or pursuit or in living a more full, abundant, and joyful life. We must first recognize and admit, and then somehow overcome limitations and fears in order to allow ourselves to learn and acquire the skills necessary, and to have the strength and self-determination to integrate that knowledge and skill into our daily lives. Sometimes these limitations and fears are rather obvious, but they can also be lurking in our subconscious or, as in the case of my swimming dreams, we can bury them under layers of shame, guilt, disappointment, and the sense of fear or doubt we get from others close to us or who are put in some position to judge us. Those fears, if unrecognized and unresolved, can then become nagging internal voices that tell us we're not good enough or that because we are not talented or naturally gifted with a skill that we cannot do this or that. Left unchecked, these fears lead to all forms of self-doubt, self-judging, and, in the extremes, to self-hatred that may lead to self-harm or hatred of others who appear to be better than us in some way, or who are deemed more talented or naturally gifted. Writing this over thirty-nine years after that fateful swim test in the Daffin Park pool I still struggle on a daily basis to remain aware of the fears and doubts that keep me from learning and practicing the skills necessary to lead a more full, abundant, and joyful life.

And, the third, and perhaps most universal lesson, is that we need others in our lives to guide us away from fear, at times dragging us kicking and screaming and at other times grateful for the support. We cannot overcome our fears and doubts alone. We human beings require each other. And, if those others who encourage us beyond our fears are full of love and joyful sharing and we can trust them, we just might feel safe enough to embrace what makes us afraid and allow ourselves freedom from that fear and the courage to acquire the knowledge and skills to live our fullest, most abundant, most joyful lives. Without my dad's insistence that I swim and not only be around or on, but in, water, I may have never known the sheer joy, rush, and fulfillment of diving into the deep end of a swimming pool, water skiing on Georgia's saltwater creeks, body surfing in the Pacific Ocean, sailing in Puget Sound, scuba diving in the Caribbean, or spending months at sea aboard marine research vessels. It turns out I did not need to be an Olympic swimmer to do all those things and achieve a joyful life; simply overcoming the fear of drowning was enough.

I wrote this book for anyone who is committed to listening, learning, organizing, imagining, and acting with and alongside others to overcome their fears, especially during the periods of rapid change brought about by the unrelenting and violent crush of our inherited and currently oppressive economic and political systems built upon the accumulation of wealth among the few and the desecration and elimination of the sacred. This audience includes public scholars, community-engaged researchers, advocates for community repair and transformative justice, and community residents faced with sudden and unexpected changes due to unsustainable economic developments. In writing this book, the gift I most hope to offer readers is a nutritious diet of story, theory, and practice that provides both the physical building blocks and the collective spiritual energy for committed individuals and communities to work together towards building resilience to face change head on and to transform the current oppressive and violent systems.

In the diagnosis of what is at the root of oppressive forces in the world today, throughout the book I call upon the metaphor of a devastating tsunami or a great flood to describe how the monetary and material greed that under-girds all forms of capital accumulation and acquisition impacts and changes all of us. This tsunami of capitalism and greed relentlessly flattens and wipes out the magnificent diversity and exquisite details from our ecological, cultural, social, and personal lives on a daily and sometimes hourly basis leaving our stripped and naked bodies exposed to political, religious, industrial, bureaucratic, linguistic, and psycho-cultural carrion eaters. As perverse and violent distortions of culture, society, and human history, these ravenous vultures rely on our devastated landscapes and bodies to keep themselves alive. So, what can we do about this? Fight? Pray? Listen to God? After all, in the Hebrew tradition, it was the intimate relationship Moses and the elders sought and maintained with Yahweh, the divine one, that led the Jewish people out of oppression.

And, this brings me back to my personal experience of overcoming the fear of drowning and those three lessons: become conscious and remain aware of the fear that keeps us from freedom, joy, and love; overcome fears and limiting beliefs set by ourselves or others by acquiring and practicing knowledge and skills that allow us to not simply conquer our fears but to achieve our dreams; and, it is only alongside others, whether family, community, or the divine, and not by ourselves, that we can overcome our fears and achieve those dreams.

INTRODUCTION

Looking out the upstairs window of the farmhouse as I lay in bed, snugged beneath the comforter, I could see the neon green buds just starting to fill the trees at the bottom of the hill across Rome Road. There was also still frost on the branches and trunks and hemlocks and grass. It was early summer in Bradford County, Pennsylvania, and it had been unseasonably chilly last night. It had also been an especially dry spring. Below the spring buds and frost on the grass, the earth was parched. Summer rains would be most welcome.

As I lay in bed slowly awaking, I heard the whirring and pumping sounds of the milk house's mechanical milkers. The milk house on a dairy farm is the place where all the precious raw milk flows into two steel bulk tanks to be pumped out into the milk truck later in the morning. On Claude and Carol's farm it is attached to the barn facing the house. As on the other small family dairy farms I had visited in the County over the past couple of years, the milk house is the hub of so much work: it contains not only the bulk tanks but also the pumps for the mechanical milking machines, sinks, the bottles and nipples for feeding the calves, and cleaning supplies for keeping the area sanitary for farm inspections by the government. It is the beating heart of the farm.

That whirring and pumping sound in the morning, better than any alarm clock on a dairy farm, meant it was sometime after 7 am. It had been a solid three hours since Claude and Carol had awoke, grabbed a quick coffee for him and tea for her, and headed to the barn to milk "the girls." This spring they had had 41 milking cows and 10 yearlings in the barn. Each of their cows had been born on their farm and had a name. In the late spring Carol had phoned me distraught when her cows started to develop strange sores on their shoulders that would not heal. Several of "the girls" still had ugly rashes and sores on their shoulders and hips now. It was still several weeks before nine of the calves would die. Veterinarians from Cornell University and Philadelphia had been by to assess the cows and take samples of the animals' skin and blood. Numerous interested academics, experts, and investigative journalists had been coming to their farm for months now with the promise to "get their story out" and help Claude and Carol as well as others in the area. However, they had yet to hear back about what any samples had revealed, and experts came and went – myself included.

Their cows started developing sores not long after one March morning when the tap water from their water well—the same water that filled the watering bowls in the barn, the tea kettle in the morning, and that washed away the barn grime after chores—had turned a milky white-grayish color with a strange sick-looking rainbow sheen on top and a peculiar sweet rotten smell of hydrocarbons mixed with sewage. If you left that whitish-gray liquid in a glass to sit for ten or more minutes it developed a jelly-like consistency on its surface. If you let it sit overnight, in the morning there was a layer of black specks at the bottom of the glass. When Carol had filled a glass of this water and let it sit on the counter to save to show to me when I visited, I could hardly believe my eyes.

Around the same time Carol and Claude's water had changed that spring, there were several new gas wells, within a one-mile radius from their farm, that had been drilled by a gas exploration company from Oklahoma. Since those spring months their water had looked and smelled normal for a while now. Perhaps, as some people from the industry and even from the State government had told Carol and her neighbors, it was just a temporary change. Disturbing and not right, but temporary. A necessary sacrifice for providing energy to the rest of the nation, they were told by the county's leaders and by some of their neighbors.

I wiped the sleep from my eyes, stretched, and headed to the bathroom for a shower before Claude and Carol returned from the barn. I couldn't sleep in any longer that day because I needed some time to write up field notes before I headed into town for meetings. I turned on the shower to hot, gave it a few minutes to warm up while I undressed, and then stepped in. Still groggy from staying up far too late talking with Carol, Claude, and their neighbor Greg in the garage, I reached for the shampoo and lathered up my hair. Then I squeezed out a bit of body wash, and as I rubbed it on my arms I noticed it did not create the typical bubbles and suds but instead kept its creamy consistency. As I was rinsing my hair, I began to notice how the shampoo was not sudsing up either, and in fact the lather felt slimy and sticky. Strange. I did my best to rinse it out. Then I smelled a sweet putrid smell, like a gas station next to a sewage plant, and my heart sunk. I looked in the bottom of the shower and through the thicker soap I noticed a grayish-white tint to the water. My skin began to feel tingly, and I could not get out of the shower fast enough. As I was toweling off I heard the screen door in the kitchen slam.

"Simona!" Carol yelled from the bottom of the stairs, "Hurry and come down. The cows started spitting and snorting when they were drinking. The water. It's come out bad again. I saw it happen."

I quickly dressed and ran down the stairs. When Carol saw my wet hair she paused with a strange look on her face, "You were in the shower?"

"Yep." I said with a lump in my throat. I now knew from experience what she had been telling me. I would never again be a passive researcher in this county, or in my life, ever again.

For two years I had been documenting changes that were happening to people's drinking water, as well as the illegal dumping of waste water, in Bradford County Pennsylvania. Between the years of 2009 and 2011, at least 1,686 *new* shale gas wells had been drilled in the County. During this time I had watched with a mix of fascination and horror when Sherry took a match and lit her kitchen faucet tapwater on fire, when black water spurted out of the kitchen faucet at Robin's house, and when strange orange liquids appeared overnight in a field and an adjacent ditch even though it had not rained in over two weeks. I had spent hours on the phone listening to farmers and landowners who had seen and felt their water go from pure, cool, groundwater that they had bathed their babies in, drank with their meals, washed their dishes with, and made available to their livestock and family pets, to rotten and stinky and all sorts of colors in one afternoon. Worse still, people, livestock, and pets whose water had changed in this way were developing sores and rashes on their bodies that would not heal. Some had experienced more severe medical issues - a burst spleen, nose bleeds that wouldn't stop, infections that couldn't be explained. One newborn whose mom drank the water while she was pregnant was born with a heart defect. In fact, when I had gotten to Claude and Carol's house earlier in the week, both had shown me the still red and inflamed sores that had erupted on their own skin in March and had not yet fully healed.

Bearing witness, though, is not quite the same as experiencing something for yourself. And, that summer morning in 2011 was the first time my own flesh had experienced the water quality changes that had coincided with the arrival of the shale gas drilling and fracking rigs. I felt shocked, violated, and fearful in the same way as when an elementary school classmate, for absolutely no reason, punched me in the stomach. Questions I had had over the past year listening to people's experiences about their water changing and working with Carol and her neighbors to do something to raise attention about it, now seemed laughably inadequate. As I looked at Carol's face, the fear I had felt for my own safety while in the shower turned into anger, and then urgency. My scientific rational mind told me not to jump to conclusions about what was causing people's groundwater to turn foul, but in the lived reality, it was abundantly clear. In heavily drilled and hydraulically fractured areas where shale gas companies were working, people's water was dangerous, even potentially deadly. And these changes to water had only started after the drilling and fracking began. This had to be fixed. People whose water was damaged needed clean drinking water to replace it. And, in farming communities they needed enough clean water to not just supply the household, but also their livestock. But who would fix this? Who would even demand it be fixed?

Before my fateful shower, I had spoken about, written about, and publicly testified about what I had witnessed and documented was happening to the people and places and water in Bradford County as it became one of the heaviest drilled and fracked places in Pennsylvania. But it turns out I had been unable to see into the very heart of what really mattered to local people affected by the shale gas developments in this rural place - the embodied reality of uncertainty, fear, helplessness, anger, change, and loss. I had not had skin –literal or figurative— in the game until that very moment. And, as I grabbed my camera from the living room to document photographs of their water that morning, it occurred to me that any images I took or words I would write or speak trying to describe what was happening to families and their water in the county would not ever be able to truly capture the emotional dimensions, physical pain and discomfort, and lives turned upside down by shale gas developments. And even if I could, what would be done?

Since September 2009 I had been listening to farmers and landowners in Bradford County as a researcher on a participatory and community-based study of the relationship between people and their environment. I had been documenting how changes brought about by the rapid development of shale gas was rapidly changing local lives and people's attachments to their land and water and one another. I had witnessed the changes to these attachments and loss of these attachments firsthand. That winter, after Carol had noticed that their water first changed in March 2011 and I had that fateful shower, I had sat with Carol at her computer to craft a letter to the Pennsylvania Department of Environmental Protection (DEP) to report the changes happening to her water and to request someone from the state come to collect water samples per state regulations.

But the DEP insisted that a representative from the Oklahoma gas company drilling for shale gas on neighboring farms be present in her home and on her land during the DEP testing. Claude and Carol refused to allow any person from a gas company on their farm. They told the DEP that the gas company had no right to be on their private property because Claude and Carol did not have any leases, easements, or other types of legal arrangements with a gas company at the time. In response to their refusal to allow the gas company to come on their property and be present during the water testing, DEP delayed and then outright refused to come test their water. For months, I had documented and seen evidence of gas company representatives and county and state elected officials from the governor to local county commissioners denying, dismissing, and outright lying about the potential environmental and health risks of shale gas drilling and fracking. But, the refusal of the State to test Carol and Claude's water appeared to be some sort of punishment for demanding that the law be followed and standing up for their rights in denying a private corporation access to their land and water.

It is no wonder then that, beyond the water and health concerns from the gas developments, Carol and other farmers felt a deep sense of distrust towards the gas companies who had been allowed to build industrial sites on protected land, fill in wetlands, build enormous containment ponds, spread chemicals on fields, and contaminate creeks and rivers through exceptions to state environmental laws that farmers would have been, and still were, being swiftly fined and criminalized for. This was not right and a double-standard, and the farmers felt a deep sense of injustice. To make it worse, as these companies got away with damaging the environment, they were also buying out local farms that had been in families for generations, purchasing large quantities of materials necessary for dairy farming (like sawdust and lime), building pipelines through family cemeteries, hiring away milk truck drivers and school bus drivers to haul water and waste, buying out local contractors who worked in local agricultural operations, and threatening rural livelihoods and the County's overall quality of life. Deception and hoarding were the gas companies' m.o.

Farmers blamed the state and federal governments for environmental destruction, double-standards, and injustice. Carol and others wondered why DEP insisted on working hand-in-hand with the gas companies to set up the process for reporting and testing household water problems when the gas companies themselves might be responsible for those problems in the first place? And, the federal government at the highest levels had turned a deaf ear to local complaints of water problems in rural areas, instead making claims that the national economic and energy benefits of shale gas developments far outweighed the risks posed to local and rural water and public health. Carol and farmers like her felt preyed upon, discarded and sacrificed by their local leaders, state leaders, and an entire nation.

In the space of several minutes – as my skin recoiled from the stinging water, the screen door slammed, and Carol's face reflected a deep concern for my own well-being –that curtain separating myself as "social scientist," "tree hugger," "outsider," and "city girl" from the farmers, hunters, and rural neighbors I had listened to and met with for the past two years was ripped away. The violence of this experience on that February morning was not immediately obvious to me, but according to Carol I immediately changed. It sowed doubts in my mind, body, and heart, about the work I had been doing for the past couple of years. I doubted the environmental, social, and economic consequences of shale gas developments and the answers I was finding to my research questions. After that morning I saw how fundamentally flawed and inconsequential some of those questions were. They did not get close to the root causes of what is systemic oppression, and certainly did not offer any tangible solutions to ending the violence against communities, between neighbors, and against Nature[1].

By asking the wrong questions I had failed so far to name or describe the precise and localized violence that was occurring, to identify the systems of oppression that allowed the violence to continue, to recognize my own role in the violence, and, most importantly, to take meaningful actions to undo those systems and mindsets that create the perfect environment for such violence to flourish. And to this day, over the months and years since that February morning, my heart has broken over and over as I have listened to and watched Bradford County's people and places, alongside other local communities and places – some of which are even more precious to me, like my hometown of Savannah, Georgia – metaphorically and physically crushed and flattened by the unrelenting pressures of private land grabs, corporate balance sheets and the calling-in of debts, local political corruption, the failure of democratic governance by and for the people, and the soul-death accompanying our alienation from one another and Nature.

As the U.S. government has granted corporations expanded control over Nature, land, and labor for both private profits and expanded political power, there has been less and less concern from government agencies about the dangers posed to human lives and community well-being as a result of all sorts of economic and industrial developments. Shale gas developments are just the latest iteration of what has become an unholy and toxic alliance between private corporations and governments and money and political power. But, in witnessing and experiencing this heartbreak first-hand I have also begun to realize that not only have I and other researchers been asking the wrong questions, we[2] have also been looking for answers and someone to blame in the wrong places. By placing singular blame and responsibility onto the actions and inactions of private corporations and governments and focusing on certain political party affiliations as one of the answers, we have distracted ourselves from our own everyday actions that are complicit in both the capture of our democracy by private corporations as well as the violence against local communities, ourselves, and all of life and Nature regardless of political party or ideology. We should be extremely wary of any such political, corporate, and government scapegoats and distractions because the sites of blame for how dangerous our lives have become may in fact be staring back at us in the mirror.

I'll never forget what one student in a class I taught

at Dickinson College said after meeting with Carol and other farmers and landowners in Bradford County, "I cannot turn on the lights or drive my car without thinking about them. These things I do everyday without thought, all I have taken for granted. We are all responsible for their contaminated water and bloody noses."

This student had become conscious of the role *each one of us plays* in this heartbreak and violence. Our resource consumption patterns, our willingness to go along with the private ownership, human domination, and destruction of land, water, air, and Nature, and our settling for low wages and non-existent social services only emboldens and reinforces private and public demands for resource control, profits, and concentration of political power. In one way or another, each one of us has a role and none of us is entirely blameless. Most of us today are participating in economic and socio-political systems that prioritize the accumulation of materials and services that demand exponential rates of extraction, production, and consumption that perpetuate violence against one another and Nature every single moment of each day. Depending on what you read or who you talk to you will hear these systems referred to with various words and phrases – Global Capitalism, the Industrial Growth Society, or Evil, among others. To de-mystify these systems, throughout this book I will simply use the word I have heard most often in listening to local communities who have been directly impacted by these systems: "Developments," and more explicitly, "Industrial and Economic Developments." But, whatever you want to call it, our continued complicity *in* these systems is *the* horror. Like the Dickinson College student, becoming conscious of my own patterns of consumption and complicity in violence against one another and Nature has not "fixed" the system, the horror, or Evil, but it has prompted me to make necessary changes in how I not only live my own life but in how I relate to others and Nature with more love and reciprocity. And, these personal changes are the necessary first steps to transforming our world together.

Yet, I have also realized something remarkable about being made aware, and then acting in honest and humble ways, about this harsh reality of widespread complicity. First, of course, we must somehow be made aware and conscious of the magnitude of the violence. This can take years or it may never happen. But, once we are aware, if we can find the courage to be self-reflective and be open about our own complicity, we just might open ourselves up to a critical consciousness that exposes the root causes of violence experienced by those living in places where industrial and economic developments are taking place. *This is something each one of us also has the courage and the power to stop.* This consciousness helps us understand what it means to *be in* solidarity and not just *act in* solidarity with both victims and perpetrators, with the oppressed and with the oppressor. Restorative and transformative justice and intentional community-making lead the way.

* * *

This book seeks to provide strength and inspiration to find that courage, imagine, practice, and act together in solidarity to build systems, organizations, and a society that honors local people and Nature as interconnected first, that recognizes the holy whole-ness of our communities, and acts out of a radical embrace of transformative liberation for all. This work of building a world that is good and free **for all** requires what James Baldwin calls in his 1963 book *The Fire Next Time*, a love that is "not in the infantile American sense of being made happy but in the tough and universal sense of quest and daring and growth."

This is a fight for our collective lives and our common home and we are going to need all of the quest, daring, and growth we can muster.

So, let's begin, together.

PART ONE

1. A LITTLE THEORY & A CALL TO ACTION

Only months after experiencing the horror and fear of September 11, 2001 while working as a government biologist in Washington, DC, I came across a book entitled Pedagogy of the Oppressed by Brazilian educator Paulo Freire. His concepts of "cultural synthesis" and "conscientization" made an enormous impression on me as I searched for answers to the motivations behind the personal and collective hatred towards the United States of America that led to all the destruction and death on that September morning. Freire's words provided a counterpoint to the mounting drumbeats of revenge, talk of a war between good and evil, and the labeling of everyone and everything as an enemy that was not 100 percent supportive of the United States' policies against "global terrorism."

What was most deeply disturbing to me immediately after that day were the xenophobic fears and physical violence that began to take place against United States citizens and residents of Middle Eastern descent or anyone who even physically "looked like" they might be from a Middle Eastern country. And, in Freire's words and concepts, I found an intellectual hope, but even more than that I was introduced to a radically different path for grappling with our Nation's past and working together for our individual and common futures. In this new future, a process of truth and reconciliation or restorative justice, in which "confronting and reckoning with the past is necessary for successful transitions from conflict, resentment and tension to peace and connectedness,"[3] replaces the destruction and death that occurred on and which has followed September 11, 2001, or 9/11. In this imagined future where fear and xenophobia no longer work as nationalistic tools of propaganda to both divide and unite people against some external threat, it is because understanding better our internal threats and sharing our very differences is where our greatest strength lies. As the motto of the South African Truth and Reconciliation Commission says, "Without Truth, no Healing; without Forgiveness, no Future."

What I have come to understand since discovering Freire, though, is that this path is paved with the Herculean, and at times Sisyphean, work of critical analysis, dialogue, reconciliation, and love in action. It also requires a greater emotional vulnerability and humility than I, daughter both of privilege and of those willing to sacrifice their own lives to maintain total control over others, had ever been taught to bear. But, those realizations came later. As I read Freire's descriptions in 2001 of how the acts of listening, understanding, and participating in the lives of others who are voiceless, or have been somehow discarded, could be a path towards allowing the voiceless to find their voices, better understand and articulate their experiences, and participate fully in their own lives, I began to imagine a way out of all the despair, confusion, anxiety, fear, and hatred.

Freire's ground-breaking participatory methods of engagement in educational settings are authentic practices for teaching and learning, developed in Brazil decades ago as he taught and worked alongside those who were the poorest and most forgotten in Brazilian society. In my search of new ways of understanding the post-9/11 world these practices seemed to serve as a guidebook towards true liberation for both those left voiceless and those who silenced or tried to control those voices; the oppressed and the oppressor. What if Freire's engagement methods were used not just in education settings but in a much broader sense? As a practical path away from what seemed to be the relentless march towards a never-ending "war on terror" and "fear of other" that inevitably leads to even greater oppression, more violence, and death.

Cultural Synthesis & Critical Consciousness

Freire's approach centers around two core concepts, cultural synthesis and conscientization. The first concept, cultural synthesis is a theory of action that describes the true liberation of all people, both oppressed and oppressor. While the second concept, conscientization, more commonly referred to, and what I will refer to throughout this book, as critical consciousness, is the psychological and social process that leads someone to become conscious of their own complicity in laying blame, patterns and choices of consumption, and how this feeds into upholding systems of oppression. In becoming conscious of these systems of oppression and our complicity in them, one also becomes aware of a contradictory, what may seem counter-intuitive idea at the heart of all oppressive systems: they are always relational and interdependent. Meaning that oppressive systems rely on the continuation and maintenance of an oppressor image and an oppressed image that are in continual struggle over their separateness and lead to increasing individual and inter-group identities (what some call "tribalism") that makes it far easier to dehumanize and demonize the "other."

This idea of oppressor-oppressed enmeshment is difficult for many in the United States, and other relatively wealthy and politically powerful countries, to accept. Especially in the United States, most of us have been taught to understand and see our nation and the entire world through a black and white, dualistic, paternalistic, and individualistic mindset. The history taught and read to this day in U.S. schools and universities about our nation's founding leaves out the collective nature of struggles for freedom and justice, and the voices and bodies of the continent's original inhabitants, victims of chattel slavery, and so many people and communities labeled as "other" who sought for their own liberation and freedom. What most people have been taught about the formation and maintenance of the United States of America leaves out the following: the bone, blood, and tears of Indigenous grandmothers, grandfathers, aunts, uncles, and children murdered in their sleep or forced from their ancestral lands and sacred places; the hands, heads, and hearts of enslaved Africans who built roads, canals, railroads, agriculture, nursed their owners' crying babies, fed their owners' families, and prompted the formation of predatory banking institutions and financial markets; and the souls and bodies of immigrants from around the world who fled war, famine, and religious persecution only to be turned away at the border, sent into war as cannon fodder, or into factories and fields with starvation wages.

Instead of silencing the "other" and focusing on duality, cultural synthesis and critical consciousness takes a more holistic view, or what theologians would call a non-dual view, of good and evil whereby an oppressor does not exist without an oppressed, and an oppressed does not exist without an oppressor. This means both oppressor and oppressed must consciously recognize and address the fact that both have a certain power (although many times politically or materially unequal) over the other—the oppressor in outward domination of the oppressed, and the oppressed in an inner and outer defiance and freedom-seeking, whether expressed or hidden, through escape and rebellion.

This latter description of what it means to be oppressed takes a kind of leap of faith that challenges our default black-white, winner-loser perspectives that have led us all too often into retribution and revenge-seeking behaviors. Instead, cultural synthesis assumes that every human being contains within them a spark of something more, a yearning for freedom, the spirit of liberation, and a belief that this spark, yearning, and spirit is always there in each one of us no matter how deeply suppressed or unconscious. And, most importantly, cultural synthesis honors and values that spark as worthy of life. Cultural synthesis also assumes that those oppressed always have agency and choice regardless of their physical or material circumstances, but that their agency and choice can be suppressed and especially withered when oppression is felt internally, eating one from within, and thus creating a psychology of low self-esteem, lack of self-worth, blind obedience to authority, and a self-identification as a victim or martyr.

It is essential to pause here and clarify that this internalized oppression *does not* mean that the oppressed person is guilty of their own oppression. Such perversion of internalized oppression as blame and victim-shaming is a dangerous trope that has and is used by settler-colonials, slavers, white supremacists, misogynists, and others throughout the world, to justify their own oppressive and violent behaviors. In United States' history, such behaviors were encouraged by Southern white leaders in the post-Reconstruction South when they called for Redemption. This Redemption then merged into the narrative for the "lost cause" of an economic system and way of life dependent on the enslavement and continued oppression of millions of kidnapped people from the African continent that was further encouraged and enhanced by the moral authority of white preachers and priests in the South after the Civil War. In the United States this is the most stark illustration of how distortions in internalized oppression can lead to the very behaviors that reinforce, maintain, and even create new and horrific forms of systemic oppression[4].

Cultural synthesis confirms that the self-expression of an oppressed person's agency and choice in the world is entirely constrained by the oppressor's embrace and maintenance of systems of oppression of all types, all the – isms, biases, and phobias that our species has dreamed up across the generations over thousands of years. The ability of oppressed peoples to assert their agency and autonomy in the world is further denied by all the structures and rules of access to law and order and bureaucracy designed to keep those systems in place. Cultural synthesis in action means no less than full emancipation or liberation of body, mind, and spirit of both oppressed peoples and their oppressors by them working together to interrogate and dismantle those systems.

The important leap that the act of cultural synthesis asks us to take is to realize that the "other," whether oppressed or oppressor, is in fact "you" and to embrace that fact with our whole selves and communities. It also demands that we recognize that "to help" many times operates from an individualistic, paternal, and external mode of control and power over, and can actually operate to deny full self-determination and sovereignty of others and ourselves. There is no "other" when we talk of cultural synthesis or freedom and emancipation in an entire society. We are all part of a whole system of inter-relatedness, a whole community. The whole system and whole community is within each of us. For all of us, whether we identify as oppressor or oppressed, this comes from the recognition and realization that each one of us has, in some way, internalized the same oppressive systems and structures that we have been born into and have been taught to maintain, not question, and fall in line with. This internalized oppression leads to all kinds of brutal ways of acting out these inner forms of oppression on our selves, one another, and even on our natural world, Nature. This pattern of internalized oppression is seen most obviously at the interpersonal level in abusive relationships between domestic partners or adults and children or humans and animals, and it is seen at the community and national level in the form of racial segregation and discrimination, gender and sex discrimination, current immigration policies and practices in the United States, destruction of ecosystems and pollution, and predatory financial and legal practices, just to name a few.

If we listen to social and eco-psychologists, they have been telling us for years that happiness is in fact not about power over others or Nature, but it is about connectivity and relationality, or reciprocity. Psychological studies have shown that it is also not about material goods or accumulation of wealth; and that, in fact, such accumulation has been shown to be a key indicator of unhappiness, depression, and anxiety. These findings may come as a surprise to us today, when many of us tether our happiness and quality of life to the type of car we drive, how big our bank account is, how many social media followers we have, what neighborhood we live in, or even how successful we are in our career, especially when we compare all of this stuff to our neighbors' stuff. But true emotional happiness is more about loving, supporting, and on-going relationships than about any of these material things. The truth is that these relatively recent studies are only a rehashing of ancient teachings that have been part of the basic operating instructions of indigenous and spiritual belief systems or cosmologies for many millennia[5].

So, then, the question for those of us looking to break out of these habitual and socially ingrained patterns of internalized oppression is, what exactly do we think happiness means? How do we identify and take concrete actions to reclaim our own agency and ability to choose our own course of action and behavior based on true freedom for all and not some unconscious or conscious power over "other" or internalized sense of powerlessness? What exactly does Freire mean when he teaches about a conscientization process and how exactly does it work to allow us to transform ourselves and resurrect our communities and maybe transform the world as well?

The Process of Critical Consciousness

This strange term conscientization, or conscientização in Friere's native Portuguese, was originally defined by Paulo Freire as a process of learning to perceive social, political, and economic contradictions, and to take action against the oppressive elements of reality[6]. Throughout these pages, I will use the phrase "critical consciousness" to refer to conscientization. But, it is still a bit of an abstract concept for most people, so it may help if I shared a personal experience with critical consciousness in my own life.

For me, the experience of critical consciousness not only began with 9/11 and my first reading of Freire, but also with an experience that made me realize for the first time how my self-satisfied identity as a marine mammal biologist and environmental policy analyst working for the federal government was deeply implicated in oppressive systems, structures, and paradigms. This all happened during my second year working as a scientist and regulator for NOAA Fisheries. It was at a meeting in Seattle, Washington between indigenous elders and leaders from the Arctic Circle, federal scientists and regulators, and consulting scientists for the oil and gas industry. The meeting was called a "technical transfer meeting." These "technical transfer meetings" were held each year to give scientists, regulators, and industry a chance to share the most recent scientific findings from government and industry scientists about the populations of marine mammals that the indigenous communities living in the Arctic rely on for survival through U.S. government-regulated subsistence hunting quotas. The meeting was also supposed to be an opportunity for Arctic indigenous elders to ask questions with regards to the "science" of marine mammal biology and to share their own experiences from the previous whale and seal hunting season. These Arctic communities, as they have for thousands of years, rely on all parts of the whale's and seal's they harvest for food and other products. Their very survival as a community and culture is interconnected with the abundance, health, and availability of their ocean relatives. As such, they have the right under the U.S. Marine Mammal Protection Act and Endangered Species Act to harvest for subsistence a certain number of otherwise federally protected species each year.

From the outset, these meetings were a lopsided arrangement of different sorts of knowledge, perceptions, and power. The government and industry scientists framed their questions and answers about marine mammals in terms of U.S. laws and implementing regulations, certain scientific assessment criteria for endangered and threatened species, and oil and gas exploration targets. The government and industry representatives had access to the funds to answer those questions. In contrast, in the same room sitting around the same table, were the indigenous participants who framed their questions and expected answers in terms of food on the table, health of their children and themselves, adequate clothing and shelter, cultural sovereignty and self-determination, access to hunting grounds, and the very survival of their families and communities. These indigenous participants had no independent financial resources to answer those questions, but rather relied on the government and industry to fund their search for answers and survival.

On the first day of the meeting, one of the indigenous bowhead whale hunters provided his first-hand observations of a unique whale behavior, and then asked for further scientific study and monitoring based on his observations. The industry scientists almost immediately dismissed his observations as anecdotal and not worthy of a scientific investigation or monitoring plan. I expected my more senior federal employees to take the side of the indigenous hunter and ask the industry scientists to find out more about his question. Instead, they concurred with the industry scientists that it was not a question that was worthy of study and even dismissed the hunter's observations as sounding more like some kind of mythology or superstition than a scientific question. Although I do not think they used those exact words, their intent to not just downplay but entirely disregard the indigenous knowledge and experience being shared by someone immersed daily in that world was abundantly clear to the indigenous elders at the table, and I watched their faces as the federal bureaucrats and industry consultants dismissed them. This troubled me deeply. I could hardly put words to it at the time while my body felt sick. I remember during one of the breaks searching out one of my trusted friends and teachers from the Seattle NOAA Fisheries office where the meeting was being hosted and attempting to put voice to these feelings. It was not right. The government and the industry should not have so much power over Arctic community lives. How could the person in the room most intimately familiar and knowledgeable about bowhead whale behavior, whose family and village would literally go hungry without that knowledge be told his observations were not important to understanding whale biology and behavior? This dismissal of indigenous knowledge and experience was, in my opinion, contrary to the purposes of the meeting. It dismissed indigenous ways of relating to and honoring the bowhead whale as part of local community, as reciprocal, as relational, and as interconnected with their daily and seasonal lives. If the government was not interested in understanding and supporting those relationships and lives, then what business did they have with all these laws, research projects, and monitoring plans? How was this benefiting the subsistence way of life of these communities, not to mention the whales? And, what I concluded then was that these complex inter-relations were so easily dismissed for two related, but separate reasons. First, the bowhead whale hunter's knowledge and experiences did not match how Western-educated scientists and bureaucrats in the meeting had been taught to perceive and analyze the natural world, namely through mechanistic and quantifiable models of wildlife populations and ecosystems. In these models from the late 1990's human threats, except as threat factors or rational decision-makers in financial markets, were for the most part not accounted for in the algorithms. And, the second reason, was that indigenous knowledge and understanding had nothing to do with answering the questions that the government bureaucrats and oil and gas companies thought were most important. These Western questions were of course tied to those mechanistic models, and thus asked about quantifiable and measurable factors that could be plugged into those population and ecosystem models. As a result, funding for research and monitoring went towards those questions and not the ones raised by lived Indigenous experience and knowledge.

This realization, especially of how rapidly Western science and analysis dismisses Nature as interconnected and relational, made me question my identity as a "scientist." And my questioning began with the very words I had learned to employ when describing my own and others scientific and environmental policy work. When phrases like "natural resources" are used, it implies to break up a living, breathing natural system into only "usable" parts or "resources" for human capital or consumption. This dismisses entire cultures and denies that every human being has a mutually interdependent relationship with Nature. Who was I to work for a government that built entire laws and value systems that laid claim to "management of natural resources" while dismissing and disrespecting thousands of years of indigenous knowledge about Nature and the parts that we cannot quantify or put on a graph? Who was I for justifying this "useability" or "value" in order that our bureaucratic and financial systems could put a monetary number on Nature in order to more efficiently manage, monitor, regulate, develop, extract, or conserve its representative parts and pieces but never consider the immeasurable value of the sacred whole? What underlying systems, structures, and paradigms were embedded in this Western lexicon and reasoning that formed the foundation of my professional identity? What type of harm and violence did phrases and words like "natural resources," "conservation," "management," and so many others cause? And, who were the victims of this Western disregard and failure to recognize the sacred wholeness of life on Earth? The answers to these questions inevitably led me to the conclusion that my professional identity and career choices were reinforcing systems of oppression that were causing harm and violence to local communities, individuals, Nature, as well as my own self. As I began to recognize how complicit I was in these systems, I also for the first time really saw how my career choices and Western-focused education in the natural sciences, the way I framed legitimate concerns about environmental destruction as a chance to "save" or "manage" the world, and my authoritative role as some kind of "expert" had caused harm and despair to both other human beings and to the Nature I was so passionate about "saving."

This one meeting, this one experience in Seattle, was the doorway that led me on this unending quest to work collaboratively with local people and communities in designing more meaningful ways to share local lived knowledge and experiences of Nature with scientists and policy makers. It also made me understand the critical need for natural and environmental scientists during such sharing to not only open their minds, but more importantly their hearts, by not just listening to document, but listening to understand and allowing themselves to be changed by, local people's lived knowledge and experiences of Nature. This meeting not only awoke my critical consciousness but it began a critical learning process that continues for me today; an endless journey of staying open to new revelations about how our Western self-satisfaction, our desires and lusts, for control (in whatever form that may take) and power over Nature and over others, is in fact the soil where the seeds of cultural and political oppression are planted. Over the past two decades I have come to understand that environmental management practices, and the ethics of natural resource conservation in the United States, have been dictated solely by Western European notions of human sovereignty over natural resources and the extractive use-values that can be bought and sold from those resources. There is little room for other values of a spiritual, emotional, interpersonal, embodied kind, that cannot be easily extracted or monetized. And, there is no room for recognition of the inherent reciprocity and interconnections within Nature and between Nature and human well-being. This has led me to see that the subjugation of Nature is the same as the subjugation of people. And, they are both the subjugation of life. There is no place for freedom, care, or love where Nature and life is oppressed. This is the soul-death of us all[7]. That meeting in the early 2000's was the first time I realized my complicity in this system of oppression; and once I saw it I could not un-see it. This experience was only the beginning of my critical consciousness process, a wake-up call, that did not end at the Seattle meeting, but began there and continues to this day.

In becoming more aware of the ways in which systems designed, constructed, and maintained to separate us from one another influences our world and our daily lives and our very survival, the process of critical consciousness has also offered me a bit of clarity on the enmeshment of oppressed and oppressor, and how both external and internalized oppression impacts my daily life and relationships. It has also kept my eyes wide open to see how the violence of our systems from within and without eats away at ourselves, at our communities, and at our interrelationships with Nature. This awareness, of what I would characterize as not just a material and psychological struggle, but very much a spiritual struggle, and the need to transform all of it is the torch that keeps my fire lit to commit to this transformation and to take action alongside others towards the goal of true liberation for all. This is how I am called to take action, and this book is an invitation for you to take your place alongside me and reclaim our lives.

2. FACING CHANGE: BRADFORD COUNTY, PENNSYLVANIA

We will begin by listening to and learning from community lives that have been violently disrupted by rapid changes as a result of industrial developments from shale gas energy in one rural place: Bradford County, Pennsylvania. These lived experiences and stories of change are presented here through description and analysis, but I have tried to avoid the voyeuristic gaze or any cultural fetishism in order to honor and respect the physical and emotional lives of individuals as integrally part of mutual and reciprocal relationships between humans and Nature that move between the past, present, and future. There is wide-eyed and critical analysis, but this is offered only if it makes sense to the lived experiences of a community undergoing rapid change. These stories of a place and people facing change will provide us with an embodied ethical and moral grounding and an emotional fulcrum from which we can together face change and build awareness of how oppressive systems and structures operate within and outside of ourselves, communities, and Nature.

I spent much of my time between 2009 and 2015 getting to know, listening to, learning alongside, and thinking about the local people who call Bradford County home today. I initially began visiting and living in this county of approximately 68,000 residents as a researcher looking at how rapid change brought about by new economic and industrial developments was impacting this rural place, Nature, and the people who lived and worked there[8]. But, as I looked harder and listened closer and developed relationships with local farmers, landowners, town residents, family dogs, the Susquehanna River, the creeks, the valleys, the mountains, and hills my identity as a professor, scientist, and researcher shifted into something else entirely and my relationship with this place changed. I fell madly in love with a place and its people. Today, Bradford County is rooted deep within my soul and is much more than just some "research site." It is a beguiling place for me, both enchanting and charming as well as deceptive and cruel. I have been profoundly changed by my relationships in the county and by the experiences I have witnessed and had for myself in this beautiful and fractured piece of Appalachia. These stories of change I share here are only snapshots and reflections of these relationships, experiences, and moments I have witnessed. There is much more to tell beyond these pages.

And, there is so much more to the beating heart of this place than its "isolation" or "insularity" or the rapid changes that have taken place as a result of the "shale gas boom" and the inevitable "bust." For the purposes of this book, understanding the historical and cultural context within which the shale gas developments are taking place is important because they serve to introduce concepts that will be central to how we critically understand the root causes of oppression and the impacts of rapid change in Chapter 3, as well as our journey towards critical consciousness and cultural synthesis that we will begin in Part II. In the words of James Baldwin in his 1966 essay, "Unnameable Objects, Unspeakable Crimes": "The great force of history comes from the fact that we carry it within us, are unconsciously controlled by it in many ways, and history is literally present in all that we do. It could scarcely be otherwise, since it is to history that we owe our frames of reference, our identities and our aspirations."

So, to prepare ourselves to listen with compassion and empathy to the urgent stories of change being experienced in this one community as a result of shale gas developments, it is important that those of us who are "outsiders" or "transplants" to Bradford County (or any other frontline impacted communities) understand that such rapid and disruptive changes to community do not just begin when the gas rigs and drilling equipment roll in, nor do those changes end when they roll out.

Weaving the Past into the Present: A Brief Borderland History

Along the northern border of the Commonwealth of Pennsylvania and just south of the small New York State cities and towns of Chemung, Waverly, and Nichols sits Bradford County. While physically located in Pennsylvania, the rocks and waterways found here, as well as the genealogy and cultural traditions of the people that live in the county today have much more in common with Appalachia, Upstate New York, and New England than any of Pennsylvania's larger population centers or the southern Pennsylvania farming communities, that lie south of Interstate 80 or the Interstate 81 corridor. Bradford County is far removed from cities like Pittsburgh, Harrisburg (the State Capitol), Lancaster,

Philadelphia, Wilkes-Barre, and Scranton. This region of Pennsylvania where Bradford County sits is known as both the "Endless Mountains" and the "Northern Tier.". When I asked Bradford County landowners who were born in the county how they would describe the place, they used words like "insular," "isolated," and "deep-rooted." When I asked outsiders and transplants, those not born in the county, they used words like "backwards" and "uncultured" to describe both the place and its people. After years thinking about this place and its people, I am not at all satisfied that any of these words are appropriate.

While the county can feel and seem insular and isolated to human lives, it is in fact geologically and ecologically interconnected and integrated with the surrounding region and the entire North American continent in complex and very important ways. The Susquehanna River that flows through the entire eastern half of the county is the central artery that interconnects and integrates land and water, both underground and above ground, from upstate New York to Baltimore as it floods and drains mountains, ridges, farms, forests, valleys, towns, and cities. As it twists and turns 444-miles from Otsego Lake in Cooperstown, New York[9] south through Upstate New York and the entire middle of Pennsylvania to Havre de Grace, Maryland where it merges with the Chesapeake Bay, the Susquehanna flows as one of the oldest river systems in the world. As far back as the Paleozoic. for at least 300 million years, the Susquehanna flowed before the current continents had been shaped and before the Appalachian Mountains had yet risen.

When I first set eyes on the Susquehanna River and

its magnificence it tugged at me in a way that I had not felt since first stepping aboard an ocean research vessel in 1996. It dwarfed my sense of self and I felt the presence of something much greater and more powerful and timeless than my tiny human existence and short-term problems. Thomas Pownall in his 1754 travels through Pennsylvania looked upon the vast unbroken forests of the Susquehanna River valley and noted: "The Vales between the Ridges of these Mountains have all one and the same appearance, that of an Amphitheatre, enclosing as it were, an Ocean of Woods swelled and depressed with a waving Surface like that of the great Ocean itself."[10] While today that Ocean of Woods in Bradford County has long been broken by timber clear-cuts, coal and hard rock mines, farms, residential neighborhoods, towns, utility and pipelines, windmills, and gas well pads, the Susquehanna River flowing east and south through the Endless Mountain forest lands continues to arouse a sense of human smallness and connection to some greater and infinite power.

In 2013 I was honored to spend a couple of afternoons with Ted Keir, the beloved patriarch of local archaeology and rock hunting, at his Susquehanna River Archaeological Center Museum in downtown Waverly, New York, just over the border from Bradford County. Ted spent his entire life exploring the Susquehanna River floodplain for treasures of natural and human history, and passionately educating others about his findings and sharing what he had learned. He told me as we walked through the cramped museum full of glass cases with everything from fossils to ancient pottery shards to Revolutionary and Civil War buttons, that he thought that some of the more ancient artifacts in his incredible museum were certainly washed down from farther north on flood waters. Ted explained to me that the critical juncture of the Chemung and Susquehanna Rivers, a place named Tioga Point, and the fertile valleys this confluence created, meant that much of what had been found as fossils and human artifacts like flint points, pottery, small carved rocks, and even parts of human skeletons, may not in fact have originated from Bradford County's Susquehanna Valley at all, but been washed down from floods in New York and deposited there. Today, Bradford County's people and their histories are complicated by these convergences and residues of deposition.

In terms of where the natural and human history of the county converge there are significant overland transportation and cultural exchange routes within the county that were laid out along geologic features, major rivers, and forests of the region centuries, if not millenia, ago. The Sheshequin Path, between the Western and Northern Branches of the Susquehanna River, used by the indigenous tribes of the area prior to and during European occupation also played a critical role in the European's colonization of this valley during the Seven Years' War and the American Revolution. And, during the late-18th until the mid-19th centuries, there is evidence that portions of the Sheshequin Path served as an important route used by Africans escaping slavery and walking to their freedom in northern states. This is just one path adjacent to and along the Susquehanna and its tributaries with so many stories connected to so many other places. More recently, rail-lines, canals, dirt and gravel roads, and paved roads and highways follow the Sheshequin Path as well as other ancient routes of exchange and travel to connect the county to the region.

Contemplating this interconnectivity between ancient geology, natural beauty and awe, physical landscape, and human history, Bradford County appears as a densely packed web of life and history spanning space and time. It is much less insular and isolated than it appears to our human eyes. Yet, we cannot discount our eyes. For me, trying to describe Bradford County in a way that honors this interconnectedness, its unique, yet timeless, natural and human history, while at the same time not dismissing the isolation and insularity it conjures in us, leads me to describe the county as a "borderland."

Borderland as a descriptor of place was a concept I first learned about reading David Hackett Fischer's *Albion's Seed* in which he defines borderlands as places of the physical, conceptual, and imaginary in which people, and their culture, are both deeply rooted in local place and constantly moving between places outside, or transitory[11]. Unlike other types of places, it is borderlands, in their interconnected and integrated history and placement, that are uniquely situated to be shaped by and to potentially shape the power structures of the states, nations, or regions that they interact with. So, as a borderland, Bradford County is a place where the center of power and the peripheries of power are sometimes upside down, and where, if the timing is right, unexpected ideas and voices are more likely to emerge to both reinforce and challenge the existing structures of power and authority.

Bradford County described as a borderland also sheds a brighter light on how this complex, colonized, and geo-politicized edge between New York and Pennsylvania has nurtured so many voices that have played such a significant, and many times unrecognized, role in U.S. history. And, it could help explain the continued role local voices play in the current Marcellus shale gas developments as they help reshape and re-imagine Bradford County as both a deeply rooted as well as a highly transitory place[12].

Born and nurtured on the edge of something that is neither inside or outside, locals of the county tend to have a slightly different perspective on what power and authority means, and therefore social, economic, environmental, political, even spiritual changes shape their perspectives of the world in slightly different ways. So, perhaps, the many negative stereotypes applied by outsiders to locals in the county–

ambivalent, stubborn, backwards, and uncultured— arose because those outsiders can only see one path or one river or one people. Whereas, sitting on the edge, the convergent point between time and place, Bradford County's people, if they choose to look, have a very different view to share with us all about their complex past and our collective futures.

Sitting on the border and pacing along the edge, there is always tension and conflict. Before Europeans actively began colonizing the lands that became Bradford County there is some evidence that their insertion of their monetary and systems of trade into the fur and gun trade in the region may have influenced territorial disputes and invasions between the southern Susquehannock and the people who call themselves the Haudenosaunee, five well-organized indigenous tribes living to the north in the northern mountains and lakes of New York. Also known as the Iroquois Confederacy and later referred to as the Six Nations, there is some evidence that the Haudenosaunee would kidnap and adopt members of neighboring tribes living along the Upper Susquehanna Valley, and through those adoptions acquire claims to hunting lands farther south, thus slowly moving their entire tribal territories south. It is likely that part of the motivation behind the Haudenosaunee quest for new hunting land to the south was a response to competition for advantages in the fur and gun trade with both the French and English traders starting to move into North America[13]. This is significant to our borderland concept, because it means that prior to the more violent land takings and colonization by Europeans during the 1600's and into the late 1700's, indigenous people and their relationships with one another and the land had most likely already fallen under the influence of outside, global economic forces.

As far as more well-documented border conflicts during the active European settlement era, the Sullivan Expedition of 1779 stands out. At the end of the American Revolutionary War the United States military conducted a campaign led by General John Sullivan in order to violently rid the Upper Susquehanna Valley of British Rangers and Tories (settlers loyal to the British crown) and particularly to eliminate the British-allied Haudenosaunee peoples. The campaign destroyed all Haudenosaunee settlements and agricultural fields and orchards in what is today Bradford County. These fields and orchards were the lifeblood of the indigenous presence in the Susquehanna Valley and so this destruction forced them, and the British, back to the north and out of the Susquehanna Valley[14]. Today, roadside historical markers located throughout Bradford County, and paid for by the U.S.

Government, portray these acts of military violence, property destruction, stealing, and murder as heroic and patriotic acts.

However, to get a true sense of the complex border violence and literal edginess of the county we need to step a little farther back in time and away from roadside markers paid for by the U.S. Government to a period from the late 1600's to the dawning of the 1800's known as the Yankee-Pennamite Wars. This was not warfare between nations, it was warfare between English colonists. This lengthy, bitter, and often violent period saw many different disputes over colonial land claims across many generations. This episode in the history of Bradford County shoots a poison arrow through the unified one-people, one-nation under God mythology most of us raised in U.S. families or who attended U.S. schools have been so dutifully taught to repeat with our hand over our heart. It was all a terrible and bloody dispute between groups of British colonizers.

It began in the 1600's as a result of the very same tracts of land being "granted" by King Charles II to the at that time separate and independent English colonies of Connecticut and Pennsylvania. And, then the confusion over who owned these same tracts of land became even further aggravated in the 1750's and 1760's when duplicative land deeds were also signed between the Haudenosaune and the Connecticut colony's Susquehanna and Delaware Land Companies (1754) and between the Haudenosaune and Pennsylvania (1768). These disputed land tracts were all lands throughout the Upper Susquehanna Valley, including present-day Bradford, Sullivan, Susquehanna, and Wyoming Counties[15].

The "Yankees" were the descendants of Puritan New

Englanders and claimed the right to lands along the Susquehanna River under their Connecticut Charter of 1662 with King Charles II. But, these Yankee settlements also had their share of internal controversy, since Governor John Trumbull was in support of the "eastern radicals" establishment of a western territory, while the Deputy Governor and other "conservatives" argued for a more conservative interpretation of the Connecticut Charter and were concerned about the "eastern radicals" endangering the Charter. The "Pennamites." on the other hand, identified as those who claimed their title to land as residents of Penn's Woods (i.e., Pennsylvania). The result was that both Yankees and Pennamites saw themselves as the legitimate title holders to the very same tracts of land leading to armed militia skirmishes between Puritan "radical" individuals and families from Connecticut and those from the Quaker-dominated Pennsylvania. There were clashes between armed and unarmed individuals and groups, legal court interventions, threats of state insurrection, as well as murder and property destruction[16].

In 1784 the conflict took a bitter and even more violent turn when one hundred and fifty Yankee families living in the river valley just east of today's Bradford County, were forcibly marched with no food or provisions farther east towards the Delaware River by armed Pennsylvania Rangers. When news of this State-sanctioned inhumane removal of Yankees spread around the Quaker-dominated region, particularly south in Philadelphia, it appears to have turned public sentiment towards the Yankees and raised concerns about the heavy-handed tactics of the Pennsylvania government.

Perhaps as a result of this public backlash, Pennsylvania temporarily softened its approach towards the Yankees and attempts at a "compromise" were made in 1787 that granted Yankees the right to lands and all property in seventeen townships within the disputed area, and confirmed that Pennsylvania claimants to those lands would be granted unoccupied lands in other parts of the Commonwealth. Many of the original Yankee land concessions were within the current boundaries of Bradford County[17].

Despite these wider moves towards some kind of compromise, instances of violence against both outspoken "wild Yankees" and against Pennsylvania land surveyors continued within what are now the boundaries of Bradford County up until the first decade of 1800. There was no clear end to the conflict except that perhaps those who were beginning to raise families and conduct business on Bradford County land seemed to have grown weary of the violence and threats. On March 24, 1812, the Governor of Pennsylvania signed into law an Act declaring what was first Ontario County, and then named Bradford County, a separate judicial unit, making it officially a part of the Commonwealth of Pennsylvania[18].

Having gone on for almost a century, the Yankee-Pennamite Wars had become more than just identity politics between Yankees and Pennamites. It also became a dispute central to political boundary-making and power, and it shaped the meaning of land as well as an emerging nation. In later years, the dispute had become dominated by wealthy land speculators from both the Mid-Atlantic and New England with the only thing they all agreed on being the absolute removal of all indigenous land rights. And while there are no roadside historical markers, these land disputes and border conflicts are to this day recorded in land deeds and county records. And, there are still many local families who proudly claim their Yankee or Pennamite heritage[19]. Many of the individuals and families in Bradford County today are the descendants of those same Yankee Puritans, farmers, loggers, lawyers, preachers, and merchants who settled in Bradford County prior to and during this tumultuous period.

But these Connecticut Puritans were not the first Europeans to claim Bradford County and the Endless Mountains as their own. The very first European "pioneer" families arrived from the northern woodlands of Upstate New York to settle in the county were of German and Dutch descent[20]. They were shortly followed by Moravian missionaries from the Delaware River Valley who founded missions along the North Branch, or Upper, Susquehanna River, notably at Wyalusing and in current-day Ulster near Sheshequin, to preach the Bible and convert the indigenous peoples in the Valley[21]. Other early Europeans who came to claim land in the county were French Loyalists who had fled Revolutionary France to seek political asylum. They selected a tract of land on the flood plain of the Susquehanna River on which to construct a French villa for Marie Antoinette surrounded by an entire French village, with the plan that she would escape from France and live out the rest of her life there. The villa and remnants of the village, including an old persimmon tree, are all that is left today of French Azilum[22].

Then, throughout the late 1700's various Lutheran, Presbyterian, and Connecticut Yankee families continued to settle in the forests and fertile valleys where they cleared forests, built sawmills, and created devout Lutheran and Presbyterian communities of worship. Decorated veterans of the French and Indian Wars and Revolutionary War were granted the most fertile lands in the county where they built homes, married and had children, started large farms, operated saw-mills, founded towns and places of worship, and were buried.

Shortly after farms became established, sawmills started operating, and towns began to grow, laborers of mixed Dutch and indigenous ancestry from Upstate New York began to arrive in greater numbers. Joining them were Irish men and women who had just recently arrived from across the Atlantic Ocean. Workers began to find their way to Bradford County and found employment in clearing the forests, planting and harvesting crops, tending orchards, constructing towns, building canals and railroads, mining coal, felling timber, and processing wood products.

From around 1830 to about 1860 Pennsylvania farm historians recognize Bradford County as part of a diversified woodland, grassland, and livestock economy[23]. Old farm ledgers from the Coddington family's farm in Towanda span the early and mid-1800's, just after the family arrived in the 1790's bear witness to this diverse local agricultural economy[24]. They are full of details about the county's agricultural abundance— apples, cider, tobacco, butter, cheese, hemp, and other crops— as well as the manufacturing and mining of iron, coal, timber, and hard rock (particularly of the highly-prized bluestone) and the growth of private businesses, banks, and railroad in the county. These early agricultural and extractive businesses and the infrastructure to support them were the engines of capital that drove the county's economic and population growth[25]. Like Ruth, her daughter Margaret, and her grandson, who are descendants of the Coddington's, many individuals still living in the county have family histories about ancestors who started the farm they still live and work on today or who participated in building those capitalist engines and driving that growth.

I have had the privilege to read and digitize these old farm ledgers and listen for hours as local residents shared with me their family histories passed down to them from uncles, grandfathers, aunts, and grandmothers. Stories from life at the lumber camps like the one at LaQuin, about rafting lumber down the Susquehanna River to markets in Harrisburg and Baltimore, about constructing the North Branch Canal parallel to the Susquehanna River, about the life, hard labor, and death in the coal-mining town on Barclay Mountain, (now a ghost-town), and about building and maintaining the railroad tracks, rail cars, and engines for conveying of lumber, coal, and other products (as well as people) to points east, west, north, and south. While these stories may sometimes romanticize the past and exaggerate feats of heroism, they also reveal important facets of how people and families who came to the county from other places related and adapted to local Nature and how they also changed that Nature for their own purposes. These are narratives of colonization and change. The stories reveal how early colonizers exploited and used local Nature. But, they also reveal how they became dependent, and even interdependent, on relationships they developed with specific forests, mountains, waterways, soils, rocks, deer, bear, and Nature. At the same time, almost all of these relationships with Nature, whether exploitative or interdependent, were under the influence of some type of regional, national, and global market, development, or event.

To further describe how a borderland like Bradford County is both influenced by these outside forces, but also influenced by the physicality, both natural and human-built, of its local landscape Bradford County's 738,800 acres (1,154 square miles) can literally and figuratively be referred to as "a space on the side of the road"[26]; not a highway, thruway, or expressway but a "road." There were probably never any completely safe or easy places to find rest and comfort along the Sheshequin Path or the other indigenous foot paths that in the past connected people and places. Today there are only two main paved roads that run into and out of Bradford County.

One road is oriented north and south (Route 220), the other east and west (Route 6) and both roads cross near the Susquehanna River in Wysox and Towanda. These two main roads are just two lanes for much of the way through the county. Neither of them are part of the interstate highway system. And, if you are heading to a specific location in the hills and valleys of Bradford County, unlike Elmira, New York, or one of the other larger towns just over the border in New York, your GPS and smart phone will be of absolutely no use. And, if you happen to take a turn off of one of these two main roads when your GPS fails, you will more than likely find yourself traveling on some of the county's more than 1,302 linear miles of dirt and gravel roads[27].

Some road names, such as Spaulding Hill Road, are associated with the Yankee surname of the families who won their original land claims. Some are indigenous names, such as Sheshequin Road, which traces part of the ancient Sheshequin Path used by indigenous travelers and hunters. Other roads bear the names of the specific streams, townships, villages, or neighborhoods they run through or alongside, such as East Smithfield. Still others, like the stretch of winding road between Athens and Sheshequin have nicknames like "The Narrows," with a place to pull over and see the river called "Point O' Rocks." In some cases, treacherous and deadly stretches of road like "The Narrows" are also referred to as "Ghost Walks" for those who have lost their lives there. These roadway names, both formal and informal, are important to understanding the history of this place because the county's history and genealogy are literally etched onto the land, allowing locals, and initiated outsiders, to "read" and map their location without that useless GPS.

To someone who is a second, third, fourth, fifth, sixth, or seventh generation Bradford County farmer and landowner, family history and the history of family land is closely intertwined and vitally important. And, these family histories and kin relations with land, more than friendly or neighborly relations, are the hub of community and social life in the county. When I first started learning my way around the county, it took about a year of close listening and observing for me to just begin to read the land through the eyes of those who had lived their whole lives there, as had their parents, grandparents, great-grandparents, great-great grandparents, and on and on. I began to understand that what I saw as endless hills and valleys and the monotonous dirt roadways that I was constantly getting lost on, made up a patchwork of family memories and stories both past and present.

Once I began to learn more of the local family stories and recognize a hill as not just another hill, but a hill and field where a certain couple was married or a hill before the farm where their barn burnt down five years ago, I was not just traveling on another dirt road but a dirt road that had a particular personality and life and story to tell. I also noticed that in learning the landscape this way I was not getting lost quite as often. In other words, by learning people's stories that had lived in the county I began to get my bearings in this place and understand how and where family stories were inscribed on the landscape and how they in turn had shaped that land, giving me a way to literally read the land and orient myself on it. I felt and saw the presence of local community in the land.

As Kathy, a retired administrative assistant at a rural electric company, told me: "See I'm rooted to this farm. My grandparents and my parents and my sister we all are. Well actually my sister came back and is living on the old farm. But I got divorced and here I am in the tenant house. So we're rooted to this place." In other words, no matter what else happens in ones' life, this rootedness to family land persists. The land is also the compass of local lives and community, a sort of built-in GPS, that even when you are thousands of miles away still offers directions towards home.

And, much of this rootedness is passed down verbally through sharing stories and different forms of gossip and rumor. This verbal communication serves an important function in the daily community life of Bradford County's residents in not only remembering, retelling, or reimagining past events, but also assessing the current state of affairs and "sizing each other up" as trustworthy or honest. This sizing up was something I became very familiar with as I started asking people in the county questions about their land, families, and shale gas developments.

"Sizing each other up" takes place regularly when sitting at the kitchen table or in the neighbor's garage after a long day at chores, at a job, or in the fields and woods. You might not notice how it works if you're not paying attention, because it mainly involves swapping stories and trying to make sense of or understand the motivations of neighbors, outsiders, and the world outside of the county. This swapping of stories, gossip, and rumors are some of the primary currencies of community life in Bradford County, and are therefore used to describe, as well as shape, much of how local cultural, political, economic, and other information is judged, exchanged, and disseminated around the county. As I learned to find my way around the county's dirt roads from the clues left by the family stories I was listening to, it became clearer to me just how essential the very act of sharing and swapping story, gossip, and rumor is to maintaining community in the county. It allows a space and time for individuals to communicate who they are and what they believe and how they judge others, and it is essential for providing the glue that holds the community together and creates some sense of shared values among individuals and differences. This is especially important in times of change and uncertainty because it allows for an orientation or re-orientation towards the world and other communities that may be seen as different than or "other" than Bradford County

It was also increasingly evident as I was invited to

sit in on some of these story, gossip, and rumor swaps just how centrally tied all the stories are to family, land, and Nature. Economics, politics, and other general topics were only important if they somehow related back to family, land, or Nature. It depended on who was present, of course, but most shared stories or rumors revolve around the grand kids, weddings, funerals, untimely deaths, birthdays, the weather, building a new pond, planting times, veterinary visits, equipment failures or repairs, creek restoration, hunting tales, and other important aspects of everyday life and interactions in the county. This realization left me with a worrisome thought that only grew as the shale gas developments rapidly advanced. If the people in the county were to lose their relationships to family, land, and Nature they could lose their stories. And, if they lost their ability to share those stories, they could lose their sense of memory and rootedness to family, land, and Nature, and the relationships to one another and community. And, if their memories and that rootedness and those relationships were lost, what would be left?

The Global(ized) Countryside

Beginning in the early 1900's the local livelihoods, jobs, and locally-owned and operated timber, mining, and agricultural businesses, while still dominant, were starting to see some competition for labor and income from outsider-owned manufacturing and processing companies. Companies like Ingersoll-Rand, E.I. DuPont de Nemours and Company, Taylor Packing Company (later bought out by Cargill), GTE Sylvania (today Global Tungsten Powders or GTP), Paxar Corporation (later Avery Dennison), and Craftmaster (today

Jeld-Wen), Leprino Foods, and Procter & Gamble.

Some of these larger corporations, namely DuPont, GTP, and Procter & Gamble, were most likely drawn to place their manufacturing facilities in the region and county because of the Susquehanna River, which offers an abundant source of water for their manufacturing processes, as well as a convenient site to dump the toxic wastes their manufacturing processes produce[28]. Other corporations such as Craftmaster, Cargill, and Leprino were attracted by the area's local raw materials – trees and cows. These corporations, along with the Robert Packer and Guthrie Clinic Regional Hospital complex (with a history closely linked to the rail-yards of Sayre), had become the largest employers in the county by the 1980's.

With this 20th Century increase in external and international investments, global markets, and development pressures, Bradford County is best described today not just as a borderland of inside-outside connectedness and rootedness, but also as a global, and globalized, countryside; a rural community in the cross-hairs of globalization and global markets facing unprecedented changes to local ways of life, ways of being, and ways of relating with one another and Nature[29]. And, although our very brief foray into the history of the county in the 1700's and 1800's showed just how much global influence had always played a role in the county, the rapid amplification and exponential growth of these developments and global market pressures from the early 20th Century to the present is completely unprecedented in the history of this rural place.

As a global countryside, Bradford County has

experienced, and continues to experience, changes in how local agricultural producers are able to make a living. Some of these changes have had dire economic and quality of life consequences for local farmers and agricultural landowners. For example, some local dairy farmers now sell their cattle for slaughter and packaging to Cargill and their milk for processing into cheese to Leprino Foods, and large wood manufacturing facilities like Jen-Weld make it more difficult for small saw mills to compete with pricing or to find raw materials. Under the logic of global market capitalism these corporations mechanize labor processes and lower costs in order to maximize efficiencies and profits. They end up hiring less workers, paying less to the workers they do hire, and paying lower prices for local raw materials. This all leads to lower incomes for workers, farmers, and forest landowners. These declining local incomes coupled with increasing prices for fuel, hay, equipment, insurance and inspections, has left some family farmers and small forest landowners having a harder and harder time keeping food on the table or operating their family businesses without borrowing money, increasing their debt loads, or taking on additional off-farm employment.

And, for some farmers and their families seeking off-farm employment means getting a job at one of the very same corporate-operated factories and facilities that are buying local livestock, milk, and timber. These off-farm jobs allow families to feed themselves and keep up with the mounting bills and extra debt in order to keep their cows fed and the tractors running. In other words, in an effort to "just get by" and to keep their small family businesses going, county residents may work in the very factories or processing facilities responsible for bringing down the on-farm and timber incomes that had made it necessary to get an off-farm job in the first place. They may also decide that the family business is no longer worth it and become entirely reliant on outside income. This depressing cycle of dependency, declining incomes, debt, and loss of local family farms and forests is made even worse for local residents when we consider the increased hazards these factories and facilities place on both public health outcomes and Nature. Large scale manufacturing facilities catering to global, as opposed to local, markets are more likely to pollute and over-consume water, degrade air quality, and increase local demands on energy for both transportation and electricity generation[30].

On the consumption side, mega-retailers, such as Wal-Mart, opened in 1994 in the county and increased the availability, and the prices, of disposable goods from non-local and many times global locations. This is another reason why the county can best be described today as a global(ized) countryside; local consumers have become more and more dependent upon the global economy for their basic everyday needs as opposed to locally producing and exchanging goods. In many cases, county residents choose to purchase from Wal-Mart and other large retailers rather than direct from local producers because of economics. Lower prices on everyday products are, of course, required in the global countryside as local residents find their incomes declining and local alternatives to the market economy like barter and exchange are no longer available. Increasingly, any self-determination, autonomy, and choice that was present among small local producers and local consumers during previous times in the county, is manipulated, controlled, and destroyed by these globalizing market forces.

Now that we have a general understanding of some of the county's borderland history, the important ways that land and community are connected in this place, and the county's participation in the past and today in the global economy, we will be better equipped to put the current lived experiences and stories of rapid changes being brought about by shale gas developments into proper light. Such historical and cultural context gives us greater insight into local people's, and our own, "frames of reference, our identities, and our aspirations." These contexts also allow us to critically see and hear the deeper reasons, or root causes, behind how industrial and economic developments have so rapidly and dramatically impacted local individuals, communities, and Nature in the past and into the future. And, lastly, these frames of reference are necessary for us to locate and evaluate our own individual and community stories of change, and then act to protect, rebuild, and resurrect ourselves and communities in the face of them.

On the Water

My very first experience in Bradford County was in a canoe on the Chemung River on a bright blue sky and slightly hazy 4th of July day in 2009. My guide on that first canoe trip was Laura, a co-worker at *Truthout*, an online newspaper I was working at while I was finishing my doctorate at the

University of Massachusetts. The post-doctoral research and teaching position I had secured at Dickinson College, a small liberal arts college in south-central Pennsylvania, was to begin in the Fall and I had decided to focus my community-based and place-based social science research somewhere along the more rural stretches of the Susquehanna River.

When I mentioned my research interest to Laura during one of our work communications she immediately invited me to visit her. She also sent me photographs of her and others, including her children, families, and elders from the Haudenasaunee Nation, canoeing on the river. She told me about these "Sojourns" that they would take down the river and about the Promise Basket that they would carry on their journey. She explained that the Promise Basket held the promises that humans made to the Susquehanna and Mother Earth to respect and honor the water and the inter-connectedness of all life for our ancestors, life today, and for the next seven generations. This beautiful story of the Susquehanna Sojourn and the Promise Basket piqued my interest in what I might find delving deeper into people's connections with the river.

But first, Laura said, I had to get out on the water. So, we started planning a canoe trip on one of the main tributaries of the Susquehanna, the Chemung River, for as soon as the temperatures were warm enough. In July, with her friend Charlie and several other people from the New York towns of Waverly and Elmira just across the New York-Pennsylvania border, and my spouse Ernie we set off down the Chemung River.

I don't quite know how the conversation started, but I

think someone asked me what kind of work I was going to be doing at Dickinson College once we were on the water. I mentioned that I wasn't completely sure yet, but that I had heard about some type of oil or gas developments being done in the area and wanted to learn more.

"Well, I don't know much; heard rumors though," one of my fellow canoeists said.

"I know a guy who got a job up in Horseheads with one of the companies -- Fortune or Fortuna, I think it is."

Another canoeist, wearing a Waverly High School Wolverines t-shirt added, "Marcellus shale it's called. They say it's a new way of getting energy. Gas or oil I'm not sure. They can drill really deep and farther than ever."

"They use a new technique to crack the rock with water," a third said. "I heard the energy companies are offering farmers big bucks to let them drill on their land."

Prior to the canoe trip that summer I had come across an alarming news article from *Reuters* that told the story about Pat Farnelli's family getting sick after drinking the water from their private water well in a place not far from our canoe trip where these new drilling techniques were being used[31]. And, it wasn't just her family, three other families, the Carters, Mayes, and Switzers, had stopped using water from their wells because the water coming out of their taps had changed color and started to smell bad. Most dramatically, the news article noted, the well cap on Norma Fiorentino's water well had blown off after methane had built up in her private drinking water well. All of these events had happened in 2008 in one town, Dimock, Pennsylvania. Dimock was a small place, home to 1,383 people, in Susquehanna County just one county to the east of Bradford County. These families lived about an hour and a half drive from the town in New York where we had put in our canoes.

The *Reuters* news article went on to tell how the water coming out of these families taps was also making some of them sick and forcing them to buy bottled water. Only one of the families could afford to install a water filtration system. The families were concerned that there was a connection between the changes to their drinking water and the presence of high levels of methane gas and possibly other substances in their water wells. They were sure that the new drilling for natural gas near their homes begun three years earlier had something to do with the changes to their well water. They wanted answers, and more urgently, they just wanted their clean drinking water back.

The article then explained that the drilling for natural gas being done in Susquehanna County was different from any previous type of oil or gas drilling in the region. This gas drilling involved horizontally drilling through shale rock formations deep below the surface—up to one mile—setting off small explosions along the bore hole, and then injecting large volumes of chemicals, sand, and water into that hole to fracture the rock which then released the trapped methane. Several years after that article, this process became better known in the news media, among environmental activists, and the general public as "fracking."

But, in this news article it was made clear that both the gas industry and the state government had concluded that this new drilling and "fracking" had not caused the drinking water contamination happening in Dimock. An industry spokesperson in the article cited "meticulous safeguards" that they were required to follow to protect groundwater. The spokesperson also stated "that any chemicals used are heavily diluted and pose no health threat." The gas company spokesperson even went so far as to say it was "impossible" that drilling could contaminate the groundwater.

And, apparently, the state government also believed that the drilling and fracking the shale rock was safe and posed no threat to groundwater or people's drinking water. Ed Rendell, governor of Pennsylvania at the time, is quoted in the news article saying, "We are very scrupulous about whether it will have an effect on the groundwater." An official at the Pennsylvania Department of Environmental Protection is quoted saying that they tested the well water in Dimock houses recently and that they "have not seen anything that would be of concern."

The denial by the gas company that there was any possibility that the problems were from their drilling into the shale rock and fracking, backed up with what appeared to be the Pennsylvania government's not finding any linkages between drilling, fracking, groundwater, or water well contamination made this seem like an open and shut case. Anyone reading the article could be forgiven for wondering why these local families were so concerned about the gas developments. After all, the state government and the companies doing the drilling and fracking had said there was no health threat and no evidence of any effect on groundwater or people's drinking water.

In early 2009 when I started scoping out the possibility of conducting research in the area, the drinking water contamination in Dimock had not received much attention in the national news media, despite what appeared to be a tragic case of people getting sick from drinking their own water and a suspicion that some type of new natural gas energy developments might be causing it. It made me wonder: Was this a much larger problem with this type of new development? People's water wells making them sick and exploding seemed like it should have been a much bigger national news story than it was.

But, in the region where this tragedy took place it was rural, there was a low population, and people were relatively poor. Similarly, in southern and western states in rural, low population, poorer communities in Alabama, Colorado, Wyoming, New Mexico, and Utah families had been experiencing similar groundwater and water well problems in close proximity to these same type of drilling and fracking operations for at least the past ten years[32]. None of those local stories had found their way into the national or international news either. From what I had learned at my time as a senior editor at *Truthout*, stories from rural and poorer communities in the U.S. tended to get far less media attention than the urban poor or middle-income suburban communities.

What struck me most about the *Reuters* news article on Dimock was that it read more like a human interest story focused on rural poor families – some on government food stamps, the article made a point of saying – with quotes from an industry spokesperson, the governor of Pennsylvania, and state regulators offering assurances that of course none of this had anything to do with the new gas developments. But, in fact, this was a tragic story of environmental contamination and injustice.

From just reading this one article on the issue of shale gas developments in northern Pennsylvania, a more urban reader or even a rural reader from another place could come away with the impression that these Dimock families were discontent with the gas developments and their life circumstances and were maybe just lashing out at this new progress or jealous of other peoples' good fortune, or seeking some type of monetary compensation. And, it was not so much the facts of the news story that could leave readers with that impression. It was the way the article had been framed by the reporters and editors to portray rural poor people in the U.S. as powerless and under the benign protection of government as well as private industry, who were, without question of course, using the law and technology to ensure that people and groundwater were safe.

I came across that article about the water contamination in Dimock not long after I had read the French 2008 best-seller by Herve Kempf, *How the Rich are Destroying the Earth*. Since reading Kempf's book I had been thinking more explicitly about questions of poverty and economic disparities across the U.S. in the context of environmental harms and climate change. In my work at *Truthout* I had begun to notice so many news articles and popular media pieces that created idealized human interest stories out of environmental contamination and injustice tragedies by re-framing the events in terms of rich against poor or framing them within a solely class, wealth, or identity narrative rooted in the logic of global capitalism, exponential growth, private capital, and personal responsibility. Why is it that a nation like the U.S.

that boasts of being the "most advanced" and "democratic" in the world, does not address more comprehensively the everyday plight of the poor in public policies and funding, especially when it comes to allocation of basic environmental and infrastructure services like clean air, water, food, housing, and healthcare?

I arrived at a potential answer: maybe poverty is not a larger national policy issue in the U.S., especially in the context of the environment, because if it was it would require a total re-calibration of our national mythology around the American Dream and dismantling our illusions of exponential and individual economic and population growth. To really take a hard and critical look at poverty in the U.S. would mean realizing that we have all been gravely mistaken in thinking our individualism and well-being is connected only to monetary and financial accumulation. It would mean admitting that we have made a fatal error in denying or ignoring the inter-connections and non-monetary values of reciprocity, care, love, Nature, family, and community. I also found Kempf's book relevant to analyzing the unequal access to information and community participation in development projects along economic, racial, ethnic, and other identity lines I had begun to recognize while working at NOAA and that I had observed and written about during my research along the urban Neponset River and Estuary in Boston, Massachusetts for my doctoral thesis, *More than One River*[33].

Those years in Boston conducting interviews and cultural observations along the edges between lower wealth immigrant neighborhoods in Boston and some of its more wealthy suburbs helped me see how political and economic leaders actively deny and manipulate the day-to-day realities of poverty, and especially its relationship to race, ethnicity, and Nature, in one of the country's most affluent cities. Instead of asking residents living in neighborhoods of low wealth and with less access to information and other resources what they needed and how they related to Nature and community, and then recognizing and addressing their needs first, the city and state leaders at the time focused instead on re-development of blighted buildings, re-locating low wealth residents, cleaning up litter and trash, and allocating public and private money to crime watches, policing, and new economic development activities along rivers, bike paths, parks, and open spaces.

In my carefully documented observations in Boston, these development activities and the use of neighborhood crime watches and community policing, while sometimes motivated by lower-wealth residents to improve the quality of life in their own communities, were predominately being planned and implemented by wealthier residents living in adjacent neighborhoods or by philanthropic organizations who sought to promote "sustainable urban development" and other "green" or "socially-conscious" activities to "beautify" or "clean-up criminal elements." These economic differences in the part of Boston where the Neponset River lies also run along historic race and ethnic boundaries. Many of the neighborhoods along the Neponset River have a mix of black families and immigrant families from Africa, Central America, Caribbean Island nations, and Asia. I watched as re-development and new "sustainable" development projects along this urban river failed to meaningfully include these lower wealth, mixed neighborhoods, and so their needs and dreams were simply not considered in any of these projects.

Sustainable development projects like I saw being promoted along the Neponset River in Boston require considerable political buy-in, expert consultation, and financial resources from both government and private sources. Rarely, though, do these projects lead to investments to improve the quality of life or well-being of the current, long-term, or low wealth residents. Occasionally these developments include investments in a certain percentage of more "affordable" housing units or in moving local residents due to their inability to pay higher rents or taxes or their dissatisfaction with the projects aims and goals. In most cases these projects lead to urban gentrification, higher property taxes, and displacement of local residents[34].

It occurred to me that the underlying circumstances around gas developments that were happening in Dimock, Pennsylvania, were not that much different than how this process of urban gentrification operates to make room for sustainable development projects in the lower wealth, less clean, or racially and ethnically mixed parts of a city. In Dimock it was rural gentrification making room for energy developments. And, just as urban planners promoted "green" and "sustainable" developments, these new energy developments were being promoted as "clean" gas and a "bridge fuel" to renewable, non-fossil fuel energy sources that would make life better for anyone who could afford it.

With this comparison in mind, as I planned for my new rural work, my vision was to design a truly collaborative, participatory, and community-based project that would have both emancipatory and transformative potential for local communities when it came to development projects. I wanted to give local residents greater opportunity to share their needs, expectations, dreams, concerns, and visions about whatever developments might be going on now or planned in the future. My idealistic notion was to follow Freire's work and engage them in a process of critical consciousness and cultural synthesis and give them a way to share their rural lives with one another and decision makers, express their relationships with Nature and community, and openly discuss the new energy developments, water quality, and any other changes and developments that they saw occurring in the region. In the end, the goal was for local people to find their voices and play a major role in determining what developments would look like in their own community.

In the beginning, my questions would be as an outside researcher in rural Pennsylvania as I had little understanding of the local social, cultural, or environmental history. These early questions were focused on finding out if what I knew of the Dimock families' stories and their suspicions that their drinking water was impacted by the new energy developments resonated with other families in Bradford County. At the same time, I was listening for other relevant histories, stories, conflicts, and emerging questions from the community itself related to their relationships to their land, the river, their water, and one another.

Staying open to other questions and stories, and not just being fixated on the new energy developments, I learned about new water quality regulations that included mandating new agricultural best practices that were designed to protect the downstream waters of the Susquehanna River and the Chesapeake Bay. In talking to locals it turned out that these new agricultural best practices were leading to distrust and resentment among local dairy farmers and forest landowners towards the Bradford County Conservation District and the state environmental protection office, as well as environmental advocacy groups. The Conservation District told me this lack of trust came from farmers not understanding the new practices or science or from them not wanting to change and being stubborn. But, in probing a bit deeper with local landowners, I found that in fact the main points of distrust and resentment came from the disrespect local farmers felt they had been shown by the Conservation District and others who had not incorporated their local knowledge of the lands and waters they knew better than anyone else and had farmed on for generations into the best practices. This reminded me of the meeting I had attended in Seattle when I had watched industry scientists and federal regulators dismiss an indigenous hunter's knowledge and experience years ago. Once again, local peoples' knowledge and experience was being discarded and treated as irrelevant to scientists and government in the formulation of science and policy.

It also reminded me of one of the important lessons I had learned in Boston: to understand why environmental policies and regulations do not live up to expectations about protecting Nature and can lead to negative impacts for local communities you really need to understand how local conflicts and both animosity and support over those proposed or existing environmental policies and regulations came about in the first place. It is in the urgency and everyday quality of such local conflicts where the real stories about the human relationships with Nature and community change lie and where, I believe, both conflicts and relationships can be transformed. So, my plan was to involve local people in not just answering some broad outsider research questions about values, attitudes, and perceptions regarding energy developments, but to also involve local people in deciding and formulating important questions that they wanted to answer for themselves and for their own community. In other words, my goal with the work in Bradford County was to allow local people to share, in their own words, how they related to Nature and the stories of change most important to their own lives.

If my project could raise local peoples' critical consciousness about their relationship to themselves, their communities, and Nature, and introduce them to new information and create awareness about the developments that could impact their daily lives, whether it was fracking or new farm regulations, maybe it could also guide them through a process of finding their own voices to tell their own stories of wealth and abundance. But it was clear from the beginning of my time in Bradford County this would not be an easy thing to do. It turned out poverty and lack and unquestioning acceptance of government and industry authority was already a well-entrenched mind-set among many local landowners and farmers. And, new economic myths of farmers striking it rich from shale gas were only entrenching that further. Two of the other canoeists during my trip on the Chemung River warned me of this.

"It's pretty much a done deal. I think the local politicians see this new gas as a way to make some big money. Plus, there's so much poverty in places like Bradford, Susquehanna, and Sullivan and it could help farmers who have been struggling for so long now. Young people are leaving," one said

Another responded, "Yeah, this could mean jobs. Well, that's what the newspapers are saying."

Dangerous Myths

Outside of news media portrayals and casual conversations with out-of-state residents on the river, stories of poverty and lack from places like Appalachia, many other rural places across the U.S., as well as in poorer nations around the world, have framed the research questions of sociologists, anthropologists, and economists for decades. This is especially the case with regards to research looking at the economic cycles of boom and bust in rural, low-income, or racially and ethnically segregated communities. Solely relying on this outside sociological, anthropological, or economic frame of poverty and lack to understand changes taking place within the everyday lives of communities where developments are being proposed or are already underway discounts the most vital, essential relationships of community and the inter-connectivity between humans, communities, and Nature that will be affected and sometimes permanently changed by such developments. These vital community relationships should be central to how all developments are planned and evaluated in the first place, not just collateral damage or part of the cost calculations, or necessary sacrifices, made for economic progress. The community changes from economic and industrial developments are much more nuanced and complicated than simply economic winners versus economic losers.

Thus, using economics as the central argument or the sole framing of public debates is not only inaccurate it can cause great damage to the local communities where these developments are happening. In fact, many of the seeds of local inter- and intra-community conflicts around shale gas developments that I observed in Bradford County were planted by news stories and by vocal supporters of the shale gas industry that created the mythology that the industry would turn "dirt poor farmers" into "farm shale-ionaires" overnight[35].

I was fascinated to learn during an interview with a local resident whose father built roads during the Great Depression throughout the county that portrayals of local Bradford County farmers as "in the dirt" were in fact nothing new[36]. In the 1930's when President Franklin Delano Roosevelt's Secretary of Interior visited the town of Athens to kick off a million-dollar road building program throughout the Northern Tier as part of the Works Progress Administration's Farm to Market Roads project, he had vowed to "get the farmers out of the dirt." But, this "dirt poor farmer" turned shale-ionaire narrative was something else entirely. As policy makers, local politicians, and experts of various types repeated this phrase, the phrase became a devastating slap in the face to many local farmers I met and spoke with. Even worse, most local farmers had experienced being mistreated and lied to by land men from the gas industry regarding the amount of money they would get from any leases or surface use agreements and the idea of becoming some kind of shale-ionaire was a joke, even if they did harbor secret fantasies of it being real.

The conflicts became worse as this mythology of farmers striking it rich was interpreted as something entirely different by town residents who did not own tracts of land and those who opposed the shale gas developments on environmental and public health grounds. With the image of "dirt poor farmers" turned shale-ionaires firmly planted in their minds eye, both groups saw "greedy farmers" as the primary reason behind the drive to develop shale gas in the first place. But, such economic myths like this had no basis in the material everyday realities of poverty and wealth in the county. These myths completely discounted the inherent value and wealth that resides in local land, soil, water, Nature, rural life-ways, and knowledge. Such myths have continued to do great damage to already fragile psyches and community relationships in places like Dimock and Bradford County. And, they have done nothing at all to protect communities from the overwhelmingly negative local changes brought about by shale gas developments.

Scholars of Appalachia and of wealth inequality in the U.S. commented to me, and I also had begun to notice how little the material poverty of the region ever actually entered into conversations by those who argued against shale gas developments and fracking. According to almost every news article or marketing flyer, whether from a gas company or an environmental non-profit, shale gas developments were never going to make poverty or inequality worse, they were only going to make people richer and wealthier. They may kill fish, destroy water, and make the air un-breathable, but locals would still get wealthy. That's why all those "greedy farmers" were such a problem if you were against the developments, and were such a gift if you were for the developments!

The spread and perpetuation of this mythology had a lot to do with the out-of-state gas developers and economic interests spending a lot of new money, including creating the American Natural Gas Alliance (ANGA) in 2008. ANGA spent 4,054,488 dollars in national and regional pro-shale gas public relations and advertising campaigns in 2011 alone[37] to keep the framing of both local and national debates for and against the developments in terms of economic winners versus economic losers. I even kept seeing this sort of framing in the research questions academic sociologists, anthropologists, and economists were asking and getting funded to answer. And so, this economic winners versus losers story, with the winners always supporting shale gas developments, gained traction and was repeated by everyone for and against the developments in advancing their side of the debate over shale gas, and later fracking. This economic framing was the primary narrative whether you were listening to politicians, economic developers, urban residents, town and city dwellers, university professors, corporate agriculture, environmental activists, organic farmers, or energy contractors. It was extremely effective at silencing other narratives, other frames, and other voices, especially local ones.

Rarely, if ever, did local people from Bradford County or other communities where the drilling and fracking were taking place speak for themselves about what their hopes, dreams, and concerns were related to the new gas developments. If a local politician, economic progress authority representative, or gas company spokesperson did mention the material poverty of the region in relation to the shale gas developments, it was in terms of an "opportunity" to save the poor and destitute, to get "dirt poor farmers" out of the dirt, and other economic rescue promises. But those promises and all those opportunities never came with a clear plan of action. Empty promises were all they were.

In fact, in my own interviews and research in Bradford County with those in the county with the most access to information and the most political and economic power—local supervisors, county commissioners, agricultural extension agents, and other county staff – there was a certain animosity, shame, and dismissal when they spoke about local family farmers or problems of poverty in the county. They seemed to truly believe that the only way to help farmers find a better livelihood and get people out of poverty was to allow more industry and more subdivision of farms. And, yes, a surprising number of these people in powerful positions even believed the area should move away entirely from an economy based on agriculture. "Farming in Bradford County is in the past," someone literally said to me during a presentation I gave to some members of the County's Natural Gas Task Force in 2009 about the work I was starting in the county.

After my presentation, in which I showed the most recent census numbers on the agricultural nature of the County, a minority of the Task Force members who mostly served the more populated towns informed me that the census was misleading. They said that Bradford County was in fact not agricultural anymore, as there were simply not that many farms left and the population was migrating out. Young people, they explained to me, would not stay. In fact, they told me, I needed to look at the growing retirement population and that the county was moving towards a tourism-based economy and away from agriculture altogether. Some on the task force also made clear to me that they thought the new gas developments would not have much of an impact on agricultural land or the farming way of life simply because there were not enough farmers left. And these Natural Gas Task Force members saw themselves as the people who would shape the future of the County.

During a hearing in the Pennsylvania State Capitol in Harrisburg I noted that a Bradford County Commissioner told members of the state legislator how he was so grateful to the state for being so quick with permitting new gas wells and not listening to all the scare tactics of the "tree-huggers and environmentalists" because such permit streamlining had made it possible for the County to roll out the red carpet for the shale gas industry. This red carpet he attributed with a whole host of only good things: keeping the Bradford County's farmers in business or allowing them to get out of farming and retire, helping people start businesses, and helping the entire County turn its economic situation around.

But, once again, reality was something else entirely. As county and state elected officials smugly walked the halls of the state capitol in Harrisburg and boasted to their fellow politicians of all the wealth that shale gas developments had brought to Bradford County and the surrounding counties, those living on fixed incomes or who were already financially struggling in Bradford County, particularly in the more densely populated towns of Towanda and Athens, suddenly found themselves without a roof over their heads and living in unhealthy and unsafe conditions overnight. When gas industry workers from other states began to swarm to the area, and were able to afford triple the rents of what locals were paying, local landlords saw the opportunity to make more money and either kicked their long-term tenants onto the street or dramatically raised their monthly rental rates. To make matters worse for this new house-less population, the hotels typically allocated as emergency housing for those without a house, were also unavailable since they were booked for months ahead of time by out-of-town gas workers. Some Bradford County residents finding themselves without a place to sleep were sent to temporary shelters or hotels in other counties by service organizations, ended up moving in with family, or in the most desperate situations living under bridges and in parks.

Eventually, there was a politically connected group of community advocates for the homeless in the County who did have success in convincing the state lawmakers that the shale gas industry's pressure on the limited affordable housing options in Bradford County was causing great hardship for those on a fixed income and otherwise in need of housing assistance. But, in the end, the disdain and shame of poverty in Bradford County was larger, and instead of truly addressing the root problems of poverty in the County local leaders chose to ignore them and continue to give a green light to the gas developers to develop the County however they saw best.

In conversations and interviews with local and state elected officials and Bradford County staff I was told that gas royalty checks would save people from poverty and all other social problems. This ignored the reality that royalty checks would only go to people in the County that already owned land, such as the County government, farmers, and forest landowners. So, those already with more would gain more while those with less would not benefit unless there was an intentional effort to allocate royalties to County residents equitably. But, instead of discussing this reality and policies for equitable economic distribution of County royalties, the local elected officials were using the talking points of the gas companies who kept promising they were going to make everyone rich from the shale boom and that the flow of gas from these gas wells would go on for the next one hundred years. Most politicians and many local landowners and residents believed these outrageous boasts without question, especially if they had land to lease to the gas companies and thought they could get rich. It was winner take all. Each person out for their own benefit without regard for the greater whole.

The Pennsylvania state legislature did make some attempt in 2011 and 2012 to begin collecting an impact fee on Marcellus shale gas wells in order to ensure that communities that are directly affected by natural gas drilling receive their fair share of funding for projects like road and bridge repairs, housing and other local infrastructure needs. But at the same time, landowners with gas leases started reporting that they had received deductions from their gas royalty checks for expenses the company had incurred in its operations. And, by 2013 landowners with gas leases and active drilling and gas extraction on their properties were starting to report that the gas companies, instead of sending clean royalty payments had started deducting expenses that they claim to have incurred during their operations.

Remember the Bradford County Commissioner who had boasted at the state capitol to Pennsylvania legislators about the County laying out a red carpet for the gas developers and how the gas companies were making the County so wealthy? Well, on January 25, 2012 he and his fellow County elected officials received a bill in the amount of $609,179.42 from an Oklahoma gas company. The bill was for assisting in community clean-up after the disastrous and deadly September 2011 Susquehanna River flood during which at least one person died, dozens were injured, thousands displaced, hundreds of homes and businesses destroyed, agricultural fields full of rocks, large debris, and trees, hundreds of bridges washed out and roads closed, and many of the historic buildings in downtown Towanda, Monroeton, and across the valley significantly damaged[38]. It turns out that the gas company's "generous" community clean-up assistance was not unconditional as they had made it appear in their photo-ops of their employees handing out "donations" of water and other supplies and equipment immediately after the flood.

Yet, it took four years after the flood before the public learned that the County had been billed and then paid over a half million dollars to the company by reading a front-page headline in the local *Morning Times* newspaper in 2016. Meanwhile, between July and December of 2011, as the river had crested its banks and left thousands homeless and lives shattered that September, that same Oklahoma gas company had drilled 21 new gas wells in Bradford County and sucked 79,921,959 Mcf (1000 Cubic Feet) of shale gas from below the

County's ground, an amount of gas worth more than $386 million at that time. According to Pennsylvania State Senator Gene Yaw's accounts of Impact Fee money, Bradford County's County and Township governments received over $157 million in combined tax revenue between 2011 and 2020.[39]

Regardless of the dollar amounts created or generated for, from, or by new gas developments and flowing to private developers, large landowners, and those supporting the gas developments, the overall communities in Bradford County and other rural counties where shale gas developments take place continue to suffer. Between April 2010 and July 2019 there was a population decline of 2,377 in Bradford County. Bradford County continues to grapple with a poverty level that has never gotten below 11%. And, in Bradford County and surrounding counties like Susquehanna County, there continues to be a growing gap between those making more money than they ever have and those who can barely get by.[40]

Looking for a Savior

Whether local county farmers and landowners were seen as greedy, felt shameful or fearful, or saw themselves as part of a new business partnership, there was no disputing the reality that agricultural and forest landowners still owned most of the land area in the County in 2009, and the majority still owned their own mineral rights. And while farming still made up the largest source of county revenue in 2009, family dairies, woodlots, and other smaller sized farms in the county had been on the decline in terms of number of farms and definitely on-farm income for decades. As we know, this downward trend was not only about the gas developments but had been part of the globalization of countryside and was part of a larger national and international shift that left small farmers behind in the name of industrialized farming and large corporate financial and trade interests. In 2009 Bradford County also had higher poverty rates than surrounding areas in Pennsylvania and New York and its young people were moving away from the county and not coming back. Without a doubt all of these realities of decreasing profits from farms, low rural employment, lower incomes, and decreasing population made it easier for the oil and gas development interests to be seen as the "savior" of the local economy.

But when I met landowners and spoke with them this wasn't what they talked about. They did not want to tell me how much money they could make with the new gas developments specifically, but instead wanted to talk about the overwhelming sense of powerlessness they felt to do anything different but sign leases with the oil and gas companies in order to pay their bills or to secure what currently looked like an uncertain and poor future in farming or other local business. My colleague, Dr. Stephanie Malin, in her work in the same region (Endless Mountains) and Pittsburgh also found that landowners felt a sense of powerlessness when it came to signing new oil and gas leases[41]. What Dr. Malin and I both heard from families considering signing gas leases on their land was that they saw it as a way out of their financial troubles and debt. The companies were acting in a savior role and landowner families wanted to believe that any negative consequences or costs to the environment and public health, if they did occur, would certainly be monitored and regulated by the federal or state government. For many agricultural landowners I spoke with, the decision to sign a lease or surface use agreement was borne out of necessity and real uncertainty about their family's future. They really believed that the government would protect them from any problems that might happen.

In other words, for these landowners it was not so much about greed as it was about feeling powerless and that they had no other choice if they wanted to stay on their farms and in their homes. Signing leases and doing what the gas companies told them was, they believed, their only choice. The gas companies had become their saviors. And, if the gas companies failed, they thought that certainly the government would save them. What is so darn confusing to outsiders is that this local belief in government as savior from health and environmental destruction contradicts recent support among these same locals in political ideologies (i.e., neoliberalism) being pushed by the two main U.S. political parties that have seen increased calls for removing government protections from public health, environmental protection, and other basic common goods and services in favor of more private and corporate decision-making and control. While voting (if they voted at all) for politicians and policies that advocated for getting the government out of people's lives, they at the same time believed that government would still be there to save them if there was some type of disaster.

Over the next several years as I worked in the County, many local farmers and landowners and politicians would even dismiss their own, or my, concerns about the impacts of shale gas developments by invoking this belief in government oversight and responsibility to protect people's water and health. There was a confidence in local people in this part of Pennsylvania that the government, either federal or state, if not local, would certainly step in and intervene if gas developments posed a danger to their water, or if there was the threat of other types of environmental destruction. Local people felt confident that it was the government's responsibility and that the government would fulfill this responsibility by protecting the environment and citizens' rights. Make too big a deal of the environmental problems, some said in the county, and the gas companies would invest their money elsewhere; never-mind the geological fact that the gas was there and not just anywhere. Ask too many questions about how the gas developments might impact your water or soil or forest and in the politically conservative county they'd call you dirty things like "tree hugger" or "environmentalist."

Unfortunately, my own previous experiences had brutally awoken me to the reality that this confidence in the government's will and ability to enforce or even follow U.S. laws, especially environmental laws, and exercise their public trust and protection responsibilities was misplaced and just plain wrong. The effects of neoliberal policies to take public trust responsibilities for clean air, water, soil, and public health out of government hands and to make the fight for community values and common goods somehow treasonous had almost entirely eroded away the government's public trust or safety net role when I began working with NOAA as a civil servant back in the early 2000's. In that role I was offered a front-row seat to very purposeful efforts to undermine environmental laws and policies that had been designed to protect human and ecological communities.

As a naïve and intimidated young federal employee, I begrudgingly took that seat and with a very troubled mind did as I had been told by political appointees and my boss. They had asked, and when I had questioned it, they had demanded that I write permits for the harassment and harm of marine mammals in the course of the dynamiting and dismantling of old, retired oil and gas rigs in the Gulf of Mexico without a revised environmental review under the National Environmental Policy Act (NEPA). No comprehensive environmental review of oil and gas development programs in the Gulf of Mexico had been done in over 10 years, so it was past time. I resisted, but in the end, I complied with their demand. As some type of thanks for doing as I was told, I received a personal phone call from one of the G.W. Bush administration political appointees in the Department of Commerce, who had previously worked for the American Petroleum Institute (API).

When he called me the first time, he emphasized how important my work was in helping them finalize the oil and gas permits and something about patriotism. (Remember, it was not long after 9/11.) He then invited me to an energy round-table with energy leaders and businesses. Shortly after that round-table, I was invited to an inter-agency planning session on new regulations to be enshrined in a brand-new Energy Policy Act related to a permit program that would allow for the development and expansion of new liquefied natural gas (LNG) port terminals and other oil and gas activities, including the exploration and development of onshore deep geological formations with horizontal drilling and hydraulic fracturing (fracking).

Little did I realize it at the time, but those interagency meetings were part of a concerted effort by the federal government under the GW Bush administration, at the behest of the oil and gas industry, API, and Vice-President Dick Cheney to derail and dismantle laws and regulations designed to monitor, mitigate, and protect water, human health, and ecosystems, when energy development activities used underground injection, such as fracking, to extract oil and gas. It turned out this new energy policy law would also ease the way for future U.S. exports of LNG as the fracking of gas and oil reserves became more common across rural parts of the intermountain west, southwest, Gulf coast, and northeast.

What now appears to have been a very strategic industry-led effort to dismantle environmental and public health protections that were part of federal regulations since the late 1960's eventually culminated in the passage of the Energy Policy Act of 2006, in which exemptions from government oversight of the oil and gas industry's use of "unconventional" practices, such as fracking, left local environments and communities vulnerable to uncertain hazards and risks related to chemical contamination of their soils, air, surface water, and groundwater. Even more threatening to the protection of local communities, this new law prohibited individual citizens and communities from even petitioning companies or the government for information about the details of fracking-related activities. The new law sought to keep "secret" what chemicals were being used and what the risks of those chemicals were to humans and Nature. This was not only dangerous to life, it codified the G.W. Bush administration policies that had been disregarding environmental and public health laws for the sake of corporate developers' returns on investment, and it paved the way for a new land and resource grab by oil and gas developers to drill and extract natural gas and oil with impunity from private, public, and tribal lands.

I would hear phrases like, "I'm sure the environmental regulators like the Environmental Protection Agency, would not let them do it if it hurt our water," from all sorts of people both within and outside Bradford County and each time I heard this, it re-ignited within me the outrage I had felt as a newly minted scientist at NOAA when I first became aware of the hypocrisy and political manipulation that occurred within our government in order to serve corporate interests and profits; to serve private interests that have no regard for protecting water, air, other living creatures, or human lives from harm. It also lit inside of me some sort of consciousness of a deeper responsibility to warn local people that they were mistaken to put so much faith in a government that would in the end not protect them. I had seen it with my own eyes.

And eventually these feelings of outrage, as well as responsibility, got me thinking about ways to bring attention to these exemptions and the shrouding of the risks inherent to fracking in ways that would raise local public awareness about the government's complicity in the promotion of oil and gas developments. I naïvely thought that once people learned of the way these exemptions were enacted through deception and cunning political manipulation that they would no longer just assume that their government would protect their communities and Nature from harm, and they would demand that the government do more to protect not only their own families and selves, but also their communities. Boy was I dead wrong.

Unfortunately, my abstract ideas of cultural synthesis and the idea that I could jump-start some sort of critical consciousness process within people by getting them together to talk and asking them the right questions were complicated by the entrenched mindsets in Bradford County, and most of rural Pennsylvania, regarding poverty and lack, individual over community values (what some call a "rugged individualism" or even "stubbornness"), and deep suspicion of outsiders. I also completely underestimated the oil and gas industry's tactics to manipulate the government, to keep their secrets, and silence those who tried to reveal them. Yet, despite my own experience and awareness about the government's failures, I still must have held out some kind of hope that at least the federal government would in fact protect us, because I also still greatly overestimated the federal government's concern for rural communities and places.

To this day, reading over my field notes, reading transcripts from public meetings, and listening to interviews, I am shocked by the appalling lack of political will, even disregard, at local, state, and even federal government levels to protect people, especially those of low wealth and living on the margins; not to mention the total disregard government had for the rights of Nature. And, at an individual and community level, there was disturbing evidence in those field observations and interviews of the learned helplessness and the way years of political and interpersonal violence had kept a local community traumatized and focused on individual survival at any cost.

This evidence made me realize that warning people and seeking to raise peoples' consciousness about our government's failures to protect us was much more difficult than I imagined. The widespread internalized oppression among rural landowners and farmers had left them identifying as and feeling like victims, as much as they would outwardly deny it, and so they were on the constant search for a savior. I quickly learned that attempting to take away their belief in the government, or anyone else, as savior was met not only with disbelief or dismissal but many times also distrust and anger.

Just Business

Throughout Pennsylvania between 2007 and March of 2012, there were 9,837 new Marcellus shale gas wells permitted. Looking at the larger Pennsylvania trends in natural gas development and production (non-shale and new shale wells), the Commonwealth of Pennsylvania had 52,700 gas wells already producing gas in 2007. So, from a state-wide and industry perspective, these close to 10,000 shale gas wells did not represent a "new" industry as much as a new type of technology used to access methane gas trapped in deeper, previously inaccessible shale rock formations.

But, the amount of water, land, and other raw materials that would be necessary to support the development, the level of financing that would be required to undertake such developments, the uncertainties and risks posed to Nature and all life, the pace of the developments, the type of workers that were needed, the amount of money promised to individual landowners, and the type of places that were targeted for shale gas development were all "new." And, one of those "new" types of places being targeted for shale gas development was Bradford County.

The two people who continue to play the most critical role in my understanding of Bradford County and what these new gas developments mean to farmers are Carol and Claude. They are dairy farmers whose farm land sits at the convergence of Bullard and Flower Creeks on Spaulding Hill in Sheshequin. Both Carol and Claude's families have lived in the county for at least the past one hundred and fifty years. They are both from Yankee families. Carol in particular became my indispensable guide and companion in helping me understand how shale gas developments were impacting Bradford County's farmers and residents both inside and outside of Pennsylvania. She also became a very patient teacher in helping me understand and decode for myself, my students, and others the values, beliefs, and behaviors of county residents. Most importantly, she continues to be a dear friend despite of, and critically because of, our different experiences, perspectives, and belief systems. Although, if you had told me that Carol and I would be friends eleven years later when I first met her in 2009, I would never have believed you.

It was a Saturday in November when I first met Carol. She sat next to the window in the back dining room of Bishop's Family Restaurant looking out onto Route US 220 that runs through the center of Ulster. I saw her through the window and thought it might be her, but then when I approached her inside the restaurant, I immediately knew it was her by her hands. Another farmer I had met earlier in the week in Wyalusing had offered this little tip: "Look at their hands.

That's how you can tell a real farmer from a hobby farmer."

"Carol?"

"Hi."

"Hi, I'm Simona Perry. Thanks for meeting with me."

I put my hand out for a handshake. And, yes, she had the working hands of a dairy farmer, a real farmer -- red, rough, cracked.

"Yup," she said, as she shook my hand.

My goal in this first meeting was to simply build trust by getting to know her and letting her get to know me. Carol spoke in a no-nonsense way and had a great sense of humor, even as we spoke of serious things. She had done her homework about the area's new Marcellus shale gas industry, the hazards, the risks, the benefits.

"It's just a business," she told me matter-of-factly. "They will do what they can to operate in the cheapest way they can to make the most money they can. They don't give a damn about the farmer or farming. But we're a business too."

She candidly described to me more than any local I had spoken with (including staff at the County Conservation District and County Commissioners) about how the gas industry in the County had already been impacting local farmers; mostly around shady land deals involving low-balling signing bonuses and royalties. She told me she had spoken with a lawyer in New York who had gotten death threats for trying to help farmers and landowners get better deals with the gas companies up there. She was very up front about what she knew, and also about what she didn't know, admitting to me that she had a lot to learn.

In addition to being a life-long Bradford County resident

who grew up on a dairy farm in the north-central part of the County, Carol had incredible first-hand insights into the current political life in the county. She worked for the local U.S. Department of Agriculture office, as well as sold insurance for a time, so she knew the issues faced by local farmers from their perspectives, and had local knowledge of the geography of the county and its people, as well as the towns just over the border in New York.

In terms of the politics in the county, she told me the story about an agricultural tax program called "Clean and Green" and how one of the County Commissioners had asked her to help him by being a spokesperson for his political and economic objectives[42]. This experience had changed her view of county politics and politicians, and government in general, she told me. She felt used by the Commissioner when he did not get his way and felt he had treated her as disposable and "dumb farmer."

"And maybe I was," she added. The details of the tax rebate program aside, the personal time and effort, even going on radio shows for him, she had put into helping the Commissioner without any respect from him made her even more suspicious and wary of government officials. Her eyes had been opened she told me. She said she had been stupid to their manipulations and their double-dealing before that experience.

"Not again. Never again," she said. She felt angry after being manipulated by the County Commissioner and helping him score political points, while he cared nothing about what it meant to her life or to her farm.

I told Carol about what I was looking for in my work

in Bradford County -- people to participate in focus group meetings to share with me and each other what their land and water means to them. I handed her a sheet of information about the project with my contact information and a form that described what consent to participate in the study would mean—any risks and rewards and how the information collected would be used. I emphasized to her how important it was for me to get her full consent, and what that meant, before she decided whether or not to participate.

"If you do choose to participate, I can ensure you that your confidentiality will be protected. However, because these are group meetings, I cannot ensure your anonymity," I told her.

She asked me lots of questions about my views on the environment and the gas industry. Although she was quite kind about it, those questions were a very clear interrogation about my true motivations. She was trying to gauge whether I could be trusted or not. I appreciated this, since I realized how suspicious it might have seemed that a researcher at a small liberal arts college in the southern part of the state would be asking questions about her farm and the gas industry.

"Why the hell do you give a crap about us? Me? Our land? Farmers in this County? What do you really want from us?" she asked bluntly.

No one had ever asked what was most important to her about the place she lived and the life she led except in wanting something from her, and thus she was inherently suspicious of why I would ask her these questions. Grasping at anything that would set her mind at ease, and build her trust in me, I began telling her more about my personal story and who I was beyond the researcher role. I told her about my education as a wildlife biologist, a little about my work and experiences in NOAA, what led me to be interested in people's connections to the places they live and work, and even a little about my hope that my research would give her and others more of a voice in local decision-making.

"I am from southeast Georgia, and on my mom's side I come from six generations of farmers and loggers. My relatives would be very wary of anyone asking them these questions too. I understand your concerns. I want to give you some time to think about it. My contact information is on both of those sheets."

As it got closer to 4 o'clock, she said she had to getback to chores. We left Bishop's Restaurant after paying at the counter and walked out into the gravel parking lot. As we walked toward her truck, I kept asking questions about where in the county she grew up and went to school. Eventually, she asked if I would like to come back to the farm with her to keep talking, see the place, and meet Claude.

"But, if you do," she warned, "You have to help out in the barn."

I enthusiastically said yes, but only if I would not be a burden. She repeated that I had to help. I said I was more than willing to learn, to be the student. I reminded her not to pay too much attention to those letters behind my name.

"Remember I am also a wildlife biologist and before that my major was animal science. And, I actually did do a short work-study in the University dairy barn."

She said nothing, but seemed to get a chuckle out of that.

I also reminded her that she knew more about farming

and her life and her own land and water and this place than I ever will, so I was eager above all to learn from her. That was why I was there. To be her student. This made her smile.

"Follow me," she said as she hopped up in her truck, and I walked quickly to my car.

I followed her truck through Ulster, over the Susquehanna River and straight up Ghent Hill. After that I was lost. There were very few road signs marking the dirt roads between the fields, barns, and stands of trees, and more fields. We turned right onto a long dirt and gravel road. It was beautiful with the trees in their fall colors. We crossed a bridge over a small creek. When we pulled up to the house, a two story white farm house with a small front porch to one side, a very happy golden retriever rushed down from the front porch, his wagging tail leading the way.

"That's Aspen," Carol said.

Aspen dropped a rock at my feet. "Her favorite toy. She loves rocks." Carol explained.

I felt a bit nervous. This was the first time I had been in a working dairy barn since college. Plus, I did not want to give Carol any reason not to trust me. I kept reminding myself to have a learner's mind and attitude as I followed Carol with Aspen trailing behind me through the milk house into the barn.

"These are our girls," she said proudly, as we entered the barn to a cacophony of mooing. I saw a thin man on the far side of the barn.

"Hi Claude," Carol shouted, "This is...uh"

"Simona Perry," I whispered.

"Dr. Simona Perry," she called out.

"Hi Dr. Simona," Claude shouted back in a tired, but friendly, voice. Then he yelled, "Dr. of what?"

"Well..." I started to answer, but before I could get more out Carol answered for me, "It's complicated. She'll tell ya later."

Carol directed me back into the milk house to help her with her chores, which it turned out, was feeding the young calves. I was relieved we were starting out so simple. The whirring of the mechanical milkers, and the prospect of having to learn how all that worked, had made me a bit anxious. Quickly Carol made me feel at ease with her humor. She told me the names of the cows. I asked questions about them. What breed they were and those kinds of things.

Finally, Claude's chores brought him closer to the side of the barn where Carol and I were feeding the calves, and I was immediately struck by his resemblance to both my Grandpa Gnann (mom's dad) and my dad. His calm and strength was my Grandpa, while his kind sternness, slim physique, and smiling eyes were my Dad's.

After spending the afternoon and early evening with her, I could honestly say I liked Carol. Her sense of humor and honesty was so refreshing and spoke to a curious mind that while cautious, was still open to learning new things and new possibilities. I wanted to know more about her. I thought she would be a great person for the focus groups of farmer women I was trying to form; although, at that point, I was still not completely sure what she thought about my motivations for asking her so many questions. I could not tell whether she believed me, and especially whether she would be willing to participate in the work I wanted to do in the County.

After chores were over, we all exited the barn through the milk house together and walked down the little path to their house. I walked beside Claude telling him a little more about what the Dr. before my name meant. Or trying to find the right words to, as I was keenly aware of how he might receive the information. I wanted to make sure it was clear, not too complicated with jargon, and that he felt assured I was not hiding anything.

"No, I am not a medical doctor or veterinarian. I have a doctor in philosophy."

"Oh yeah? What kind of philosophy?" he asked.

"I ask questions about how farmers like yourself find meaning in the world around them. Especially the natural world-- your water, your land – and how that translates into public decisions or policies about managing that water or land."

"Are you working with those people down at the Conservation District? Because they don't know what the hell they're doin' down there," he asked and stated calmly.

I smiled, "No, although I have talked to them. But I am not working for them. As a matter of fact, I am more interested in working with you and Carol than them. I am conducting a study as part of my appointment at Dickinson College down in the southern part of the state to understand farmers' knowledge of their own lands and how things have changed over time so that you might have a greater voice in what the Conservation District actually does."

He looked at the ground as we continue walking, "Ha! You think they'll care?"

Then, right before we reached the bottom step of the porch,

Claude stopped, and asked, in a serious tone, "Where is the funding for this here study coming from?"

"Mellon Foundation."

He immediately stepped closer to me, "Isn't that a bank? What does a bank want to know about us?"

And although he spoke in a calm voice, I admit I was intimidated. And, I also knew that was the point. He definitely did not trust me. And, why should he? But, I did not move, and I began to try and explain how the money is not from the Mellon Bank, but a private philanthropic foundation focused on supporting scholarship on human-environment relationships. Until, thank goodness, Carol approached and told Claude to cut me a break. I was relieved. Without another word or a good-bye Claude continued up the porch steps, opened up the door, and walked inside the house.

Carol kindly invited me into the house, but I told her I should get back to where I was staying because it was quite a drive.

"Thank you, I do appreciate the invitation. I will be in touch very soon. Just think about the project. Take another look at the consent to participate form. Your voice and experiences are so important and really should be shared. Others can learn from you. I would love for you, and even Claude, to participate," I tell her, "and, you have my phone number if you have any questions or think of anything."

"Alright. Don't let him get to you," she said.

"Thanks. I know I have learned so much from you today. And, thank you for showing me your farm," I added.

I said good-bye to Aspen and got in my car. Carol approached the car before I closed the door. "Do you know how to get where you're going?"

"Kind-of?"

I told her I was heading south towards Wyalusing, and she gave me some directions that were basically: the same way we got up on the hill in the first place is the same way you get down.

Turns out I got lost trying to get down to the river. The landscape just looked so darn similar wherever I looked —with dirt road after dirt road and field upon field—and no signs or distinct markers. I could be going around in circles, and I would never have known it. I got lost because I was also distracted by what I had just learned and experienced, and especially what I had said to Claude and Carol about the research I wanted to do in Bradford County. I was worried about their judgments of my motivations and how I had responded to their questions. I so wanted and needed their trust, and I needed the trust of so many more local people like them to be able to ask the types of questions I wanted to ask about this place and, importantly, to have them begin asking their own questions. I was anxious about whether I would be able to get this type of trust among county farmers and landowners.

Despite the distracting thoughts, somehow I got down that hill to the bridge crossing the Susquehanna River between Sheshequin and Ulster. From there it was easier. I crossed the bridge and made a left at the light and drove South on Highway 220, past the Bishop's Family Restaurant, to Route 6 going East through Towanda and a strip of retail known as the Golden Mile, and South again towards Wyalusing. The cabins I was staying at were on the other side of the Susquehanna

River from Wyalusing, in Sugar Run. They belonged to David and Melody, who also owned Endless Mountain Outfitters on the Susquehanna, and had moved to the county over ten years ago. I arrived back at the cabins in the dark. Because the Susquehanna River serves as a center line through much of the Eastern half of Bradford County, I had crossed the river three times getting there, weaving above and through the river, creeks, hills, and valleys.

I unlocked the screen door to the cabin, put my bag down inside, and sat on the porch in the stillness and solitude trying to quiet my mind of all the anxiety and doubts about what I was doing in this place and the unease I felt at prying into local peoples' lives. What right, really, did I have to ask questions of these people in the first place? And, especially, what kind of arrogance did I have to think that my project here would make a difference in local lives or to the magnificent river that flowed just feet from where I sat? What if asking these questions actually caused harm? Across the road and through the trees, I could barely make out the moonlit water of the Susquehanna as it flowed south. I suspected at that moment that just upriver Carol was talking to Claude about me and whether I could be trusted.

Gaining peoples' trust was the most difficult part of working in Bradford County. As I talked to different types of people— farmers, county commissioners, town residents, township supervisors, county staff, students, teachers, forest landowners— I started to understand how the social networks and relationships between people moved and the ways in which gossip and rumor played such an important role in that movement. This understanding allowed me to see how talking to or being seen with certain individuals within the community might mean that other individuals within the community would be more or less trusting of me. This was the reality of conducting community research in a small rural community and trying to gain the trust of as many people as I could. It meant making some difficult choices about both who I spent my time with and where I was seen. In addition, it made me think more about what I realistically expected I would be able to conclude about people's relationships to one another, Nature, and the changes they were experiencing as a result of the shale gas developments based on what would likely be my limited ability to access a diversity of lives, experiences, and perspectives.

The conundrum was, as with all community research, that I would get in-depth interviews and focus group participation only from those individuals and their social networks who ended up trusting me and giving me their full consent, and that in the end this would somewhat limit the general applicability of any conclusions I would be able to make. As the pace of shale gas developments began picking up in the county, and more and more people were wanting answers and sensational stories, including international newspapers like *The Guardian* and large U.S. publications like *Time Magazine*, on topics from water contamination to health concerns to the impacts to farming, this lack of generality made me unable to offer any such answers or stories with any type of certainty. I am sure this left more than a couple of news reporters frustrated, as it left me feeling inadequate to the task.

But, as I kept reminding myself, the specificity and

richness of people's everyday lives, family dynamics, daily work life, relationships with Nature, and other details of County experiences that I was able to access was absolutely critical to understanding the cultural dimensions of how humans and Nature were mutually interdependent. And, it would be this type of baseline understanding, information, and context that would allow for a more complete understanding of how changes brought about by shale gas developments in the County impacted individual lives, the whole community, and Nature over time.

In the focus groups, thanks to Carol and others who decided to put some level of trust in me, I was eventually able to bring together individuals who were low-income to middle-income dairy and crop farmers and higher-income forest landowners. To my delight they were predominately people who were born in or had multi-generational ties to the county and their land and they were mostly female. On the other hand, the broad representation of the community I was able to get to participate in one-on-one interviews and meetings expanded the type of experiences and perspectives I documented and made me much more confident in the conclusions I eventually drew from the work.

Shifting Frames of Reference

James Baldwin once said that history is "present in all we do" and to what "we owe our frames of reference," identities, and aspirations[43]. If this is true, and if, as Wendell Berry has pondered, "local place" is where the true meaning of belonging in community is found[44], then how does history, local place, and sense of community fit into our understanding of rapid changes in the face of the shale gas developments in a local place such as Bradford County? Will these new industrial developments fit within existing frames of reference, identities, aspirations? Or, will local people have to shift those frames, and therefore their understandings of their histories, identities, aspirations, and thus their relationship with place and community to fit into those developments?

Population and economic statistics prior to 2009, when the development of Marcellus shale gas in Bradford County really took off describe a rural agricultural place with a declining, aging, relatively poor, and racially homogenous white population. According to federal agricultural statistics, Bradford County as of 2007 received most of its total revenue from agriculture (up until 2010, the County reported $150 million in cash receipts from farming businesses), while manufacturing had been the greatest source of employment in the County. And, like with farming, the natural resources in the county have played a significant role in why manufacturing businesses originally located in the County and why they continue to operate to this day; with one in ten jobs being in the forestry and wood products industry.

In 2008 all of that started to change. When I first put a canoe in the Chemung River in July 2009 there were 102 vertical gas and oil wells within the county. In 2021 there are close to 2,100. There is no doubt these gas wells, and all of the impoundments ponds, pipelines, compressor stations, and industrial facilities that have come with them have brought a scale and pace of change to the county that has not just caused damage to people's drinking water, contaminated their waterways, changed the forest and farmland landscape, but has threatened peoples' trust in a handshake and one another, shaken their faith in a government and system of laws that they thought would protect them and their children from harm, and fundamentally altered their belief in the strength of relationships with family, neighbors, and community, as well as with Nature and the essential life and livelihoods it has always provided. While much has always been changing in this borderland county and globalized countryside, when I arrived in the county in 2009 there was a feeling that these changes could crack open the very bedrock of everyday life and rip apart the very fabric of community.

Throughout history Bradford County's financial wealth and overall prosperity has been intimately connected to its dense forests, fertile soils, geology, and abundant waters. It has been home to generations of families whose sense of place and economic livelihoods have been tied to the products generated and extracted from Nature. One study estimated that between 1,533.53 acres and 3,327.76 acres in Bradford County could be taken up by new gas wells and access roads alone, which does not account for impoundment ponds, pipelines, and other related gas infrastructure.[45] What does it mean when industrial developments threaten to destroy those forests, soils, geology, and waters? What does it mean when family cemeteries are threatened by pipelines and farming livelihoods are no longer feasible?

Local residents I spoke with in 2009 told me that in the past there had been outspoken opposition by Bradford County residents to the citing of more factories and hazardous waste sites along the Susquehanna River in the County. One of the reasons for this was a concern over existing water and air contamination problems at the Dupont and GTP facilities in Towanda, one of the largest towns in the County. I also heard from both Laura and a staff person at the Bradford County Conservation District about organized local opposition to a hazardous waste incinerator that had been proposed along the Susquehanna River in the late 1990s. The Conservation District Director at the time told me he did not understand why local residents who were so opposed to a hazardous waste incinerator going in along the Susquehanna River ten years ago and were able to stop it, were not just as, or more, outraged and organized against the gas developments that were operating without appropriate environmental safeguards for water, air, and land in place[46]. Conversations like these piqued my interest to find out more accurately how the local community had perceived new economic and industrial development projects in the past as well as today.

First, I wanted to know if this perception of the Conservation District staff was in fact accurate: locals were not as concerned about the new shale gas developments as earlier industrial developments. And, second, if it was true that locals were not as concerned, I wanted to know what made the new gas industry developments different from previous industrial and economic development projects in the eyes of Bradford County locals. Was it because they considered the extractive value of the land more important than other values? Were they in fact poorer now than they had been in the past and now much more willing to sacrifice clean water and air for money? Was it because most of the natural gas developments were occurring on private land? Was it because the development was spatially dispersed? Was it lack of information? Was it apathy? Were local people tired of fighting against industrial developments? Did they believe that there was nothing that they could do to stop the shale gas developments? Or, was there something else?

In March 2010 I was sitting in my office on the Dickinson College campus when the phone rang. I picked it up.

"Hello, this is Simona."

Without missing a beat, the voice on the other end responded nervously and breathlessly, "Hi, this is Heather *(not her real name)*. My husband and I just had a meeting with our lawyers about the surface use agreement with the gas company. Unfortunately the agreement has something in it that prevents us from discussing the gas developments on our property with anyone, including any problems we might have in the future. I just don't see how I can participate in your study and meetings. I talked to my husband about it and he does not think it is a good idea."

I sat there stunned, starting to feel anger rise up in my throat, as I mentally processed what she had just said. I thought to myself, "This is their land and water which they relied on for their livelihoods and well-being, not the gas company's!"

I knew from our previous meeting on her dairy farm a week before, where I had asked Heather to participate in a focus group with other farmers, that within the last year she and her husband, also a township supervisor, had just signed lease renewals to their subsurface minerals and new surface use agreements for pipelines and other infrastructure to a gas exploration and production company out of Oklahoma City. When she had told me about these agreements with the gas company she had been excited about the financial opportunities she felt these leases and agreements offered to her family. They would now not just be dairy farmers, but the expectation was that they would also be royalty owners of Marcellus shale gas wells and receive enough money to not only cover annual expenses, but also pay-off debts from the farm, and maybe even buy new farm equipment to enhance their farming operations.

As we walked from her dairy barn to her house she had told me, "We are supportive of the gas industry developments in the County because it offers a way to pay our taxes and farm debts, while at the same time keep our dairy farm going. It is a way to continue doing what our families have done for generations despite the changes in our County and country that have made it more and more difficult to sustain a working farm." And, she continued, "Of course we will still need good water and land to grow hay and corn, so I am also cautious about how these developments might impact our business. I *would* like to participate in your meetings to understand and share with others about our experiences."

So, this first meeting had left me feeling hopeful about farmer participation in my work in the county. What had changed? Had she stopped being concerned?

The initial conversation I had with Heather at her farm was important because it helped me understand the mix of expectations and concerns local farmers had about the new gas developments. At the meeting she had shared her feelings about her land and the county with me, and her expectation that the gas developments would support both her land and the county. But, she was also concerned, and cautious, about the risks the developments could pose to her water and soils. And, she wasn't the only farmer or landowner in the county and region who had expressed these mixed feelings of both positive expectations and serious concerns regarding the gas developments.

Many locals I spoke with in the County who farmed would speak plainly of their concerns about the risks the gas developments might cause to their water, soil, and air; however, with the promises of taxes and debts paid-off and money coming in to continue farming operations, farmers also wanted very much to believe everything that the gas developers told them. And what the gas developers told everyone, including local politicians, local news reporters, and state environmental regulators, was that their operations were completely safe, there were no risks, they were "environmentally-friendly." They assured everyone that they took all precautions to protect water, soil, and air and so there was absolutely no need to be concerned.

In my office, back on the phone, Heather continued, "The lawyer told us there was some type of non-disclosure clause in our surface use agreement and that if we talk to anyone about anything going on with the gas companies on our land that the agreement would be null and void. That means we would get no money and be asked to give back the signing bonus."

Her voice cracked, and there was a hushed sob from the phone. "What we do for a living is more important than all of this. We've had a good life without all the money. I am so, so sorry."

"You have nothing to be sorry about," I responded in a

lame attempt to set aside my escalating anger and disbelief to comfort her.

"I am worried that if I participate in your study it will hurt our farm," she continued, "I am scared about what is going to happen to our land, to our cows if there is an accident or spill. I have so many concerns and questions about how all this might affect us; access to our fields, our water wells, what happens if there is an accident or spill? What if our life is no longer even possible because of this? Then we will have to rely on the government to protect us. My husband says they are heavily regulated like our farms --to protect the environment -- so he is sure that we will be protected by the government if something goes wrong."

The gas developers had masterfully used the public's beliefs and assumptions that the government was responsible for protecting the environment and human health to their advantage. Then, when developers could not convince people that their activities were one-hundred percent safe and clean, they made claims that federal and state regulations were terribly stringent and onerous, appealing to most local farmer's disdain for on-farm regulations, and therefore everyone would be protected even if there was some type of accident or contamination. Of course, they conveniently left out the fact that their industry was exempt from federal and state clean water, clean air, and hazardous waste disposal regulations. Something the entire oil and gas industry had lobbied for and received over the previous ten years to pave the way for this new type of onshore energy development that relied on horizontal drilling and fracking.

And as I listened to Heather tell me that she could not

participate in my study, or even discuss with others any of the gas developments taking place on her land, I realized gas developers were now attempting to hide the risks and hazards of their activities behind non-disclosure agreements with local lease-holders. The companies were using contractual threats and corporate lawyers to convince landowners not to publicly discuss their concerns nor to publicly reveal any contamination or negative impacts they observed on their own land. It was insidious.

Heather's voice shattered behind sobs. This time those sobs were tinged with anger. But not the type of anger that I was feeling towards the developers and the horrific trap they had set for her family. No, Heather's anger was completely directed at herself.

"How could I have been so stupid? I am so ashamed and scared. This is not right."

I would hear words of self-deprecation, shame, and fear cross many farmers and landowner's lips when they shared their uncertainties and deep concerns about the presence of the gas developments in the County over the next couple of years. And, I would begin to understand that this expression of shame and fear was not simply about the gas developments. These deep emotions and feelings of helplessness among many local farmers and landowners seemed to come from old unhealed wounds that pre-dated these new developments, but whose rotten skin and scabs were being freshly ripped off because of them. And, it could be hard to empathize or be compassionate at times because their emotions would sometimes come out as blustering self-righteousness or anger and distrust of me personally. At other times, though, there would be distraught self-flagellation, apologies, or tears like Heather expressed. I had already seen the outlines of this shame and fear over the past five months before her phone call. But, Heather's phone call, brought the violence of re-injuring such unhealed wounds into clear focus.

This was much more than one woman with low self-esteem or regrets over a decision made about money. There was a lack of confidence in individual self-determination and agency among many of the local landowners I had spoken with. At the community level, this phenomenon of personal shame and low self-esteem has become a recurring theme in not only my work with Bradford County landowners but with other communities experiencing rapid changes from industrial and economic developments. So, instead of framing my questions around the material aspects of boom and bust economies and material poverty or lack of wealth and other resources, I asked questions to better understand the causes of internalized feelings of poverty and lack in the county and region. How did local people interact with others and perceive themselves, their communities, and the world in ways that might leave them feeling poor and lacking in material wealth and other ways? One of the environmental causes that arose had to do with the county's physical location and its digital isolation, and how this led to a lack of access to a variety of different sources and types of information. As close as Bradford County is to New York State and some fairly large cities in northeastern Pennsylvania, like Scranton and Wilkes-Barre, the county lacks major highways, reliable cell phone service, reliable and inexpensive high-speed internet service, and independent news media. As I have described before, the county is an isolated place in northern Appalachia.

Having noticed this isolation early on, much of the previous studies I reviewed in planning my fieldwork in Bradford County looked at the lives of isolated rural communities in West Virginia, North Carolina, and Kentucky. There are similarities with these other rural Appalachian communities particularly when it comes to how people identify themselves, one another, and outsiders. For example, I learned that previous studies in Appalachia had shown that the deep sense of learned helplessness, victimization, and low self-esteem I was observing and documenting as I began conducting focus groups and more interviews throughout Bradford County was common across Appalachia and in other rural areas in the United States.

Could this be the source of these feelings of poverty and lack in Bradford County as well? Could these feelings of shame and fear, along with the mix of distrust yet hope in environmental regulators, and these legal threats from gas developers be at least some of the reasons why the person working at the County Conservation District did not think local people were concerned about the environmental risks posed by the gas developments?

Locals might not publicly express their concerns about the shale gas developments because they had not only mixed feelings, in terms of economic relief and environmental concern about the developments, but they also felt ashamed, fearful, unable to make a difference in the face of an industry that would go to such great lengths to deny their concerns and silence them if and when there were any problems. On top of what appeared to be a local epidemic of low self-esteem and lack of self-confidence, my phone conversation with Heather revealed that gas companies were putting gag orders into contractual agreements with local landowners and farmers. This was the very first time I had heard that.

On the other end of the phone line, Heather was silent. She had stopped crying. I felt responsible somehow and wanted to reassure her since I was the one who instigated this painful revelation. I had only met her once when she had graciously showed me around her immaculate barn and we had gone inside the kitchen of her home where she had expressed to me her excitement to participate in the project. At the time, she had especially seemed drawn to the idea that the project was going to be with women from other dairy farms, some of whom she knew, and some of whom she didn't. So, I took a deep breath and searched for the right words to comfort her while at the same time trying to keep my own shock and anger at what she had just told me in check.

"I understand why you cannot participate and why you feel it is not safe, particularly in a group setting," I told her.

And while I did not say it out loud, I also understood that recording an interview with her was probably not wise either, given what her lawyer had told her.

Instead, I offered that she could call me whenever she wanted and gave her my cell phone number. I also tried to reassure her that our conversations would always be confidential and her anonymity kept.

"Thank you," she replied.

And then, before we hung up, I asked her, "Would you mind if I contacted a lawyer about the non-disclosure agreement in your surface use agreement? I would not reveal your identity or even location, of course." I felt it was the least I could do. Plus, I wanted to know if such a non-disclosure clause in a surface use agreement would actually be able to hold up in a court of law.

"Of course you can ask your lawyer. I would be interested to know what they say. Thank you!"

I hung up the phone as the angry lump in my throat turned to hot tears in my eyes.

Selfishly I was certainly angry that the gas companies putting gag orders in landowners' agreements might mean the end to the type of participatory study I was attempting to organize in the County. But, what made my blood-boil was learning about the non-disclosure agreements. It confirmed that the gas industry would go to extraordinary lengths – using legal contract language and tactics in individual leases and agreements – to keep their secrets and silence anyone who might ask questions, have concerns, or witness any type of damage or contamination related to the shale gas developments. This was not one company, or one bad actor, such legal tactics were done with a team of people dead-set on keeping people quiet. Those silencing tactics coupled with the shame and low self-esteem I heard in Heather's voice and words shook me to my core long after that phone call.

If farmers in Bradford County already felt a sense of powerlessness when it came to the gas developments due to pre-existing feelings of low self-esteem, shame, and fear, what would this literal gagging of people's own experiences and their search for facts do to them? How would local people be able to find out that they shared the same concerns as their neighbors? How would they know that there were risks and hazards that needed to be addressed before gas developments should take place on their own land? And, what sort of developers would demand a farmer sign away their rights not only to their land, water, relationship to Nature and rural way of life, but also to their freedom of speech, safety, and security?

During and after that call with Heather the queasiness that overcame my stomach was very similar to what I had experienced ten years before when the government asked me to ignore environmental law I thought I had been hired to uphold. The nausea I had felt when I had instead written those permits allowing the oil and gas industry to continue their developments in the Gulf of Mexico. I have learned that this physiological response is a reflection of the sickness of systemic oppression, others might call it injustice, leaving me nauseous with disgust, but also anxiety. Bearing such witness time and again to local people being told they have no choice or agency and being silenced when it comes to economic and industrial developments in their community, I have grown impatient.

But, maybe this sick feeling in my belly wants to also teach me patience. Morning sickness perhaps? A prelude to deeper transformations in worldviews and ways to work together? This sinking feeling and nausea I feel in my own body most often occurs when those who I care for and love are being harmed in the most callous way by either other human beings in the name of money and greed and domination, or by the ravages of disease from addiction, mental illness, or cancer. I realized in the moment when I hung up the phone with Heather that I would need to revise my approach to how I would conduct and share my research in Bradford County.

What also began emerging in me was how to reconcile my previous complicity, as a federal scientist, in helping the oil and gas industry manipulate and re-write our nation's laws to remove protections for environment and public health. The weight of what I had taken on in working with people in Bradford County who were in some ways feeling the consequences of my failure to previously stand up for the common good and my own ethics was extremely heavy. I was not sure I could see it through, and I did not know what it all meant exactly. All I knew for sure after the phone call with Heather was that I would continue my work in the County as a witness. Bearing witness to the everyday, personal consequences of what happens when a nation secretly disregards its own laws to protect its citizens and Nature for the sake of individual greed, corporate return on investments, and our addiction to fossil fuels.

A month to the day that Heather and I had had that devastating phone call about her non-disclosure agreement, I visited her farm with Carol to see the new well pad that had been constructed next to one of their pastures in the past month. I told her that the landowner rights lawyer I had spoken to said she and her husband could probably fight the non-disclosure clause in the agreement if they wanted, and that it would most likely be inadmissible in a court. She still did not feel comfortable participating in my study, and I completely understood. Off the record, she shared more of her story with us. If anyone came to the farm and asked who I was, I was a cousin from the South named Samantha. We sat on a berm being built around the new well pad on their farm and Heather and Carol, who had known each other since they were young, reminisced about shared friendships and stories of their land and the county. It was a meaningful conversation and it was clear that Heather had accepted the changes happening on their farm land as a result of the new gas developments. It was also clear that the gas industry was permanently altering her relationship to her land. But, as I had watched her do many times, Carol told Heather she could call her if she wanted to talk about the gas developments going on around their farm. Because, as Carol said, even though Heather's relationship with her family's land was under threat and in the process of changing in unpredictable and potentially harmful ways, it should not mean that her relationship with other farmers, with her neighbors, and her community should also be threatened.

Perhaps another reason why outsiders thought that local people were not concerned about the risks of the shale gas developments was that by 2008 an estimated 90 percent of landowners in Bradford County had already leased their subsurface mineral rights to an oil and gas company. Many of these leases it is important to note were not a new thing but actually renewals of leases that had been in place for more than 30 years. Unlike some parts of western Pennsylvania and the United States where the coal, oil, and gas development rights have been severed from the surface rights, the majority of the mineral development rights in north-central Pennsylvania where Bradford County is located were still predominately owned by local farmers and landowners. In these arrangements, the gas companies were lessees of the subsurface mineral development rights and the surface owner legally maintained the right to control their property's surface uses as the lessor until they signed a separate legal agreement allowing companies to use the surface of the property. For as long as most people could remember there were just a little over one hundred scattered vertical wells with small two- to five- acre footprints, one major interstate pipeline, and a gas storage area in the county. The majority of landowners with subsurface mineral leases had never seen those leases activated for exploration or development nor did they know other landowners who had. So, as a result, without well pads, pipelines, or other facilities they had never been asked to sign surface use agreements, or to grant unfettered access to their lands to gas developers. That all began to change in 2008.

Up until then most of these landowners had simply used their lease signing bonuses, which had been five to ten dollars an acre every five years on average, to pay off some of their taxes or other annual expenses. Now that the new shale gas developers were offering them more money, though, many landowners, especially dairy farmers, saw this new development as equivalent to having someone come and offer to quarry a rock outcropping on an acre of your land and then using the proceeds to buy a new piece of farm equipment or pay off any debts. To these local landowners, shale gas development was a legitimate extractive use of their land. It is no surprise then that many local landowners saw themselves as business partners in these potential gas and oil developments for decades, thus Carol's belief that they should be thought of as just a business and Heather's belief that allowing their land to be used for gas developments would lead to economic relief for their family and farm. As mentioned earlier, the county, despite being rural, was not new to industrial and manufacturing activity. Bradford County has also had a long history of extractive industries like coal, lumber, and hard rock mining. Many landowner families came to the area to participate in such industries in the late-1800's and early 1900's. The extractive uses of Nature had been how many local people related to their land and water. This certainly contributed to the perceived lack of concern by local residents about the impacts on Nature from shale gas developments. But these new shale gas developments would take much more than an acre, or even several, of a farm and the developers would end up asking for unfettered access to surface rights and silence from landowners when something went wrong. This was different than any other type of business in the county.

That phone conversation with Heather, and especially listening to the later conversation between Heather and Carol about maintaining community relationships despite the changes and all the uncertainties about the gas developments, affected me greatly. These two moments mark for me the point in my work in Bradford County when I became committed to being more than just a researcher in this place. Although it has taken me years to accept, I began then to let go of any notions that I was just here to document, conduct a participatory project, and leave. From then on I saw my role in the county as a witness and accomplice in the liberation of these local landowners from the tyranny of a gas company's predatory behavior and from a nation's disregard for any kind of protective covenant with its people and Nature. While I did not necessarily share the extractive relationships with Nature these landowners had I also began to understand the important role they had played as caretakers and stewards of the county's forests, soils water, air, and rural way of life.

In the end, local people in the County were and are deeply concerned about the damage that shale gas developments have done to their county and their relationships to their land, family, water, neighbors, and community. But confounding those concerns are the underlying feelings of shame and fear among many locals, the continued empty promises of the extractive use values of shale gas to individual landowners, and the gas company's tactics of silencing landowners. These feelings, promises, and silencing have made it easier for the gas companies to develop and significantly alter the landscape and an entire rural community without any regard for the mutual interdependence of Nature and place, and the social ties of community that hold neighbors and their community together. Heather, her husband, their farm, their land, their water, and all the farmers and landowners and places I have grown to know and love in Bradford County are treated (if they are thought of at all) by the gas company executives, and political and economic proponents of shale gas, as a column of liabilities in their business ledgers.

The True Costs of Doing Business

Time after time those in local communities with the fewest resources and less wealth are those who end up bearing the brunt of not only the economic losses, but the hazards of environmental contamination and public health consequences as well. In Bradford County the deep oil and gas formations that were most attractive to the oil and gas developers were called the Marcellus and Utica Shale Plays.

As I learned more about what Carol had referred to as the business of onshore fossil fuel companies and their service contractors, I also learned that Bradford County was not an anomaly; most U.S. energy developments were located in rural, agricultural, and relatively poorer places. Public land in the Western states aside, the history of private land use in these rural places had led to little or no comprehensive land use planning or zoning, and the vast tracts of already cleared cropland and grazing land made these locations very attractive for the development of previously untapped and harder to reach deeper oil and gas rock formations. So much of this new energy development is planned in areas where we grow the majority of our current (and future) food supplies and in areas where our drinking water supplies originate from. If working farms and woodlands and watersheds are destroyed and displaced by oil derricks, gas wells, and fracking rigs who will feed us? Who will clean, replenish, and protect our drinking water?

Despite the geographic and geologic realities that place rural agricultural areas in the cross-hairs of fossil fuel developments, the U.S. government has never done a comprehensive analysis of the consequences of these developments – the increasing environmental, infrastructure, and public health burdens these developments place on rural and agricultural landowners, their families, communities, our food, or our drinking water[47]. These are what I refer to as the consequences to Nature and bodies and the consequences in minds and hearts and are what economists refer to as external costs or externalities. These costs have yet to be accounted for in national energy policies or analyzed in any environmental and social impact assessments of the fossil fuel developments into deeper, harder to reach shale rock formations using techniques like horizontal drilling and fracking. In fact, it is even worse than that.

For the past twenty years the U.S. government has allowed shale gas and oil companies to deduct all external costs as business expenses and write them off in the expected liabilities column. On top of this, these companies have also received government subsidies for these developments. The federal government, as well as state governments, have also streamlined permitting and risk assessments to ensure these companies would not have to be held responsible for such external costs as drinking water becoming contaminated, babies being born with birth defects, unexplained rare cancers, and entire neighborhoods falling into sinkholes.

Despite this lack of government interest, oversight, and willingness to hold gas and oil companies accountable for the real costs to rural communities, the past ten years have seen new social science and health researchers that have continued to document the everyday, real-life perspectives of rural families across the U.S. who live in the midst of these gas and oil development activities. This research has revealed disturbing trends related to the mounting external costs and the devastating losses that continue to affect rural communities and Nature[48].

According to applied anthropologists, rural sociologists, and community health practitioners in Pennsylvania, Colorado, Wyoming, Arkansas, West Virginia, and Texas, these rural people have lost land and water supplies and their rural way of life, and are sometimes suffering from debilitating physical and psychological illnesses as a result of living in close proximity to these industrial facilities. When shale oil and gas developments occur, the rural lands and waters that local people have lived, worked, worshiped, and recreated on –some for close to two hundred years, and in the case of indigenous communities thousands of years – are no longer under their control. Instead, domestic corporate, foreign, and multi-national corporate business interests assert their control of the land and water. These private interests disregard the renewable and infinite potentials of the plants, soils, groundwater aquifers, rivers, and streams, and the unique local knowledge dwelling in these rural places. Instead, oil and gas development interests are motivated solely by how to maximize short-term profits. They are focused on the costs of extracting what lies one thousand or more feet below ground, the costs of getting that subterranean resource to regional, national, and global markets, and the return that they can make on their initial investment as soon as possible.

In a cruel twist that only adds psychic trauma to the terror of rural community loss of land and livelihoods, the increasingly threatened rural way of life for these communities is portrayed as irrelevant, old fashioned, disposable, and backwards by local, state, and national governments, the global oil and gas industry, the news media, and urban culture. In place of this threatened rural way of life, both industry and government continue to make promises of economic opportunities and wealth for rural communities, whether from newly created jobs or newly tapped energy resources. This image of rural ways of life, and thus local people and communities, as poor and lacking continues to cloud the perceptions of outsiders and the general public. And, most critical to the work of facing change, resurrecting our communities, and transforming our world, these images of poverty and lack have also too often become the self-identity rural people and communities ascribe to themselves. They feel and judge themselves, their livelihoods, their communities, and even Nature as lacking and in poverty.

It is no wonder then that rural people across the U.S. who are living within these new oil and gas fields and along expanding transportation corridors along which the oil and gas must travel to reach manufacturing facilities, market hubs, and export terminals, have expressed acute feelings of anxiety, loss, homesickness, and helplessness as a result of the rapid changes they are experiencing. Even worse, the activist organizations whose stated missions are to improve the lives of people being impacted by different developments by advocating and legally fighting for better environmental and health safeguards also rely on economic myths by amplifying the stories of poverty and lack and harm to raise money for their advocacy and legal fights in the name of these poor rural communities.

The well heads and pipeline routes expanding across America's rural agricultural lands are only the most visible signs of a much deeper fracturing of rural communities that first began during World War II and that coincided with the turn away from whale oil, wood, and coal for our energy, manufacturing, and transportation needs towards more wide-spread use of gas and oil. These fractures have been deepened and proliferated, especially within the minds and souls of rural communities, by outside images of rural families in poverty and lacking in wealth, and rural ways of life as lacking in culture and in need of outside intervention. The interview I did with the daughter of one of the young men who was part of building the first paved roads in Bradford County to "get the farmers out of the dirt" comes to mind, as do so many other interviews, focus groups, hours of public meetings, and the thousands of pages of documents I stayed up all night reading. Somehow all these costs, all these consequences, must some day be accounted for.

Consequences to Nature and Bodies

By October 2011, 1,900 Marcellus shale gas wells had been drilled in Bradford County. As of July 2021, there were 1,442 Marcellus shale wells in the county owned by six separate gas companies that had the potential to actively produce natural gas and other products. According to monitoring reports from the county, each time a well is horizontal drilled and hydraulically fractured between three to five million gallons of water are required over a 24- to 48-hour period. In the second half of 2008, the Susquehanna River Basin Commission (SRBC)[49] saw an increase of over 200% in the number of applications for water withdrawals and consumptive water use permits as a result of all the new exploratory Marcellus gas wells being drilled within the Susquehanna watershed[50].

To meet the growing needs of the shale gas companies in Bradford County, the SRBC had permitted 33 water withdrawal locations in the county, the PA DEP had permitted the construction of 85 water impoundment ponds throughout the county, and as of April 2011, the gas companies had put in place 142 water pipelines to get fresh or recycled water from withdrawal locations and impoundment ponds to well sites throughout the county.

According to Pennsylvania's Water Rights Act of June 24, 1939 the PA DEP has the responsibility to protect every citizen's right and access to clean drinking water by reviewing applications for surface water withdrawals to ensure that new or expanded withdrawals: "Will not conflict with water rights held by any other public supplier, is reasonably necessary for the present purposes or future needs of the public supplier making the application, will not interfere with navigation, will not jeopardize public safety, and will not cause substantial injury to the Commonwealth."

All of this fresh water extracted from the Susquehanna River and its tributaries is then mixed with various chemicals and chemical compounds to create the hydraulic fracturing mixture that is used to fracture the shale and hold the fractures open to extract the gas[51]. Of those three to five million gallons of water used to drill and conduct initial hydraulic fracturing at a single well, between 10% and 30% returns to the surface as flowback. The remainder of the water remains underground for an indefinite period of time, with some of it coming up to the surface slowly over time as produced waters[52].

Due to their high concentrations of salts, heavy metals, and radioactive materials the flowback and produced waters are treated as "residual wastes" in Pennsylvania[53]. That means these contaminated waters required special handling in order to prevent the waste from ending up in the soil, surface, and ground waters and causing both short and long-term contamination. In a cytotoxicity study in 2015 that tested these flowback waters from Marcellus shale fracking in Pennsylvania, scientists found elevated levels of barium and strontium that malignantly transformed cells, formed tumors, and caused other alterations to healthy cell pathways in laboratory animals[54]. And, according to a review my Dickinson College students and I did of PA DEP violation reports from Bradford County between January 1, 2010 and October 29, 2010, 214 inspections resulted in 421 violations that included chemical spills, inadequate casing of wells, improper flowback (brine) pit construction, lack of proper sewer hook-ups, and uncontrolled erosion and sedimentation. These violations pose a substantial threat to the waters of Pennsylvania as well as the health of people living near or around areas where Marcellus shale developments are taking place.

Towards the end of 2009, a few advocacy groups and conservation organizations across the region were becoming more and more concerned that mishandling of residual waste, or contaminated waters, plus the large volumes of water consumed and chemicals used in the process of shale gas development would place increased pressure on the Susquehanna River basin's surface water and groundwater resources and cause increased conflicts with other human consumptive water uses and ecological services and functions of the larger Chesapeake Bay watershed. And, while spills and contaminated fields were turning up almost every day across the counties where shale gas developments were happening, there were at least two events between 2010 and 2011 in

Bradford County that confirmed all of our worst concerns.

The first event occurred in late August 2010 when a landowner noticed methane gas bubbling up along the western bank of the Susquehanna River in Bradford County at Sugar Run in Wilmot Township[55]. DEP found that the methane gas bubbling from the Susquehanna River was the result of Marcellus drilling two miles away[56]. The second event occurred on April 19, 2011 at a natural gas drilling site in Leroy Township when thousands of gallons of hydraulic fracturing chemicals and water blew back from a well at the Atgas well pad that was in the second stage of hydraulic fracturing. The chemicals flowed from the well head for more than twelve hours before being contained. Before they were contained the chemicals broke through the earthen berm containment, flowed into a freshwater pond, flowed onto fields where cows were grazing, and eventually flowed into Towanda Creek, a tributary of the Susquehanna River. Amphibians in a nearby pond were found dead after the release and surrounding drinking water wells were contaminated[57].

As I began spending more time in Bradford County throughout 2010, I met farmers who had some of the first shale gas wells drilled on their properties. One of these was Sherry's family. By the time I visited Sherry at her home, the dairy barn across the driveway from their home stood empty. They had sold all of their cows after the gas company had used their main pasturing area to construct a new gas well pad. The pasture area, and now industrial well pad, was located on a small hill above a creek right behind Sherry's house. She took me on a very short walk up the driveway to the pad and an already drilled gas well. As we stood on the well pad, she told me how she had seen the company dig a pit directly in the ground where they then put the waters and solids brought up while they drilled. After they were done drilling, she said, they covered the pit. As we walked around the pad site, I noticed the soil eroding down the hill into the creek. Back in her house, Sherry told me she had become accustomed to bottled water and quick showers after chemical fumes and explosive levels of methane were discovered in their drinking water after the gas company had come back to "clear a blockage" in the gas well. To demonstrate, she lit a match under the tap in her kitchen as she ran the water. Flames shot up.

These individual experiences of environmental and drinking water contamination in Bradford County were amplified by widespread appearance in 2010 and through 2011 of large plastic containers for holding water, called "water buffalos," on the sides of more and more homes throughout the county. These water buffalos were in some cases paid for by gas companies after the landowner complained of undrinkable well water or the PA DEP made a determination that the well water was contaminated by high levels of methane or other substances after drilling or fracturing of a nearby gas well. Still other landowners who could not get a determination from PA DEP but felt unsafe opening their faucets for fear of explosive methane levels entering their homes or other chemicals that may have seeped into their drinking or bathing water since they were now developing rashes after a hot shower paid for the water buffalos out of their own pockets or through charity organizations or donations that had been collected to assist families who had lost their drinking water in the area.

Like in Dimock in the county just to the east, there began to be deep conflicts in Bradford County over what the changes in people's water meant. Since Pennsylvania had never had regulations on private water well quality or strict standards on who can drill a private drinking water well, there was public uncertainty about whether the water contamination had been there all along. Did the drilling cause it? Did the fracking cause it? Did a spill cause it? Is it natural? The gas industry, and the government under lobbying pressure from the industry, exploited that uncertainty for their own purposes to deflect any concerns or even questions about the possibility that their gas developments might impact drinking water. All of the uncertainties, whether about water quality, emerging health concerns, or the amount someone's neighbor was paid by a gas company for an acre, in turn created uncertainties about the future, and individuals in the community began feeling fearful and anxious, whether they said they were for or against the new gas developments. But it was changes people were seeing, smelling, and tasting in their drinking water that seemed to be raising the loudest alarm bells.

The McMickens, Phillips, and Spencers, all young couples with small children during the start of the Bradford County gas developments, were some of the first people in Bradford County to experience how these uncertainties affect not only one's drinking water, but also your psychological and physical health, economic investments, social life, and future dreams. On March 24, 2011, Jared McMicken told a *Morning Times* reporter, "The whole thing is about us getting good water when this is done with. That would be the best we could wish for at this time." Jared's statement came a full eight months after the families had first noticed that their water was coming out of the tap muddy and discolored and they had contacted Pennsylvania DEP with a formal complaint and asked for water quality testing to look into the nature and source of the contamination.

The families suspected it had been caused by new shale gas wells drilled and fracked on a hill above their property, but because that gas well was farther away than either the State or gas company distance that triggered a pre-drill water quality test, their water wells had not been sampled prior to drilling. Even without that baseline water quality test, the DEP came and tested their water wells. And, in October 2010 the DEP issued a determination letter to all three families that stated those water quality test results did in fact show that their water wells had been contaminated by the gas drilling activity.

The Paradise Road families who lost their drinking water as a result of shale gas developments created a cause celébrè in local newspapers. Write-ups in Wyalusing's *Rocket-Courier* and Towanda's *Daily Review* newspapers, along with dramatic photos of the family's large modern homes with 100-gallon plastic water containers sitting on the front lawn, and the fact that they had small children and one of the women was pregnant, added to the drama and pulled at the heart-strings of other residents. And, it prompted the gas company that had been drilling above their land to issue repeated statements of denial.

The families sought to get compensation for their losses from the company through arbitration, as specified in each of their subsurface mineral rights leases with that company.

But the company denied that the water changes were due to their drilling activities and refused such arbitration. In fact, the company stated to the news media and in court documents that pre-drill water quality testing done throughout their company's operating areas in the Northern Tier by a DEP-certified independent laboratory had shown numerous issues with the local groundwater present before any drilling activity began. What the company left out of those statements was that such testing had not in fact been done on the Paradise Road drinking water wells prior to drilling. One outrageous statement of denial by a gas company representative laid blame for the contamination not on the gas drilling itself but on seismic activity in Canada.

When I finally had the opportunity to visit the Phillips family in March 2011, what struck me first was the difference between their home and the farmers' homes I had been visiting across Bradford County over the past year and a half. They were modern, spacious, and newly constructed. Mike Phillips worked as a teacher at the high school down by the Susquehanna River in Wyalusing. These were not farm families. They were living a suburban life in the country.

Mike told us he had personally spent several years building his beautiful log frame house with his buddies. He was so proud of that house. And, it was beautiful. Then he pointed to the little shed that matched the exterior of his home. That, he told us, was the water purification system that had been installed by the gas company after the state had determined their water well had been contaminated by the gas drilling and after they had unsuccessfully tried to locate and drill a new water well that would not be contaminated.

Apparently, he told us, all the groundwater around their home was now contaminated. So, while the gas company publicly denied they were responsible for any changes to their water well, they had also been drilling for new water wells and had installed a water purification system. One of the problems they had now, Mike and his wife, Jonna, explained was that their utility bills were through the roof, especially in the winter when they had to keep the water in the shed from freezing.

On that early Spring day when I finally had the chance to meet and listen to the Phillips family, they had already been publicly dismissed by the Oklahoma gas company that had developed shale gas wells above the ridge behind their homes; despite this dismissal, the company had also paid to install a water purification system on their home. They were frustrated and in despair about the dismissal of their concerns by the gas company, the lack of urgency and any long-term solutions to the restoration of their drinking water by the state government, as well as the overall failure by the state to protect any of the Paradise Road families and assist them in getting reparations from the company. They had also become well aware of the predatory machinations of local politicians and lawyers that were based on greed and power, despite the fact that a lawyer was helping them get some relief from the company that had caused the contamination. Mike said all of this had culminated in huge amounts of psychological stress, feelings of being all alone, and insomnia. He described this stress as feelings of helplessness, depression, anxiety, and constant worry. To make matters worse, the Phillips' young baby, who Jonna had been pregnant with at the time the water contamination began, had been born with a heart defect and was about to undergo heart surgery in the next month to save her life. The deep uncertainties about their own experiences with regards to why this happened and who was going to make it right, and the devastating loss of their dreams and their neighbors' dreams, and the fear of losing their child were all so overwhelming.

Not long after I met with the Phillips', they learned that the Court Petition to compel arbitration had failed in April, and they decided it best to settle for a monetary amount of $1.6 million instead of continuing to fight for the restoration of their water. Significantly, though, in their settlement the families demanded that they not have to sign a non-disclosure "toxic secrets" agreement that would have forbidden them from speaking about their experiences and the settlement. After the monetary settlement was reached all of the Paradise Road families packed up their belongings and left their homes. In 2012 the gas company that had destroyed their drinking water took over the deeds of all three homes and the surrounding acreage. Not long after purchase, the company proceeded to rip down the family home that Mike and his buddies had built with their own hands along with all the hopes and dreams that effort had manifested, and, as Mike wrote to me in 2020, "they put it all into a trash dumpster. The water could never be fixed."[58]

Consequences in Minds and Hearts

The tragedy for the Paradise Road families with the loss of their drinking water and health consequences to a newborn child were compounded by the other unseen and hidden impacts of the gas developments rapidly occurring across the

County. Traffic fatalities had increased. The County jail had filled to capacity. Homelessness had become an increasing problem as rents were skyrocketing, and long-time renters in Towanda were getting notices from their landlords to get out or pay up. Schools were seeing increasing numbers of students from families relocated as part of the gas developments enrolling in some of the county's schools. Even individual farmers and private property owners were alarmed to see the proliferation of neon flags on tree limbs, roadsides, and fields. More than one landowner I interviewed said they walked their land at least once a week to remove these brightly colored markers.

There was an exodus of public employees from various County departments, including the Sheriff's office and Conservation District, as they were offered higher wages by the gas industry and gas related contractors. At the annual 4-H livestock auction, a farm family purchased new dairy cows, as the highest bidder, after recently purchasing new milking equipment from the proceeds of their first several months of gas royalty checks. The shale gas developments had become the filters through which people in Bradford County interpreted and perceived the world around them, including one another. These changes were also generating great uncertainty and psychological and social consequences that began to alter the everyday lives of Bradford County landowners and their relationships with themselves and one another.

One such story illustrating the subtle yet profound ways that these social psychological consequences arose as a result of the changes being brought about by the shale gas developments comes from Sheila's experience returning from Oregon to her family's farm. Sheila described to me that when her father signed a subsurface and surface lease with a gas company out of Oklahoma for a Marcellus shale gas well and associated infrastructure to be developed on the family's property he did it for the good of his family, the future of his family's Century farm[59], and what her father believed to be his personal financial best interest. But, she said, it had all turned into a nightmare after the gas well was drilled and neighboring families living on the road where the gas well was located found their tap water turning black and producing a smell they said was "hard to describe."

When Sheila, who had started growing and selling organic vegetables from her family's land at a roadside farmstand, found out that there had been problems with the construction of the gas well she wondered, and worried, that the changes in their neighbors' water could be the result of the drilling of the gas wells on their farm. During an interview she told me through tears, "I mean even neighbors whose water wells have been contaminated by our gas well, they are so gracious. They don't even say anything. I would be so angry. I was worried about that. Like I started telling them, 'I am so sorry.' They said, 'You didn't do it. It's not your fault.' But I AM so sorry. Our families have generation-after-generation relationships."

Sheila's experience with shale gas development illustrates the ways personal and social anxiety, deep distrust, and feelings of guilt and harm had seeped into her relationships with neighbors, friends, and even family. It is indicative of how these personal and social consequences rippled through an entire neighborhood, town, and county to create widespread anxiety, distrust, guilt, and shame, and in some cases resulted in the breaking apart of social and family ties. However, as in all local communities impacted by rapid change not all individuals experienced these changes in the same way; even though sometimes they may even use the same words and language to describe their experiences.

For example, in 2010 the owner of the Red Rose Diner in downtown Towanda told me: "If these trucks were all painted green, you would think we were being invaded!" This man interpreted this "invasion" as an occupying force, and his personal response to that force was to try and sell his business, move from the county, and avoid confrontation. But others I spoke with who also called this an "invasion," interpreted it in quite different ways. They saw it as an opportunity to join the invasion and get a job in trucking. And, still others I spoke with interpreted it as an "invasion" to be overthrown by public protest or legal challenge. Perhaps one of the greatest sources of psychological, social, and political stress in the county seemed in 2010 and 2011 to be the continual and sometimes heated conflicts over what type of "invasion" the gas developments were, and therefore disagreement over what should be the appropriate local response to that invasion depending on whether one saw it as a conquering army, a friendly occupying force, or new job opportunities.

Like we already saw in the case of Heather, many had similar mixed feelings about what the gas wells meant in terms of the potential improvements to their land or farm and the risks to their land and water. This led to emotional stress and feelings of shame, anxiety, depression, and fear.

When such complex and contradictory perspectives about the gas developments were expressed in social and public ways without any outlets for asking questions, getting answers, or repairing the damage done, these individualized emotions began to be expressed as anxieties and fears about not just the gas developments but about a family's future or the county's collective future. Local newspaper coverage of the plight of the Paradise Road families and front-page images of water buffalos next to people's homes amplified and normalized these anxieties and fears.

Landowners I interviewed who were most enthusiastic about the gas developments and did not want to speak about any negative changes that could be happening, would still express to me in private their deep concerns about what the future held for themselves and the County since the gas industry had arrived. In my twelve years talking to people in the County I never met a 100 percent enthusiastic local landowner in a private setting. Even though someone was enthusiastic about the gas developments, they would still speak about losing their rural way of life or their attachment to their land because of the changes happening to their own or their neighbors' agricultural fields, their family cemetery, their water sources, and their favorite hunting spots. It seemed that one primary difference between the landowners who expressed higher levels of enthusiasm and the landowners who were more cautious or concerned about the developments was that those most enthusiastic believed that those feelings of uncertainty, fear, or sense of loss were necessary, and most likely temporary, "sacrifices" in the name of "progress."

One devout Christian man even expressed to me that he believed not developing the shale gas below the county was selfish because the entire nation needed more affordable, domestic sources of energy. This man said this was a sacrifice he was willing to make for the rest of the nation, and he thought others should also be willing to do the same. In a similar vein, another just as devout Christian man whose ancestors had worked in the early lumber camps of the County expressed to me that allowing the industry to develop his land was his "patriotic duty."

Like the extractive values towards Nature most landowners and farmers in Bradford County hold, these feelings of "sacrifice" for the nation and patriotic duty, are also deeply rooted in the social values, identity, and history of the County. Some of the first permanent settlers and founders of Bradford County were retired veterans of the American Revolutionary War and the War of 1812, and today, the majority of Bradford County residents have served or have family that have served in the U.S. military during wartime. Like poor rural families throughout the US, for such families with less means in Bradford County, military service was always seen as a way out of poverty and a path to economic stability.

A disturbing manipulation of this patriotism was the way the gas industry used the values, identities and histories tied to a family's military sacrifices and experiences to appeal to local peoples' sense of patriotism. When visiting County landowners to convince them to sign agreements for lease of their gas and oil rights, company representatives used this patriotic appeal to their full advantage by even telling hesitant lease signers, "Signing is the patriotic thing to do." In turn, these sacrificial and patriotic narratives were also invoked by family members, neighbors, and local and state politicians to justify the patriotism of signing a gas lease and emphasizing the positive aspects of leasing to themselves and one another. Some residents even used patriotic duty to pressure their neighbors, fellow church goers, and family members into cooperating more fully with the gas developments. Hearing about their neighbors' willingness to sacrifice for the nation reminded them of their own patriotic duty, and made some landowners I interviewed and observed believe that they had no choice but to agree to allow gas companies to explore and develop their own land and the rest of the county lest they be labeled as "un-American" or "unpatriotic." This is just one example of how social pressure operated among landowners to support the new gas developments despite the very real concerns about the threats and risks. Similar to the non-disclosure clauses or gag orders in individual landowner agreements, and much like the post-9/11 war on terrorism, this appeal to patriotism served as an extremely effective tool by gas developers, local officials, and other proponents of the gas developments to quell concerns and silence dissent.

By the end of 2010, just as the signs of people experiencing problems with their drinking water began to become more visible and public, there was a noticeable increase in these social pressure techniques as individual anxieties about the threats the gas developments posed to people's water and health rose. Various social persuasion arguments for the gas developments, whether appealing to patriotism, sacrifice, or economic opportunity, were all designed to deny any problems and get full compliance from local residents. Much of this was accomplished by making it socially unacceptable to refuse to allow a gas company to develop on your land or to even raise questions about the environmental health and safety of the gas developments. Such persuasion techniques and arguments pitted neighbor against neighbor, and even family member against family member. Importantly, though, this fracturing of neighborly relations and families was not typically played out in public, or even in lawsuits. It just festered under the surface. Until that is a gas company sought to discredit individuals in the County who had spoken out about their personal experiences of being negatively impacted by the gas developments, whether through chemical spills, declining health of humans and animals, private well water contamination, or financial misconduct.

In one of the more harrowing examples of how these pressure tactics operated to ensure compliance with the gas developments and to not question its safety, township elected officials, and not gas companies, became the enforcers by actively spreading rumors about residents' personal behaviors, violating state meeting laws, publicly supporting the gas company over their own community leaders, and creating deep fractures within the township with one side blaming the gas industry and township supervisors for threatening the community and ignoring landowner rights, and the other blaming an individual landowner for threatening the gas industry and standing in the way of progress and township business.

The landowner who was at the center of this conflict

was Bruce Kennedy. Bruce had held positions on the school board, was involved in the church, and his family had owned businesses and farmed in the township for five generations. He had signed leases and agreements with the gas companies and when I first met him in 2010. At that time, he was supportive of the industry's presence in the County. But then, during the spring of 2011, two separate chemical spills related to pipelines and pumps from the gas wells occurred on Bruce's land.

Both spills were dismissed by the gas company as insignificant and even as having "never happened." And, PA DEP, while they were initially involved in the investigation to the cause of the spills, did not follow through on doing soil testing to verify the extent of the spill or the substances involved. Perhaps what had angered Bruce the most, though, was that the gas companies had actually accused him of sabotaging their equipment and causing the spills in the first place.

When I met with him again in the late summer of 2011, he told me that he only had three words for the gas industry in Bradford County, what he called "the 3 D's": Deception, Desecration, Denial. It was the denial part he explained to me that had caused him to vent his disappointment and dismay by hand painting a blue, white, and black wooden prayer sign, lease the town square, and erect it there for all to see. The sign read:

DEAR GOD
Oh Lord, Please save Our Town.
I love my earthly home.

(1) 6" Pipline LEAK (1) DIESEL FUEL SPILL
(1) HYDRAULIC FLUID SPILL
(2) BROKEN HEARTS
HOME OF OUR GRANDCHILDREN
Please help, I ask in Jesus name.
Collins Rd – Okie Acres Farm – Bruce D. Kennedy

During an evening of despair and severe stress in June he had sought comfort by sitting next to his sign in the space he had paid the town to lease. As he was sitting there, five state police cars were called to the scene. He was handcuffed and taken to the County mental hospital for evaluation. After five days of in-patient care, and with no prior history of mental illness, Bruce was diagnosed with "bipolar disorder." After hearing about this, I consulted with a clinical psychologist and the Pennsylvania Mental Health Consumer Advocate and was advised that such a diagnosis sounds impossible in such a short time frame with no prior history, and that his unusual behavior previous to his arrest seemed to them a severe stress reaction, not a psychotic episode necessitating handcuffing and hospitalization. Nevertheless, the damage had been done to Bruce's reputation and credibility.

Then he received a bill in the mail for township road work related to the gas developments. The township was now claiming that he had threatened gas contract workers when they were using his land as a staging area for construction, thus preventing them from doing their work. The contractor doing the work had billed the township, so the township was simply passing along the bill to Bruce. Bruce decided to fight and dispute the township bill in public at a Smithfield Township meeting on August 2, 2011.

At this dramatic and heated township meeting at which gas company representatives lurked in the back of the room, and long simmering conflicts re-emerged to pit neighbor against neighbor, the room grew silent when James Wilcox, a visibly shaken Bradford County native, Bruce's son-in-law, and retired veterinarian came forward to defend Bruce. The gravity of his words captured not just the oppressive nature of this one terrible episode and the ways the gas developments were tearing apart this township and a man, they poignantly captured the social and community consequence being felt across the entire county:

"We don't need to kow-tow to this big business and let it run us out of the community that we've worked so long and hard to keep. And I just feel that there's been drastic injustice here for him to be charged for this roadwork. I think as a community we need to work together. We don't need to lower our standards for these big businesses that want to come in and dominate things on us. I think they can do this business they just need to do it right and we need to work together as a community to make sure they do it right."

Bruce and his family's experiences with the shale gas developers operating in their community make clear the difficulty in solely relying on economics to pinpoint exactly how shale gas developments impact local communities. Yes, there is an economic boom time and there are also economic busts. There are also clear environmental and public health consequences that one could put a monetary value on, I am sure. But the psychological and social costs of living through these economic booms and busts make such monetary evaluations not only less relevant but dehumanizing. People's psychological, physical, and community well-being, whether related to concerns about environmental contamination, local values, beliefs, and perceptions about their land and water, rural or urban livelihoods, or about their right-to-know about risks in order to make informed choices, should never be monetized. It is clear reading the sign Bruce Kennedy painted that his psychological distress was prompted not by loss of money or economic advantage, but by the damage the gas developments had caused on his family's land, which he described as breaking his heart and threatening his grandchildren's futures.

Solely economic evaluations of how developments impact and change local communities become even more dehumanizing when you consider the deep emotional attachments people have to their homes and certain places. In focus groups I hosted in Bradford County in 2010, farmers and landowners who were asked about how they were experiencing the rapid changes taking place on their land and in their homes, spoke about these place attachments in deeply emotional terms. Like Bruce, landowners in these focus groups expressed deep feelings of loss, fear of loss, and even a sense of impending death related to their experiences related to the new gas developments. In their stories of their land, homes, and special places throughout the County, group members called forth reminders of historical social and close family ties to land and certain places in the County. They talked about how these places were connected to their individual and social identities and values, how the threat of losing these places led to psychological fears and anxieties, and how they worried that this loss of place or home would also impact community togetherness and lead to irreparable disconnection between people and place.

These landowner conversations about place being threatened, or what one group described as invoking "Land Ghosts," revealed how the sense of place people experienced with the County was not only about specific locations but was also "deeply rooted" in memory and expectations around the past, the present, and even the future. Continuing dialogues in these groups involved their need to not only acknowledge but also reckon with these "land ghosts", or ghosts of place, before they felt able to face the rapid changes they were experiencing. The lesson for all of us perhaps is that we must first welcome these ghosts of place, and admit how they haunt us, when we are in conversations about economic and industrial developments before we can act to protect our communities from the negative and existential crises that can be brought about by the rapid changes that can precipitate from such developments.

* * *

These exemplary stories of how shale gas developments have brought rapid changes to families in the town of Dimock, and to the lives of Heather, Carol, Claude, the families on Paradise Road, Sheila, Bruce, and countless others in this one rural Pennsylvania County begin to fill in the outlines of how everyday lives are fractured by complex and overlapping environmental, cultural, psychological, social, and family consequences. The rapid changes in land development patterns, water quality, air quality, health concerns, alongside the psychological and social pressures to act as the developers and neighbors want, and the serial denials and failures of companies, governments and elected officials to address local concerns and threats, and even answer basic questions, related to shale gas developments have, at least in the case of Bradford County, led to a series of events that have left people with more questions than answers and deeply suspicious and fearful. The questions, suspicions, and fears relate to how the government and economy functions, what the future will be like, and the very meanings of land, water, air, health, home, and community. Such lingering questions amplify uncertainties and make it difficult for any of us to face change and begin to imagine a future that honors and commits to protecting our community's interests before development's interests. So, what do we do to decrease the uncertainties, find some answers so that we can face change, resurrect our communities, and transform the world together?

Bruce's son-in-law bravely spoke to this truth as he stood before his township neighbors, elected officials, and gas developers: "we need to work together as a community to make sure they do it right." But, why in the first place do they "do it wrong"? Why do developers continue to cause harm and oppression in communities? And, why is this fight even necessary? Why do "we" find it so hard to come together as community? In the next chapter we are going to dive deeper into some of the root causes that explain why and how developers of all kinds actively work against the liberation and self-determination of communities. This chapter will equip us with the critical tools and supplies we will need for the rest of our journey.

These tools include critical awareness and consciousness of how the current systems of oppression we all live within operate. We will recognize how many times our own behavioral and thinking patterns are implicated in these systems that are enabling economic and industrial developments to keep us un-free in the first place. Once we recognize these patterns, we can begin to see how such systems are created and maintained by the very same relationships that keep developers and our communities in constant struggle against one another and that this is what prevents us from cultural synthesis and true transformation. This critical consciousness and awareness of root causes and our own complicity in them is one of the most important tools we can take with us on the journey. In many cases, acceptance of this reality will allow us to face change, re learn the world, and, as Bruce's son-in-law said, "work together as community to make sure they do it right."

3. ROOT CAUSES

We have seen just some of the unhealed surface wounds and fractures at the individual and community level that are further infected by rapid changes from one particular type of economic and industrial development, shale gas, in one particular type of place, a rural and relatively poor Pennsylvania county. In the worst circumstances, if left untreated, these infected and inflamed wounds and fractures may metastasize into widespread community disruptions and deeper dissatisfactions that can in turn lead to political power struggles and violence. But what are the forces that allow such changes that lead to endangerment of people's homes, livelihoods, family and social relations, health and well-being, and relationships with Nature in the first place? What keeps communities and individuals when they are facing these rapid changes at the same time and space separated in their struggles to protect and improve their quality of life? What prevents people from working together or staying together to stop or remedy threats to their well-being and Nature? What are the causes of separation from each other, from ourselves, and from Nature? In the quest for the answers to all of these questions we are laying the foundation for practicing critical consciousness and the recognition of systemic oppression and inequities, as well as making a case for the broader, and sometimes much more difficult work, of cultural synthesis.

By the time we arrive at some of the answers, we will start to see the faint outlines of the work ahead—to relearn the world, to transform ourselves, to rebuild and resurrect community, and to commit ourselves to love in action for the common good and liberation of all. In the end, we will be guided by our collective imaginations to fill in those outlines, but not necessarily always staying within the lines. This exercise of our imaginations will change us permanently, and for the good.

To better understand why and how rapid changes brought about by economic and industrial developments negatively disrupt peoples' lives and their sense of well-being, this chapter briefly explores how global and regional capital markets (i.e., global capitalism and the Industrial Growth Society[60]) operate to extract resources from and exploit communities, and promote and demand individual values and monetary transactions over communal values and reciprocal exchanges. In our search for understanding, we will also look at how science and economics has framed the "curses" of abundant local resources and Nature when it comes to communal values and how this leads to our dis-association not only from Nature, but from one another, and therefore to relinquish the power and strength of these communal values and inter-relationships. This "curse" framing is part of how the choice of language and the words used to describe developments and the disruptions they cause create and maintain oppression mindsets that perpetuate duality, victimhood, deficit, and lack, and keep us all trapped in systems of dependency and oppression rather than autonomy and freedom. And, finally I will guide us back to why we are taking a closer look at these root causes in the first place — our individual and collective liberation from systems of oppression – through a reminder of how remaining connected to, or reconnecting with, local places, recognizing and fully articulating our senses of place and home, and honoring, and demanding that others honor, the mutual reciprocity and interdependence we all share with Nature, is essential to the work of dismantling structural oppression.

The (Ill)Logic of Global Capitalism

Whether urban or rural, there are certain characteristics that all economic and industrial developments, especially in the U.S., have in common in the way that they are promoted and maintained today. Chief among these characteristics is an uncritical and blind acceptance in the superiority of global capital markets and the techno-bureaucratic policy systems and processes of Western science and "reason" that governs them, what I will refer to as the *ill-logic of global capitalism*: the most dangerous epidemic not only our human species, but all life on Earth, has ever faced.

This sick logic, whether it began as and continues to operate to uphold patriarchy, religious dominionism, or manifest destiny, has morphed into a global financial and political system that has led to the complete disregard for the inter-connectivity between Nature and human life and thus neglect of the welfare of all life. The result is the denial (sometimes subtle, sometimes forceful) of reciprocal and generative forms of exchange and communal values. This is the rotten heart that made me feel nausea and repulsion against my own identity so acutely during that technical transfer meeting in Seattle and all the shame and anger I felt when I realized that Western science, bureaucracy, and my own mind-set had stood for oil and gas development interests in the Arctic and not for the knowledge, values, sovereignty, and well-being of Indigenous communities in the Arctic and the inter-relationships with Nature that their culture embodies. A decade later, this sickness is the impetus behind the urgency I felt in Bradford County, Pennsylvania that local voices – not my voice, expert voices, or celebrity voices – be the ones to demand to know why their water was being destroyed and their children were getting sick.

Such sickening characteristics of economic and industrial developments are present regardless of where one falls on the political spectrum in the United States. All of the dominant and powerful political ideologies in the U.S. today have bought into the mythology that global capitalism is a "tide that lifts all boats." In fact, this "tide" of global capitalism is more like a tsunami that smashes all boats into toothpicks (except those who are able to buy super-yachts) killing all life in its path. The tsunami of capital flattens, maims, perverts, destroys, and drowns ourselves, those unique local places, the stories of resistance and freedom, and all the different forms of social, political, economic, cultural, and spiritual life-ways and philosophies in order to wipe the Earth clean of all that is dear and precious in our lives and continue the march towards "progress" at any cost. As Sonali Deraniyagala wrote in her devastating memoir, *Wave*, detailing her anguish and deep grief after she survived the 2004 tsunami on the southern coast of Sri Lanka while it killed her husband, both of her young boys, and her mother and father:

"I suspect that I can only stay steady as I traverse this world that's empty of my family when I admit the reality of them, and me. For I am without them, as much as I am on my own. And when I hold back this truth, I am cut loose, adrift, hazy about my identity. Who am I now?"[61]

This metaphor will seem all the more apt as we delve in later chapters into what it feels to face change head-on, the disorientation and disembodiment of loss, and the endlessness of grief.

One example of this ill-logic and the propaganda of rising tides lifting all boats can be found by taking a critical look at the urban and suburban planning concepts of "Smart Growth" and "New Urbanism." The very power of these development concepts is in their ordinariness. In their mundane character they make integration of capitalistic concepts into everyday realities seamless, more readily acceptable for those with wealth and access, until they seem to become preferable to everyone who can gain access. The two development concepts of "Smart Growth" and "New Urbanism," although their legacies are somewhat different, have been used to describe a way of designing, planning, and constructing residential and retail development projects whose broad and amorphous goals claim to make cities and suburbs more "livable."[62]

When I moved to the Washington, DC suburbs of Maryland as a 27-year-old starting a new job in the federal government my then-husband and I purchased a not-yet-built townhouse in one of these developments, a pair of New Urbanism Towns called Kentlands-Lakelands, in Maryland. To home-buyers, one of the main draws to these developments is the mixed retail-residential uses that allow you to walk or use public transit from your house, instead of having to get in your automobile to commute or run errands. As a result, many of these developments, like Kentlands, offer more sidewalks and walking paths, easier access to public transit, and attempt to convey a "small town" urban feel. One of the marketing hooks used by both New Urbanism and Smart Growth developments towards middle and upper middle-class individuals and families is improved well-being through things like better work-life balance and shorter commute times. Obviously, the main audience for this marketing are those who can already afford this all in the first place.

While we did not move into Kentlands until 2001, these planned developments had already been underway in the rural outskirts of many East and West Coast cities since the late 1990's. In the dim lights before and the blinking lights right after 9/11 there were renewed concerns about public safety and failing transportation and social service infrastructures. These concerns mixed with larger global and economic forces (i.e., the war on terrorism, global capitalism, relaxed lending policies, and neo-liberal trade agreements) and previous decades of racist housing and zoning policies and dis-investments in city neighborhoods and local communities translated into mounting fears and anxieties among middle to upper middle-class residents related to "unsafe neighborhoods," "blighted properties," "crime," and "decreasing property values." Many times, as it has been throughout the U.S. history of housing policy, these fears and anxieties fall along racial, ethnic, or religious lines, and are dog whistles for segregation.

Ironically, the global economic forces playing havoc on local economies and livelihoods (alongside shifting age demographics) in rural places across the country have turned out to be an enormous bonanza for real estate developers. Formerly productive farm and timberland, especially in the Eastern half of the U.S., by the late 1990's had already failed or was beginning to fail to be a viable source of income for small agricultural producers. The globalization of agricultural commodities alongside the centralization, mechanization, and privatization of processing facilities, increased corporate monopolies on seeds, herbicides, pesticides, and fertilizers, and a whole host of government health, safety, and environmental regulations had made it easier and easier for large private corporations to dictate the how, where, and who of farming in the United States. This centralization also meant smaller, local, many times family-run agricultural businesses could not compete with the larger corporate-run operations leaving smaller sized family-run farms and cooperatives no longer able to break even. More and more local family farmland less than fifty miles from the center of Washington, DC was no longer plowed, planted, and harvested, and left large tracts of agricultural land in this region either up for sale or one phone call away from the auction block.

This real estate development opportunity also was a win for municipal leaders and city planners. It got them off the hot seat to immediately address infrastructure failures, racist housing and zoning policies, and dis-investments in urban neighborhoods and communities while at the same time adding new property to County tax rolls. These new real estate developments would allow for those relatively wealthy, upwardly mobile, dissatisfied residents to move into their New Urban and Smart communities and live happily ever after. As Levitt and Sons had done four decades prior in New York, New Jersey, and southeastern Pennsylvania, these real estate developers began developing and selling new towns and suburbs to families looking for "the better life."

When I look back at some of the sales and marketing materials for Kentlands, as well as other Smart Growth and New Urbanism developments, I see colorful images of neighbors and families interacting with one another in various dream-like peaceful settings – the playground, the coffee shop, the trails, the "main town" area, the community pool, private backyards, patios, and decks. On the surface all of these contemporary promotional images seem eerily reminiscent of the post-World War II era promotional photographs advertising the first planned suburban and urban residential developments built by Levitt and Sons in the 1950's and 1960's. Levittowns that sprung up along the East Coast also boasted shopping centers, sidewalks, backyards, schools, churches and synagogues, and various amenities for residents. Of course, in these earlier types of suburban developments the main focus was on automobiles, nuclear family life as defined as one man, one woman, and two or three children, separation of home life as the woman's domain from career life as the man's domain, and different forms of segregation based on skin color, gender, and even religion.

In contrast, Smart Growth and New Urbanism developments like Kentlands are focused on promoting public transit and mixing residential and retail uses and live-work spaces. Unfortunately, though, that's about as far as the differences go. Because while these new forms of urban, suburban, and exurban developments may be required to offer a variety of affordable housing options in order to meet local zoning requirements to secure permits or financial backing, the majority of them never fully commit to truly inclusive community standards or affordability over the long-term. In fact, the common use of developer tactics such as multiple builders, predatory lending practices, market exclusion, and zoning variances can dissuade or outright prevent ownership by people of color, same-sex couples, diverse families, religion, and any number of variables, including economics. So, segregation and exclusion remains a disturbing reality within these newer developments in 2024 despite the intentions of some urban planners. Real estate speculation, exclusionary and undemocratic zoning processes and policies, and sky-rocketing land prices in the United States continue to inflate costs and create barriers to community access and home ownership. This continues to result in gentrification, racial and economic exclusion, and lack of safe and affordable housing within and between urban, suburban, and rural areas.

Despite the progressively named concept, Smart Growth in practice has become just another economic development project that has figured out how to make a return on their investments by diversifying and updating their audiences, as well as using promises and appeals to improving social and environmental welfare to more quickly and easily secure local permits, zoning variances, and government grants. Re-branding or re-naming economic developments can only hide for so long the predatory nature of capital markets and the techno-bureaucratic system of laws and policies that perpetuate destruction of people and Nature, and the inter-connectivity of all life. These developments do nothing to address inequalities and injustices in our local communities, protect Nature, or challenge systemic oppression.

I saw further evidence of this during time I spent living along south Boston's Neponset River. The way the developers and proponents of "Smart Growth" and "community development" in Boston treated local neighborhood residents at community meetings and the false promises they made about equality and inclusivity offer real-world examples of how the ill-logic of global capitalism can threaten people's sense of autonomy and self-determination, as well as create an atmosphere of distrust. While attending one of the 2008 local neighborhood "visioning" sessions facilitated by a local design firm about the development of a "Smart Growth" development touted as a residential/retail/entertainment/transportation hub in the traditionally working-class South Boston neighborhood of Hyde Park, one older resident told me during a break-out session, "Seems like they already know what they want to do. I don't know why they are wasting our time pretending they want our input now."

It was clear to her that the hosts of the meeting, a community development corporation and the City of Boston's Department of Neighborhood Development, had already made their decision to build the development in the way they wanted regardless of what she or any local residents felt about it or had to say. The meetings, instead of truly being a chance for residents to voice their concerns and alternatives, were instead an effort to sell the development plans to residents and get after-the-fact "buy-in." Even worse, the meetings had been advertised and staged to appear as if all local residents would have a voice in what was going to be developed and how. But when we arrived at the meeting site they did not allow for the kind of collaborative "visioning" that local people attending had expected. This led to greater distrust among local community residents of these sorts of economic developments and even fear of losing the neighborhood quality they treasured. Residents with very legitimate concerns about how the project would impact the Neponset River, how it would impact those residents on low or fixed income, and how it might change the entire neighborhood's overall quality of life and character were not given any meaningful chance to imagine together another alternative or even give their consent for the development in the first place.

In living in one of these real estate developments as it was being built I remember there were always promises being made and broken. Most notably in Kentlands those promises included more live-work opportunities in order to reduce the carbon footprint and life disruptions of big city transportation burdens, lower cost housing options in order to reduce the displacement of local communities, and setting aside more green space as parkland and nature trails. But, after living there two years most people still commuted to work, there were still more and more cars on the highway, low or fixed income residents were unable to afford to live there, and the majority of "parkland" or "green area" that had been set aside for natural areas and nature trails had become new single family homes, another police substation, or fenced tree-less playgrounds.

Late "buy-in," broken promises, lack of community consent does not matter, though, beside the unstoppable sick logic of these developments driven by quick capital return on private investment, County revenues, monetary accumulation, and the safety and security of certain types of people. And, what should trouble anyone reading this the most, is the blinders we all wear, especially those of us who fashion ourselves as progressive-minded or conscious, as to the blasé and shrugged shoulders with which we accept these developments. So many of us and our friends and neighbors are implicated in these development schemes too: the local farm families who were looking to unload a tax burden or pay off bank loans and other debts, the real estate developers seizing the control of the land and the money, the new college graduates, families, and small business owner seeking to buy a new home or retail establishment in a safe, convenient, or "respectable" location, and the local school board, soup kitchens, and social services that may see expanded funding as property tax revenues go up. These developments are only enabled by our current systems of taxation, banking, housing segregation, and infrastructure failures. Without addressing these underlying systems, without meaningful input and local consent prior to planning of such development projects, and without the inclusion of a diversity of thoughts and different local life-ways, these economic developments flatten and erase the complex values and meanings of local neighborhoods, communities, places, and Nature. Until those things are addressed, the cold, inhumane ill-logic of capital, even when it touts "livability" and "progress," will win out against diversity, equity, and just ways of living and finding meaning in common values and Nature.

The dominance of the ill-logic of global capitalism is emboldened and strengthened by its political ideology, neoliberalism. Neoliberalism, broadly defined as a reliance on financial market forces, deregulation, corporate control, and increased global trade, successfully cloaks itself in progressive or friendly-sounding language like "Smart Growth" or in the case of shale gas developments, "Clean Energy" and "Bridge Fuel." Neoliberalism relies on global financial authoritarianism and cruelty against those who ask too many questions of those in power, who take action for those in need, stand up for communities on the margins, and who work towards solidarity and common well-being for all people. Neoliberalism is a threat to democracy[63]. But since the late 1970's neoliberal ideology has been the mindset on both the Left and Right of the U.S. political spectrums that deludes and anesthetizes any systemic critique just enough for capitalism's tsunami to flatten diverse local communities, cultures, and Nature across great stretches of the U.S., all the while making us think it is in our best interests. Now, over twenty years into the 21st Century, this ideology is infiltrating our daily lives in ever more unprecedented and frightening ways. The proliferation of on-line marketing platforms and social media applications uploaded onto our hand-held cellular phones that we carry on our bodies everywhere we go means the in-humane logic of capital markets, monetization, and techno-bureaucracies not only travels with us wherever we go but seems to increasingly intervene in our daily lives via Artificial Intelligence-enabled social media notifications and global positioning. These AI devices and technologies fully engulf not only our minds, behaviors, and decision-making, but our physiology and entire histories and life ways as well. Neoliberal thinking and capitalism increasingly define our relationships with ourselves, one another, and Nature, as well as with the past, the present, and the future.

As personal life lessons have taught me, we cannot ever truly run away from our fears or our grief. We must admit to them and face them. We need to make preparations to seek higher ground, develop contingency plans, and learn to see the world in different and new ways if we are to survive against this tsunami of global capitalism and its ugly political mind-worm — neoliberalism. As these forces continue to flatten our local communities, destroy unique and interconnected forms of life, contaminate our bodies, and devastate our psyches and social relationships, we must resist the numbing and shock and become even more conscious of the rising waters. In order to survive and rebuild we must set aside our ego-mind, our need to control and understand what scares us, our need to feel comforted and entertained and distracted, and instead be ready to reach out to others across our fears and anxieties and work together. To do this mindfully, we must also recognize and be attentive to the loss and grief within ourselves and others that will be an inevitable part of this journey. We must find ways to construct ships that will not just lift everyone but be spacious enough for everyone to participate in charting the course towards our individual and collective liberation.

Resource Curses and the Common Good

When people tell stories about losing their drinking water, whether in Pennsylvania, West Virginia, Michigan, or

Mississippi we all need to listen more closely. Then we need to act. No matter how painful, it is critically important to listen first, and not turn away or think that someone else will swoop in and fix it if we send in our donation to this or that charity organization. This active listening allows us to better understand the losses being experienced. Witnessing gives us deeper insights into what happens in the social, cultural, and psychological lives of individuals and communities when local people realize they have lost something that they for so long have taken for granted. Once we begin to truly listen and witness these losses, we will become conscious enough to realize what we need to do to act together for the common good.

When people lose their water they want answers. How will I afford to buy bottled water? How will I wash my kids' laundry? How will we bathe? Who will pay for my child's medical bills? How could this have happened? Who is responsible? These questions can lead to socio-cultural and psychological shifts that amount to an existential shift in people's relationships with the material world, qualities of life, and social, political, and economic systems. These questions raise a wide range of emotions: outrage, anger, denial, depression, helplessness, fear. They also lead to various direct and indirect actions: lawsuits, national news coverage, criminal investigations, boycotts, film documentaries, podcasts, social media campaigns, legislation, policies, research projects. In some cases, though, these questions can also lead to something deeper – existential shifts that then lead to a greater conscious awareness of the most essential things in life. An awareness of how individual actions, whether those of oneself or others, affect "common goods," like water, and what we, as individuals and communities, can do to prevent anyone else from ever losing their drinking water again.

The classical concept of "the common good," as expounded upon by political philosophers across the centuries, from Aristotle to Rousseau, focuses on that which benefits society as a whole rather than the private good in which only individuals or certain sections of society benefit. This early philosophical idea of the common good is a precursor to the concept of "common-pool resources" or "public goods," as used by ecologists and economists throughout the late 20th and early 21st Centuries. Under the spell of the ill-logic of global capital and financial markets economists have used the concept to monetize, commodify, privatize, and colonize certain communities and Nature, giving us such benign-sounding phrases as "ecosystem services."

In their 2010 political ecology and ecological economics thesis, *Recovering the Commons: Democracy, Place, and Global Justice*, Herbert Reid and Betsy Taylor offer a bold analysis of how mainstream Western politics, through capitalism and neoliberalism, continue to enable the destruction of local culture and community connections and thus operate to erode or eliminate the commons altogether. I identified this process of commons elimination and erosion in action when I interviewed and observed scientists, local residents, school teachers, environmental and social activists, politicians, and others during my doctoral research looking at the restoration of the lower Neponset River in Boston. To the dismay of some of my academic advisers from the natural resource disciplines, this critical, cultural, and humanistic research about the practice of restoration ecology and the study of ecosystem services concluded that barriers to progress on the Neponset River's restoration and protection had not been due to lack of money or resources or because local people did not care about the environment or did not understand the science. Rather, the largest barriers to the river's restoration and protection involved the very planning processes and systems that the scientists, experts, various environmental organizations, and local governments had actively created and maintained; processes and systems that did not allow all local residents to meaningfully participate in restoration or protection of the river. This meant that those studying and planning for the river's restoration were either not aware of, did not think important, or were actively hiding the full diversity of histories and experiences that neighborhood residents had with the river as an important personal and cultural space, and as Nature. There was no way for local residents lacking wealth, political connection, or membership in an organization involved with the Neponset River, residents who many times had different knowledge of and personal relationships with the river and its lands, to have their perspectives heard and incorporated into planning. The river's restoration and protection, rather than being treated as an effort to restore and protect a local community commons, was instead treated as a "research," "clean-up," or "development" project that was being directed and planned through public-private partnerships with non-local consultants and that had become just another line item in the government's budget, a grant project, a blighted property campaign, or a potential real estate amenity.

With this focus on private interests (both local and non-local) and financial concerns, there had been no regard for the historic, personal, and cultural significance of the river and its lands as a personal refuge or community commons[64].

Related to this idea of the common good, or public commons, is the concept of "tragedy of the commons" or "resource curse."[65] Much of the scholarship around these concepts is written about how natural resources are treated in a market economy. For example, the tragedy of the commons, based on European economic models of human behavior, says that humans will always act independently and rationally without consideration for the long-term best interests of society. This, the logic goes, makes the commons, common-pool natural resources, or public goods more susceptible to over-exploitation and depletion. According to this way of thinking, economists use their logical assessment of human behavior to determine that if we put a dollar value on these common goods and call them "services" the profit motive will act to protect them from over-exploitation. However, in the real world, unlike these hyper-rational economic models of human behavior, we humans are in fact complex, relational, and irrational, and concepts such as "tragedy of the commons" mislead us into some inhumane world where "survival of the fittest," rather than the humane pro-evolutionary qualities of reciprocity, sharing, and community well-being, is the driving motivator behind all human behavior for the past millennia. As Noam Chomsky posited in his Dewey Lecture at Columbia University on December 6, 2013, *What is the Common Good?*: "a concern for the common good should impel us to find ways to cultivate human development in its richest diversity."

As Chomsky asserts, in contradiction to the tragedy of the commons story-line, concern for the common good is a value that should be a guide in finding our way out of global capital's devastation towards cultivation of human diversity and richness. However, in part due to the strangle-hold that this "tragedy of the commons" myth and ill-logic of global capitalism has had for over 40 years on the U.S. economic and political system, what I found during my ethnographic research in the shale gas fields of Pennsylvania is that the inherent values held within the common good was a rarity in the minds of average citizens. As a matter of fact, today in the U.S. a concern for the common good, as Chomsky describes it, is not at all common. Sadly, bearing this out is scientific evidence from experimental and ethnographic studies that show pro-social or cooperative behavior is a much more common characteristic outside of the U.S. and other Western, industrial, so-called democratic societies[66].

Many times, when documenting landowner expectations, responses, and decisions related to the development of shale gas in Bradford County, individual gains or losses, particularly personal monetary and financial, were described as the first and only considerations. There are many reasons behind this, not least of which are the current political and economic conditions brought on by the fall-out of global capitalism on agricultural livelihoods and communities mentioned previously in the context of Smart Growth developments outside Washington, DC. But, instead of new townhomes replacing farms, we find shale gas facilities and related infrastructure replacing farms. Small family dairy farmers who are no longer able to make an income because they have to pay more to get their product to market than they make in their monthly milk check, may be forced to sign an easement to their land for a gas well, water impoundment pond, compressor station, or pipeline just to pay their taxes or monthly household bills. These individual - some would say survival - decisions combined with the oil and gas industry's targeted local propaganda campaigns that utilize the ill-logic of global capitalism and neoliberal ideology of individual profit accumulation while also ratcheting up economic, social, and political fears with calls for patriotic sacrifice makes a concept like "common good" blasphemous, no matter the psychological and cultural toll such decisions may have on families, local communities, and Nature.

But, what about those who lose their drinking water, whose cows get sick, or whose cropland becomes contaminated because of the individual decision of someone else? Personal existential shifts may lead to a greater consciousness with regards to how individual actions affect others and "common goods," like water. But, do we have time to wait for these individual, person by person, shifts in consciousness to play out? And, do we even have the stomach to see the suffering that will occur in the meantime? In fact, with the onslaught of global capital's insistence on logical human behavior, efficient markets, commodification of Nature, individual wealth accumulation, and calls to sacrifice and patriotic duty in places like Bradford County, it may take many thousands of these personal shifts in order to create a groundswell of recognition with regards to the values and intrinsic rights associated with common goods in order to reclaim and rebuild community values and galvanize local communities to work together for their common good.

Loss of Community Values

Despite the ill-logic of capitalism and the dominant self-motivated (as opposed to commons-motivated) focus regarding risks and rewards about industrial and economic developments that seem to have a stranglehold in places like Bradford County, it is even more moving and heart-warming to witness the existential shift that occurs when an individual's self-focused motivations quickly and dramatically change to being more of a concern for the commons and the common good. It is critical to understand that this shift does not happen without a great deal of uncertainty and negative consequences for individuals and entire communities. The very personal and sometimes heart-breaking realizations that what appears to be so good for one person or family can end up being so harmful to other people or an entire community bound together across generations can be seen in Sheila's words about her neighbors:

"I mean even neighbors whose wells have been contaminated by our well pad they are so gracious. They don't even say anything. I would be so angry. I was worried about that. Like I started telling them, 'I am so sorry.' They said, 'You didn't do it. It's not your fault.' But I AM so sorry. Our families have generation-after-generation relationships."

Could Sheila's words denote the beginning of a shift from individual and self-motivated decisions towards recognition of how those decisions impact the common good? Behind Sheila's despair could there be the flickering light of awareness about the richness of human development inherent in the common good? Do her words provide a passage out of the devastation on our community connections and flattening of the commons that the tsunami of capitalism brings? Could such intimate, personal, and devastating experiences of losing access to land and livelihood, anxiety at losing the trust of generational neighbors, fear of drinking water being destroyed, and collapse of any confidence and trust in a government to protect people and communities from the risks of the shale gas developments, somehow open doors in search of local, longer-term societal well-being? Could such new awareness of how individual actions are implicated in neighborly relations and community well-being lead to a broader societal and ecological consciousness about local-global connections between ecological, economic, and life processes of reproduction, production, and consumption, that motivate local efforts to revitalize community values and protect and preserve the commons?

I believe the answer to all these questions is, quite tragically, "yes." Tragic because if this is the only way for people to recognize the importance of community values and the commons it will take millions of Sheila's losing something so dear to them before such a shift in consciousness takes place; and, I weep at the thought of such staggering losses, the trauma, and the grief that will take place before this shift. But the reality, in what I have witnessed within front-line communities most impacted by rapid changes of different sorts, is that such losses and the existential shifts that precipitate from them are one of the surest paths to transformation from individualistic to more collective, community-centered, value systems.

My friend Carol in Bradford County is even more

SIMONA PERRY

pessimistic than I am. She believes people have lost their
sense of community values permanently and that even their
personal experiences of loss and grief will not lead to raising
peoples' consciousness enough for them to shift to a focus on
community values. At least, within the social networks she
knows best – small family dairy farmers— that is what she has
observed.

"Why is there not urgency for neighbors to help one
another?" she asked me during a phone call several years ago.

"No idea," I mumbled.

"In the past," she went on, "When a barn burnt it meant
that the community would rally around that tragedy and build
a new barn for the family that lost it. Today, though, when
a person loses their clean drinking water from their private
water well there is no community rallying around that person
to replace or fix their water."

"But what about the organizations and even individuals
doing water drives to get water to people who have lost their
drinking water?" I asked.

As she quickly pointed out, and rightly, those water
drives in Bradford County and other rural isolated areas of
Pennsylvania impacted by shale gas developments were more
often than not organized by people that did not live in the
local community, they were not locals nor neighbors of those
who lost their water. Many times the people, donations, and
organizations that raised the money and provided the water
were located in urban places like Binghamton, Manhattan,
Philadelphia, Pittsburgh, and Scranton. This, she said, proved
her point about her own social networks not rallying around
one another like they had in days past when someone's barn

burnt down.

On that same phone call we talked about the cases when alternatives to well water, like water buffaloes or advanced water filtration systems, had been supplied. But, in these cases, it is typically the gas companies that have supplied the systems after lawsuits (or threats of), a court order, or in some instances as an effort to keep a family quiet about their water problems. In none of these cases were local neighbors organizing or advocating for a new source of drinking water to be provided.

"Well, it wasn't for not trying," I reminded her.

Early on, in 2010, there were efforts by some in Bradford County (including Carol) to get more attention on the issue by attending and speaking on the water problems at County Commissioner meetings and by getting stories in the local newspaper. This community effort was swiftly silenced, though, with a bureaucratic change in how the County Commissioner meetings were run (limiting the number of people who could speak and the amount of time they had to speak) and by gas company donations and industry-related ad-buys in two of the primary local newspapers, the *Daily Review* and *Rocket Courier*. Carol conceded that they had tried, and it was true that some neighbors had been there, but she also reminded me that besides herself, the most vocal people in those meetings were all implants and outsiders or people who had traveled from outside the County to be there. Those fighting the hardest to fix the situation and get help for the community were outsiders, and not the people she considered to be her Bradford County neighbors.

In that same phone call, we also briefly touched on the

rare cases in Bradford County and rural Pennsylvania, when municipalities or private water suppliers talked about hooking up households with contaminated water to a municipally operated and managed water supply. But we both agreed that this last fix to people's water problems is certainly not a community-initiated and motivated solution. And, it may not be a fix that has the best interest or consent of the community. As Carol pointed out, when a municipal water supply is added it actually changes the entire relationship a household has with their water supply by making it a service that has to be paid for and that you then have to rely on others to provide. So, this intervention not only depends on government and outside help, it will also require that those who have lost their water, the very people who have felt loss and damage, now pay to have clean drinking water. For a dairy farm with forty to over one hundred cows, the costs would quickly become prohibitive. The idea of hooking up those who have lost their water to a municipal water supply is not the neighborly, community-initiated action that strengthens or reinforces community values. This will certainly not lead to systemic transformation of local community values, or move communities towards self-determination or resiliency.

As we saw in Chapter 2, in rural places where shale gas and oil developments are taking place and where most families rely on water from private drinking water wells, people have seen changes in their water quality that they have not seen in five, ten, or even fifty years. And, this is only one county in one state. Looking at loss of drinking water across the U.S. the picture is even dimmer. And, as Carol insisted in our phone call, in most of these places there is no locally-rooted community, neighborly effort that is consistently and effectively solving these existing and new water quality problems. Even where they exist, local government and state government efforts to assist communities and families have been fraught with corruption and legal delays. So, in the end, while ever so slowly there are shifts towards recovering and re-establishing community values, Carol is correct that in the case of clean drinking water for communities in the U.S., at least for now, these values are absent and do seem permanently lost.

Still, I do hold out hope in Bradford County, as I do for other communities like my hometown of Savannah, Georgia. Hope lives within individuals, like Carol, who are continuing to fight with all they have for their community, not hope in the sense that some outside human force will come and rescue all of us or intervene in this disaster. This hope reveals itself in the words of Bruce's son-in-law, who said during the East Smithfield Township meeting:

"I think as a community we need to work together. We don't need to lower our standards for these big businesses that want to come in and dominate things on us. I think they can do this business they just need to do it right and we need to work together as a community to make sure they do it right."

It is in that re-commitment to work together as local community where we may recover and resurrect community values and the processes necessary to arrive at what is best for the common good. At least it is a starting place.

The Words We Use

As a writer, I am obviously drawn to the words people

use to share their experiences with one another. And trained in the social sciences, I am also fascinated with what these words can tell us about how people internally process those experiences and how this in turn shapes their views of themselves and the world around them. For example, what can the words someone uses when I ask them about what they think about a new bike trail being built adjacent to their home along a local river tell me about how they identify themselves in relation to the place they live, to their neighbors, to recreational amenities, and to the river?

The words each of us use to describe an existing petrochemical plant, a new residential development, a shale gas well, or any place in our environment reveals our relationships and even our lived experiences with such developments and places. And, as many psychologists, philosophers, and even some of our parents have tried to teach us, there can be real-world consequences to the words we use; whether you are engaged in casual conversation with a neighbor on the opposite political spectrum as yourself, or whether you are lying in bed at 3 a.m. replaying some troubled interaction you had with a family member during the day.

For Pennsylvania's northeastern communities living with shale gas developments, when not paralyzed with uncertainty or fearful of loss, they most often use two words when describing how shale gas developments are impacting them: they are a "sacrifice" or they are an "opportunity." When they use the word sacrifice it is to say something like: "we have sacrificed our drinking water for the oil and gas industry to extract fossil fuels from our farm." When they use the word opportunity it is typically to deflect from the risks and negative consequences of the developments.

In the context of shale gas developments, the meaning local people ascribe to sacrifice varies. Some people describe it as a necessary sacrifice imbued with moralistic intent bigger than themselves (i.e., the martyr sacrifice), while others describe it as a psychological and physical injury to themselves, their family, or Nature (i.e., the victim sacrifice). But, regardless of the type of sacrifice, the mind-set of making a sacrifice or being a sacrifice within the ill-logic of global capitalism means that something is being done to make you or your family or your community or Nature give up something dear and precious in the name of profit or dominance or "progress." This is true even if you find some moral reasoning to justify why the sacrifice is necessary.

Certainly, making moralistic statements about losing their drinking water for "domestic energy independence" may help someone rationalize making a sacrifice or maybe even give them a sense of moral superiority under difficult circumstances. This is a form of cognitive dissonance that allows us all to experience some sort of short-term individual comfort. But, in the case of economic and industrial developments, whether shale gas or mixed-use residential or a new tourist attraction, the decision to give up their drinking water or access to Nature and affordable housing has not been theirs to make and therefore there really is no moral standing. No one chooses to give up their clean water, clean air, or health for undrinkable water, unbreathable air, nose bleeds, and cancer. This is what makes the use of the word "sacrifice" to describe these circumstances so deeply problematic, harmful, and violent. Using the word sacrifice to refer to economic and industrial developments turns individuals and communities into martyrs and victims and not only removes their choice to live or die, but also removes their individual and community self-determination and autonomy. Making sacrifices to satisfy global capital and monetization not only washes away diverse local knowledge, communal values, the common good, and our mutual interdependence with Nature it also threatens our very lives.

Another thing about words is that they always have a history. Could it be that the language of sacrifice (and the psychology that accompanies it) in Appalachian and rural places such as Bradford County, and many urban communities too, comes from lengthy pasts involving corporate and government land grabs, economic and social isolation, racial, ethnic, and gender segregation or subjugation, military service, and false dependencies in the name of economic progress, natural resource extraction, and certain types of livelihoods. Each one of these past uses of sacrifice was in the service of colonization, war, wealth accumulation, and global capital not local self-determination or locally-rooted community values and assets. While such isolation, segregation, and false dependencies have been documented, analyzed, and politicized in urban contexts, across most of the rural U.S. these histories remain under-analyzed, hidden, distorted, and unresolved.

We see this rural under-analysis and the distortions most obviously in the images and caricatures of rural people and communities portrayed in mass media, popular books, movies, and in conversation with urban outsiders when they portray rural people as lacking culture, being illiterate or uneducated, being unhealthy and addicted, and living in poverty with no resources or financial assets. These are very old stereotypes and still commonly used caricatures that have been used for generations, and have become part of the internalized self-identity and psychology of many living in rural places today.

One of the most profound realizations I had when I first began working in the northern Appalachian hills of Pennsylvania was the way people (especially children and young people) spoke with me that consistently made themselves out to be of low self-worth, lacking in self-esteem, and without any self-confidence. Such a sense of low worth and lack accompanied by a reverence to human authority or elected officials, to patriotism, to those who were more educated and those with more wealth and power, makes it easier to find the perfect sacrifice. This psychology of sacrifice makes it so much easier to lead lambs to slaughter. Such internalized lack among Bradford County locals had not just been cultivated and encouraged but was a necessary ingredient for feeding the ravenous beast of global capitalism.

While such psychologies of lack and past sacrifices cannot be undone and they leave permanent scars on individuals and communities, we can and must reconcile with the way in which these sacrifices were extracted, and then take actions to stop future sacrifices by re-framing. To reconcile with sacrifice means to understand that people have not always had choices or that the choices they may have had at one time have been taken away from them for another purpose. Most times the purpose of extracting sacrifice is in the individual interests of power and money that have nothing to do with the local community and are contrary to community values or local self-determination and autonomy. To change this historical trajectory and sacrifice narrative we must re-frame and re-center where the power to make choices and decisions comes from in the local community context. In practical terms, this means centering any talk of economic and industrial developments around informed consent, power sharing, respect for local community and Nature, and conscious community engagement.

To move beyond the word "sacrifice" means giving local people freedom to exercise choice and giving them the power to act on those choices without outside manipulation or propaganda. In social and health science, this is similar to what we refer to as informed consent. If you do not have consent from an individual you want to interview as part of your research study or medical trial, you do not ask that individual to "sacrifice" themselves for your research. We have numerous examples throughout the history of the world where such lack of consent has led to disastrous and deadly consequences for individuals and groups. Not obtaining informed consent is unethical and a violation of human rights. Industrial and economic development projects being allowed to carry on destroying human lives and Nature without such informed consent is also unethical and inhumane, and needs to be more boldly categorized as such.

Moving beyond "sacrifice" means identifying and recognizing the diversity of local knowledges, Nature, common goods, and community values and honoring and respecting the power they wield and should maintain – all with consent from local communities. This means respecting

Nature and local community knowledge and values as worth more to us protected and whole, rather than gambled away or auctioned off for coins in the global marketplace in the name of capitalism, political ideology, energy, technology, entertainment, individual accumulation of wealth or power, and endless wars. It also means that power to choose and to take action is shared and mutual, and not used as a way to extract sacrifices from a community or Nature. Eventually, once we expect and demand consent and shift the power dynamics away from individuals and the few towards community values, we can then move beyond sacrifice. Once this shift is actualized, there will be space for developing stronger social ties, recognizing local cultural, social, and Nature-based values as preferable to global market values, demanding that local values are never for sale to the highest bidder, taking care of those in our communities that cannot take care of themselves, building and supporting resilient individuals, families, communities, and Nature, and above all else, honoring our shared humanity and the inter-connectivity of all life.

As my parents always told me when I was growing up, words have real consequences; eventually we tell ourselves we are a sacrifice long enough and listen to others telling us that we are a sacrifice long enough, and we become a sacrifice. Or, more appropriately in the case of Bradford County and many other communities impacted by economic and industrial developments, we become victims without choices. And, let's be clear, most front-line communities impacted by industrial and economic developments *are* victims of techno-bureaucratic systems of governance that were intentionally designed to allow for efficient development and extraction of local resources, including labor, without any interference from independent and confident local people who are demanding that they have a choice and voice. So, one of our first practical steps in rebuilding, transforming, and protecting Nature, ourselves, and our communities is to stop using the word sacrifice and act against it in practical ways. Let's throw off the shackles of sacrifice to the ill-logic of capitalism and reclaim our voice, our power, our choices, and the strength and wisdom inherent within our local communities and Nature.

So, what about this word "opportunity?" Opportunity is typically the word used to downplay negative disruptions and any questions about the risks posed from shale gas developments. It's the "but" that follows all the negatives. In Bradford County, when someone begins talking about so-and-so losing their water, the farms with cows getting sick, the number of homeless sleeping under the bridge, the number of farms going out of business, the children with nose bleeds, there is inevitably someone who counters with "but what about the opportunities." What this phrase is referring to is the industry propaganda that with shale gas developments there would be more jobs and new businesses to enrich the local economy. We have little evidence that such jobs and businesses do in fact follow these energy developments or that they boost local economies[67]. We do have evidence of the water loss, sick cows, homelessness, farm losses, and childhood illnesses.

If we look up this word "opportunity" we will find that it is a synonym for "chance." Opportunity at the local level offers individual landowners, local businesses, local politicians, or perhaps a group of landowners a chance to gain wealth, pay off debts, or win a contract. But a chance is not a certainty, and like in poker or bingo, it all depends on the hand or the card you are dealt. It turns out those poker game vibes I felt so strongly during the pro-gas rally Laura and I attended in New York State were not just my over-active imagination. The shale gas developments had in fact turned out to be one long poker game, with only a few winners and many, many losers.

Now, don't get me wrong, there could be more wide-spread "opportunities" for entire local communities to raise their standards of living or to build stronger safety nets for their most vulnerable if wealth from gas developments stayed in local community coffers, but this could only happen if commitments were made to the common good and community values at the outset. Without commitment to focus the money from developments on reducing wealth inequalities, structural biases, and strengthening existing local social structures, local assets, local economies, and protecting Nature, the money flowing into local coffers only continues to serve individual wealth accumulation, centralize power further, and keep wealth in the hands of a few. It turns out that this community notion of "opportunity" is not exactly what politicians, local and state officials, state educators, academics, and oil and gas corporations are speaking about when they say shale gas has brought "opportunity" to rural Pennsylvania. What they mean is the chance to grow their own wealth based on encouraging individual competitiveness over collective good and in spite of the short and long-term risks and uncertainties involved[68].

Like my dad's poker games from my childhood, the opportunities offered by economic and industrial developments romanticize the inherent risk-taking aspect and the relatively short-term pay-off of such developments for the chance to be the big winner. Unlike my dad's poker games, not everyone can afford to even enter the huge stakes involved in these sorts of developments. Still, the allure of the chance to win seems to motivate those with the most to lose to go all in and ask for another hand to be dealt even though they could lose their water, their home, their children's inheritance, or their very life. People become addicted to this "opportunity" of winning and they will fight until the bitter end for their chance, even when the stakes can cost them their life. So, the next time someone makes a statement about all of the "opportunities" a new development offers to a local community remember they are actually talking about an addiction to opportunity and the life and death game of chance.

So, instead of using these two words, "sacrifice" and "opportunity," when thinking about economic and industrial developments, I suggest that we think instead about starting to use the word "possibility."[69] I especially like how Werner Erhard defines possibility as a declaration of what we create in the world each time we engage with the outside world. The word possibility, unlike sacrifice or opportunity, asks us to consciously engage and re-engage with the world, ourselves, and communities. In this way, "possibility" implies that threats and risks of any development project needs to first be assessed, local assets need to be recognized and appreciated, spaces and places for open community dialogue and dissent should be created, and that change must be faced head on. Casting these developments as "possibilities" sets out a framework for local consent, commitments to community values, and critical engagement with the short and long-term local consequences of developments. So, next time someone starts to tell you about all the "sacrifices" they have made for a development project or the "opportunities" that a development project has brought to their local community, make sure to ask them: What new "possibilities" have these developments brought?

Unfortunately, many people I've met and worked with across rural Pennsylvania and urban neighborhoods have never participated in meaningful community dialogue nor constructive dissent, so the idea of any sort of conscious engagement remains a foreign and misunderstood idea. Most people cannot even imagine it. This lack of familiarity and imagination makes it very difficult for individuals living in local communities up against a powerful and wealthy real estate developer or oil and gas industry to enact possibility within their own lives, much less within their local community and neighborhood. It is critical that we begin to learn, share, and practice dialogue and dissent in generative and practical ways in order to counter the extraction of "sacrifice" and the addiction to "opportunity." In Chapter Four we will go deeper into learning, sharing, and practicing conscious engagement within our own communities in order to create new possibilities.

Place & Home-sickness

When I step outside the door of my home in downtown Savannah, Georgia I still miss that Tony Yatro's sign that hung across the street on the corner of Habersham and Liberty

Streets. It was a large sign that took up the entire top half of the corner of the red brick two-story building. Y-A-T-R-O was spelled out in big red letters on a white background. One of my earliest memories of going into Yatro's store and lunch counter involved sharing a grilled cheese sandwich and ice-cold Coke with my uncle. I must have been four or five years old. I remember delightfully gobbling up the grease as I sat dwarfed in one of the over-sized booths with their maroon-colored leather seat cushions. I can still smell the acrid cigar and cigarette smoke, and taste that greasy, burnt toast and cheese washed down with the sweetness of the Coca-Cola.

Yatro's has been gone for decades now, as well as the hand-painted commercial advertisements that used to adorn the walls of buildings across the City of Savannah. But deep and lingering associations and memories of such places and visual symbols still exist because they are significant to our lives. When these places are no longer there or are threatened with destruction, we feel a sense of loss and at times grief. These feelings of loss and grief are a frequent precursor, as well as affect of, emotional stress and other disruptions to individuals in communities that are facing rapid changes, whether from industrial and economic developments, wars, or natural disasters.In the case of Savannah, this loss, grief, and disruption is related to predatory institutions of higher education. Tony Yatro's two-story red brick building across from my childhood home is now owned by the same non-profit arts college that has been responsible for the gentrification of most of downtown Savannah and our severe lack of affordable housing since the 1990s.

Like losing a parent, close friend, or companion animal,

the feelings of loss that precipitate from losing a sense of place include nostalgia for times gone by that are accompanied by emotions ranging from depression to fear to anger to dissociation to grief. In the case of developments like shale gas that result in not only visible changes to our built environments, natural landscapes, and ecosystems, but to the hidden world of underground aquifers, air quality, and our physiology and psychology, these feelings and emotions can be immediate and acute. This is what I found during focus groups and interviews in Bradford County as hundreds of new gas well pads were being excavated and constructed, forests cleared for pipeline right of ways, and enormous water retention basins were being put in. As Carol put it, during one of our focus groups in the County:

"That's why we're feelin' this death-feeling because change is a-coming. It's like you want to hold onto it [meaning of place] and you know it's not going to be there."

During this same group meeting, Laura also noted the dread she felt in the pit of her stomach as she slowly began realizing as she was listening to everyone talk in our group meeting about the photographs they had taken of what was most important to them—their farm, their water, freshly washed clothes on a clothes line, their children's and grandchildren's health, a burial ground, a family cemetery, a barn, a tree. She attributed this feeling of sickness in her stomach to realizing that those precious things and memories could so easily be destroyed forever by the gas developments.

Carol added to Laura's sentiments:

"It feels like we're losing our love. The things we love the most may be taken away. That's what we're all saying with this."

Such complex feelings (both emotional and physical) of loss, fear, betrayal, regret, guilt, anger, and despair that emerged during those County focus groups, as well as during private interviews, were eerily similar to the well-documented psychological phenomena of community loss and trauma experienced in the aftermath of large-scale environmental and human-caused disasters in which our sense of place, security, and well-being is quite literally carried away or buried[70].

Places, and the questions we ask ourselves and others about our relationships to places, whether they be public parks, the view out the front door of our home or apartment, or our own backyard, can be used as a type of Rorschach test by social scientists and psychologists to better understand human-ecological connections, relationships, perceptions, and even detect psychological disorders. Understanding how local residents interpret places and their histories, what are known as place attachments or senses of place, may also help us understand why conflicts about places, whether rivers or forests or farms or city blocks, arise and persist. The strong feelings that can imbue places also reveals clues to not only why those conflicts persist over time but also how such place attachments become entrenched within people's value and belief systems about others who hold different attachments to a place or no attachments at all.

For example, along the highly urbanized Neponset River in south Boston, I found that sense of place was closely linked to local residents' interpretations of proposed economic developments and environmental restoration and clean-up plans for the Neponset River. The deep differences in senses of place among local residents and between residents and outside consultants and developers were implicated, at least partly, in the sometimes fierce opposition that local residents expressed to various private and public development and environmental restoration and clean-up projects along the river[71].

I have always suspected that one of the reasons that sense of place is such a prominent indicator of conflict and its persistence or degree in our society today is that for some people, although not all, place has become synonymous with the idea of "home," which can be deeply enmeshed with our personal identity or sense of self. When places that are associated with "home" are destroyed or threatened with destruction or significant change, people can fear losing their identity, and sense of who they are, related to the built or natural environment, something I have heard people describe as a type of home-sickness.

To look more closely at this, I asked Bradford County farmers and landowners what "place" meant to them and asked them to take photographs and write a few lines for each photograph. In response, they took photographs of a country road to their home, an aerial view of their farm, a tree that their father planted, a field of moss, a gazebo where the bats used to roost, their children and grand kids. When sharing their photographs with others they spoke of "home," "family," "memory," and "who I am." Contrast this to the representative from an Oklahoma gas company, and at the time the largest owner of shale gas and oil leases in Bradford County, who told County Conservation District employees on a phone call in 2010, "There are just too many damn trees in this County!"

Now everyone has a different definition of what a place means to them, and certainly how it intersects with their memory, personal identity, or what they call family and "home," but there is no doubt that when most of us hear about or see for ourselves a place that we are attached to being threatened we will have certain feelings about this and some of us will want to do all we can to stop that threat or reverse the damage. The important thing I have grown to appreciate by studying sense of place phenomena, though, is that it is neither a monolith nor one-dimensional. Different people will have very different values, beliefs, attitudes, and associations with the exact same place based on many physical, aesthetic, social, cultural, political, historical, and psychological factors. When places are undergoing rapid changes and there has been no recognition or honoring of the very different and sometimes conflicting meanings that place holds within a community this can lead to intractable conflicts within and between those communities. It can also lead to conflict between local residents and outsiders or developers and those who support and enable those outsiders, leading to rebellion and dissent. This can lead to what security professionals call an insurgency, which in the final stages can culminate in social and political transformations and revolutions.

Revolution, despite what some would have us believe, does not require violence in order to lead to transformation. By activating personal or community senses of place and reclaiming those local places in all their particularities and diversity, we can also create an important intervention against the tsunami of global capitalism. By directly acknowledging the "slow" and epistemic violence of toxic geographies, environmental harms and injustices,[72] and naming the deep feelings of attachment and identity around local places, communities can act to contradict and push back against the flattening effects of developments that single-mindedly focus on capital markets and monetization and seek to destroy the connections between local cultural and ecological landscapes, identity, memory, and local community.

Like that Oklahoma gas company representative who saw the trees in Bradford County as an obstacle to the construction of gas wells, most developers dismiss and even intentionally erase the importance of local places, including the essential and interconnected histories and ecologies between local places, people, and Nature. Because of this, those of us who live in local communities and love those communities as the ties to land, family, and Nature that they are must insist that our conversations and actions in facing rapid changes and protecting and resurrecting our communities begin and end with recognizing, honoring, and respecting these localized, diverse place-based interconnections and memories. As human-beings, local places are essential to our feelings of who we are together and as individuals in that togetherness, and therefore local places are tied up in our sense of individual and community well-being, our relationships with Nature and one another, and how we find the knowledge, wisdom, and strength to face change and resurrect our communities.

* * *

Now that we have a better understanding of how

our bodies, our minds, our local communities, local places, and Nature are being threatened and flattened by global capitalism, the denial and distortion of the common good and community values, and the very words we use, our initial preparation for the journey of critical consciousness ahead is complete. The first step we will take on this critical consciousness path is learning how to evaluate our own habits of mind and behavior when it comes to how we face change in our lives that will prepare us for the later steps into what being in community means for each of us.

PART TWO

4. FACING CHANGE TOGETHER

Instead of all this effort analyzing and focusing on the developers, the oppressors, these root causes and forces that insist on flattening and erasing our local places, communities, and Nature, I challenge each of us in the second half of this book to spend our energy courageously developing and acting out our commitments to critical consciousness, cultural synthesis, and liberation in our daily lives. What if we actively sought out others who were willing to develop, share, and act with us on these commitments, and together we created a plan of action using our mental imaginations, our souls, our bodies—our heads, our hearts, our hands— to face change, resurrect our communities, and transform our world together? Is it possible – arguably necessary – but we are first required to find the humility to understand how we may be personally complicit in supporting these root causes of the destruction of others as well as ourselves. Many of us for various reasons want to skip over this step, but there is no short-cut around it if we are ever to liberate ourselves, resurrect our communities, and work towards transformation together. This first step is analogous to what Buddhist teacher and monk Thich Nhat Hanh has called "returning home."[73]

Returning Home

In the previous chapter I introduced the concept of sense of place as a concept synonymous with the concept of "home," self-identity, family, and community, whether in rural Bradford County or urban Boston or Savannah. Because of this association with home and specific types of identity, these place attachments and senses of place can also serve as an accelerant for various conflicts in the face of rapid changes. Acting as an accelerant in this way, sense of place and attachment can serve as one of the root causes that can lead to some of the devastating consequences related to industrial and economic developments.

But, what if this concept of "home," our self-identities, are actually not the most important aspect of understanding sense of place? What if focusing so much on connecting the concepts of "home," "homeland," "identity," and private property rights with the concept of place has become a tool of systemic oppression and suppression; acting to erase the important connections between local community, local families, local groups, and local place that further divide us from one another and consolidate power into the hands of the few? There is certainly evidence throughout world history of this political manipulation of people's individual attachments to and ownership of place. We can see aspects of sense of place being used by Roman legions, by English monarchies, by Nazis, and by countless settlers, colonizers, and missionaries with horrific and genocidal results. In other words, this focus on sense of place is not just an interesting social-cultural-historical-psychological phenomena precipitating from people's connections through generations and time to different landscapes or environments. It is, instead, like many psychological phenomena, a useful tool in service to political and economic systems, as propaganda to keep individuals and communities perpetually in conflict against one another and distracted from their common yearnings for freedom and liberation.

One of the Buddha's fundamental teachings is that "home" is actually a place within each of us and is not, in fact, what we would think of as a place outside of ourselves. Jesus taught something very similar throughout his life when he spoke of the role of prayer and God's unconditional love for us[74]. Learning from these philosophical and spiritual teachings has made me pause in my intellectual and research considerations of where home is and what it truly means to feel home sick for local places and memories of places. Have I been searching for home in the wrong places?

I suspect most reading this have been taught that home is outside of ourselves, that it relies on others, and that it is mediated by things like family of birth, political power, laws, access to money, wealth, and land, war, famine, and even new virtual technologies like Facebook and Zoom. But what if none of those things are actually where our true home is found? What if our true home, as Buddhism teaches, is the simple awareness of our own breath? What if, as Jesus taught, the way to find home is through prayer and acceptance of God's salvation? If that is the answer- home is our very own breath and our prayer and relationship with the God of our understanding- what is stopping us from returning home? Is it all an illusion that a sense of home, or identity, sometimes ego, is outside of ourselves and somehow controlled by others and circumstances beyond our control? This illusion is the very definition of oppression. To take this essential first step of returning home – to what is referred to in Buddhism as non-self and not ego-self, and in Jesus' teachings as loving God with all our heart, mind, and strength and loving one another – we must rid ourselves of that illusion[75].

I have come to believe that to be able to even begin to work with others in resurrecting and transforming our communities, we need to first return and tidy up our own homes with complete humility and honesty. There is no community resurrection without first developing a clear and sober understanding of how our own bodies, minds, and hearts have allowed the destruction of our communities to get this far in the first place. The root causes of systemic oppression and the forces working to keep those systems in place have already taken too many lives, confused too many minds, silenced too many hearts and voices, and destroyed too many of our most sacred places for us to keep looking outside ourselves for answers or a solution.

You might want to think of my words in this chapter as those of a midwife or a hospice nurse, someone by your side as you make this journey and take each step in this cycle of blessed beginnings and sacred endings. There are some dark and scary corners in all of our homes that require us to find illumination and wrestle with the shadows[76]. From time to time I will remind you to breathe, to take stock of your innate knowledge and connections with yourself and Nature, provide some probing questions and guidance based on personal lessons and experiences about the obstacles I have encountered in my own journey, and share the possibilities that lie ahead. But, while I am here as a guide and hopefully comfort, I cannot take any of the steps for you. It is essential that you engage your entire self – body, mind, and heart – in locating the door to your true home and entering, taking stock of the dirt, debris, and darkness that has accumulated, and with the broom of critical consciousness clean away the years of neglect and commit yourself to routine cleaning.

Breathe

Consciously breathing, in and out, is a simple way that will allow us to calm our minds enough to find the door and open it to peek inside our true or non-selves. We can then begin to ask personal, self-reflective questions that will raise our critical consciousness related to our fears and anxieties around change and loss. With a more relaxed mind, we may ask ourselves questions such as: How do I face rapid changes in my own life with the awareness and critical consciousness necessary to reclaim my connections to place and Nature, to community values, and to the common good? How do I recognize and embrace my own confidence and enhance my community's power and embrace new possibilities even in the midst of uncertainty, fear, and loss? And, how are my personal connections to community and to Nature different from or similar to others in my own community and to other communities?

In Chapter 2, we saw how the root causes of systemic oppression and the disruptions brought on by rapid changes from economic and industrial developments bring about life-altering and sometimes deadly changes to individuals, families, communities, and Nature. These changes are felt inside our bodies and minds and can be observed within the very fabric of Nature – water, air, soil, and all living creatures. In the face of such rapid changes the anxiety grabs ahold of us and we hold our breath, forget to breathe, which only multiplies and deepens our anxieties and fears. We feel like we are sacrificing and losing everything most dear to us. We feel powerless and alone. We may feel like we are losing our minds. We call on others to fight for us on our behalf. And, sometimes in the face of such suffocating, breath-less change we may actually feel emboldened and more powerful, and actively work to down-play and deny the powerful forces that are out to harm us. We may construct a fortress of denial and self-deception to guard ourselves against the violence, loss, and grief. We may scapegoat and blame those who are not like us or who we categorize as "other" or "them." But if we can find our breath for just a second, if we can become conscious of that breath, our bodies and hearts may guide us to do things in a much different way than our oxygen-starved and anxiety-ridden brains are currently telling us. And, the first thing we are guided to do differently is to simply breathe. We should always begin with breathing.

Once we can breathe again and our minds start to relax, we will see that it is not only possible but urgent that we learn to face change in our own lives, and all that may mean, with critical consciousness. As we examine how we have faced change unconsciously in our lives in the present or past, we can clearly see how this has led to all the disregard, blame, and shame we have heaped on ourselves, the individuals we encounter in our daily lives, or groups of others that may not share similar values or viewpoints or may just look and act different than ourselves.

In the face of developments that bring on rapid changes with devastating consequences for individuals and communities, it is important to cultivate and maintain our critical consciousness in order to recognize and truthfully address the root causes from the very intimate, personal level all the way to the external, global level. At each level these root causes have built and continue to reinforce the oppressive systems that have allowed for these types of developments to metastasize and cause harm in the first place. As long as we fail to admit the root causes and how they operate at that personal level, the spread of oppressive systems will continue unabated. Until there is an overwhelming groundswell of individuals working on activating their own critical consciousness for the common good we will forever be caught in webs of oppression, continue to blame ourselves and others, and never take action to break free and realize true liberation for all. Each of us plays a vital role in starting this groundswell from our own lives.

Facing change in this personal way requires a commitment to the practices of self-evaluation, contemplation, and discernment which we will find naturally arise from breathing. These nonself practices allow us to examine our lives in relationship to how we have faced change in the past, or how we are running away from change, either currently or in the past. In this examination we can identify, admit, and become aware of our unconscious and implicit biases, feelings, ideologies, and behavioral patterns. It cannot be said enough that the reason for dredging up these uncomfortable, many times unconscious feelings, thinking patterns, and behaviors is that these are the very ingredients that serve as catalysts for the dangerous stereotypes that justify the demonization and blaming of anyone categorized as "outside," "other," or "different." Because of the oppressed-oppressor enmeshment that maintains and reinforces systemic oppression, this sort of critical consciousness work is urgent, mandatory, and necessary[77]. Whether we identify ourselves, or have been identified by others as "expert," "ally," "helper," "privileged," "settler," "colonizer," or "oppressor," or as "marginalized," "uneducated," "victim," or "oppressed" it is important that we all return home, breathe, and begin this first step on the critical consciousness journey.

Hitting Bottom

I have a confession. I am a change addict. I have always loved the exhilaration of sailing from one life circumstance to another, never aware of the sadness and loss I was leaving in my wake. It sounds heartless and cruel to write this, but as a young woman I was so restless that I changed my relationships and interests on a pretty regular basis without much thought to the pain and confusion I may be causing others (and later myself). Since a child, I have always loved to learn new things and this turned into a pattern in my life of when I got bored, when circumstances and ideas no longer struck my fancy, I would just move on. In jobs, if I was dissatisfied for some reason, I would find a way to quit – sometimes without another option. I always sought out jobs and different work that kept me traveling and moving from one circumstance to another, one place to another, one interest to another. As a white woman from a fairly well-off family I always found a comfortable landing, even if it meant relying on my parents or a boyfriend for a few months. But, as a young woman I was oblivious to the role my race or class privilege played in allowing me to satisfy my restlessness and addiction to change without discomfort or any real danger. And, as with most addictions, I was using the cover of constant change and restlessness to run away from a whole panoply of interior discontents and discomforts that included overwhelming emotions, spiritual disconnection and misgivings, parental and societal expectations around career and gender roles, and many others.

While I was working in Bradford County I began to feel the ways in which my addiction to change had stunted my emotional maturity and impacted my personal life— both in terms of my physical and emotional distance from my family and loved ones and my relationship with myself. This was the first time I became aware that all the constant change-seeking was playing a destructive role in the quality of my life, my work, my relationships, and my sense of who I really was. I remember telling Carol around 2011 I felt like a potted plant; never putting down roots, always going from one place or circumstance to another in my car. I never felt like I was part of any one community, always on the periphery or outside of any community that I could have been a part of. I had begun to grow tired of constant change and desired to put down roots and really be a part of some sort of community of people who understood me.

I kept thinking about this amazing summer immersion course on intentional communities that I had taken during my undergraduate years at the University of Massachusetts in Amherst. Ever since that summer of 1993 I had been fascinated, inspired, and humbled by the individuals in these communities who I personally met across the northeast U.S. that had committed their daily lives, and sometimes all of their worldly valuables, to nurturing a community, and world, that was not about their own self-interests and ambitions but about some greater whole and the common good. I did not always agree with their ideological beliefs, but in the most long-enduring intentional communities around the world, like The Farm, Sirius Community, and Findhorn Community it was fascinating and inspiring to learn about all the different ways people had creatively and consciously addressed the inter-personal conflicts that would inevitably arise with a beautiful, although not always comfortable, mix of vulnerability, humility, truth-telling, love, practical knowledge, and intuitive wisdom. I was also awed by their commitment as individuals to, when necessary, change their personal perspectives and behaviors for the sake of a whole and beloved community, as opposed to letting toxic group-think create just another community of "like-minded" people[78]. Looking back, I am certain that the seeds of my community work and this book were first collected during that summer for later planting.

In 2012, I could no longer ignore the call to find open ground in which to plant my root-bound self when I had to leave my fieldwork in Pennsylvania and a research scientist position in New York to focus on caring for and just being present for my parents back in Savannah, Georgia as they both faced serious and life-ending health problems. I knew without a doubt I needed to literally return home. If not for myself, then for the ones who had given me so much.

Initially dad had been diagnosed with prostate cancer in 2010 while my fieldwork in Bradford County was just beginning. When he was rushed to the emergency room after collapsing in his office one afternoon, the doctor told my mom and cousins that he had probably had prostate cancer for over 10 years. It had already metastasized to his bones. That was a really frightening time, but I didn't plan to go home for at least a few more months, and it seemed like my dad's nieces and friends were there for him as much as I could be.

In retrospect, though, I regret not going home right away. Not for my dad, but for my mom. My mom, twenty years younger than my dad, had lived with a diagnosis of bipolar disease for over thirty years by then. She had loyally worked alongside my dad in his real estate business since they married in 1971, making sure the bills were paid, licenses kept up to date, and many other aspects of the business. In addition, she also made sure their 162-year-old historic home, the only house I had ever lived in before graduating high school, was always in tip-top shape and ready for the next gathering of friends and family.

But, after dad's diagnosis with prostate cancer, mom began falling more frequently and it became increasingly apparent that she would soon no longer be able to work in the office or to safely climb the stairs in their home. The damage to her body and brain from her life-long battle with bipolar disorder seemed to be getting progressively worse. Exacerbating my mom's physical decline was the stress she was experiencing over my dad's cancer diagnosis and the anxiety she felt about losing him.

Making mom's situation all the more heartbreaking was the miraculous recovery she had made in 2009 after she was overdosed with psychiatric medications while under a psychiatrist's care. I sat by her side for three weeks while she was in an induced coma as doctors tried to stabilize her nervous and circulatory systems. She had to re-learn how to talk and walk at a rehabilitation facility for another month. Several years after her recovery and just two years after dad's cancer diagnosis, mom faced her own fatal diagnosis, cerebral ataxia, a degenerative neurological disease.

To most people dad appeared to be doing just fine after his cancer diagnosis and the initial scary symptoms. But my mom and I were beginning to notice some early-stage cognitive decline that he masked and denied. His cognitive issues troubled my mom most since she lived and worked with him every day. I was living elsewhere, so it was much easier for me to put dad's problems out of my mind – especially since he was a master at faking being alright. He was still in the office by 8 a.m. each day, took my mom out to dinner each night, and went out dancing on the weekends. What troubled me most at that time was dad's complete denial about the danger my mom was in when it came to her physical decline and the possibility of her falling down the stairs. It was clear that I was needed back home and I began spending more and more time in Savannah.

This period, in late 2012, was the first time in my life I had to confront changes in which I felt helpless and not in control. My addiction to change was starting to shift, and I began to not just understand how others experience change with deep fear and anxieties, but empathize with those experiences. I thought more and more about the families I had met in Bradford County, and the friends I had made there, who for four years had been sharing their feelings of fear, anxiety, and impending loss. Now I saw more clearly how the rapid changes brought on by shale gas developments, the loss of their livelihoods, of drinking water, of a healthy family, had turned their world completely upside down. At the same time, I was over 600 miles away from Bradford County and more helpless than ever to do anything about what they were experiencing, not to mention what I was beginning to personally experience. It was an emotionally and physically overwhelming time. And, I had few healthy coping mechanisms.

My entire life I had used change as an escape hatch from boredom, difficult relationships and circumstances, looking more closely at myself, you name the excuse. I had used and sought out change because I had felt control over it. But having to face the reality of two parents with fatal medical diagnoses was entirely different. My mom's illness was rapidly progressive and there were no available doctors in the Savannah area who could treat, or much less understand, her care needs or advanced therapies. And, my dad refused to accept the reality of mom's illness nor his own, and would hold it against me personally when I made the decision to put her in a nursing facility where I hoped she would be safer from falling and get the round-the-clock care she was starting to require. I felt out of control, helpless, and angry.

To add to these devastating circumstances, my Uncle Lauvon suffered a hemorrhagic stroke that he never recovered from in early 2013. My dear uncle, my godfather, and the person who was my mom's closest relative had been such a great source of comfort to me throughout my entire life. I am convinced he was a genius. He taught me everything I will ever need to know about solitaire card games, crossword puzzles, the dangers of cigarette smoke, and the intricacies of vodka cocktails. He had lived in a ground-floor apartment in our home since 1995, occupying the space in our home where my grandparents had lived before him. With mom in a nursing home and suffering with a bout of terrible depression on top of cerebral deterioration, I suddenly found myself taking on her role, rubbing my uncle's feet and talking to him while he spent what seemed like endless weeks hooked up to machines in the intensive care unit at Memorial Hospital. I also grew closer to his best friend and roommate, Rick. Rick and I became co-decision makers on whether we should allow for an invasive procedure to keep Lauvon alive or whether he should be admitted into hospice care to die with dignity. While this decision was heart-wrenching, it was not a difficult one for Rick and I to make, as Lauvon had told us in the ICU that he did not want to be "locked up" in a nursing home like his sister, my mom, was.

It was this awful cauldron of loss, sadness, anger, guilt, and resentment as I witnessed the death, and impending death, of those people who were most important to me in my life that brought me to my knees in the face of change. I was unable to keep up with my work obligations in New York and what had become personal obligations and commitments to the Bradford County residents I had been working with for four years. So, on top of all the crushing life and death decisions and loss I experienced in 2013, I also began to realize that I would not be able to continue the face-to-face fieldwork with the people and places in Pennsylvania that I had learned so much from and grown to love. I felt guilty that I was abandoning them and the work, so I denied that I could not continue my fieldwork and tried to shift my focus to something I thought would be more manageable from afar. It never was.

Another blow to my research work was having to turn down invitations to participate in public speaking events. These events had boosted my self-confidence during my time at Dickinson College as a post-doctoral scholar and then as a research scientist at RPI. The decision to leave biology and the natural sciences to pursue work studying and teaching about the social dimensions of Nature and environmental and social conflict had been a decision that many people close to me had either actively tried to dissuade me from following through on, or had just been confused by. These public events gave me some much-needed (although certainly self-serving) confirmation that my decision was the right one. But, then, just as interest by others in my research and community work in social sciences was growing exponentially, I had to turn down invitations to speak. It was such a huge blow to my ego and confidence to have to say "No" over and over. In addition, the guilt that I felt around abandoning Bradford County, all the people I had worked with so closely, led to anxiety, depression, and insomnia.

But, despite all the No's and the changes which I felt no control over, I knew I had to say Yes to my family. I had fear and dread about the declining health and well-being of my parents, sadness and grief over my uncle's death, and a good amount of anticipatory grief over losing both of my parents. In my mind, and even my body, I was in fear and dread about change for my family and for my own future, but when I listened to my heart it told me without a doubt that what I had to do: face change and the future, wherever it might lead.

I chose to listen to my heart. As difficult as it was, I knew I had to return home and be there for those who had given me so much in my life up to that point. This decision has forever changed my relationship with change. Sometimes it is not enough just to recognize and face change with consciousness and presence of mind, sometimes facing change requires us to make hard choices, change our behaviors, and reckon with those unconscious obsessions we have worked so hard to hide. For me, this reckoning happened after my uncle died and I began to admit that my dependence on alcohol to fall asleep at night, ease depression, cope with daily stress, and then wake up each day, was untenable. My physical, mental, and emotional reliance on alcohol was also ruining my ability to communicate and be in loving relationships with myself and others. Unless I had just put down the drink in my hand or was pouring another one, the anger and impatience I felt towards my mom and my dad would erupt in ugly and vile ways. Of course, this anger and impatience was misdirected away from its true source – my disappointment in myself in not being able to continue my work in Bradford County and my anger at myself for not being able to fully control the circumstances we all found ourselves in, nor their eventual outcomes. Thanks to my husband's impatience and threatening to leave me because of how I was behaving and treating everyone around me, I did begin to admit that there was some correlation between my ugly behavior and my drinking. And, for almost eleven months in 2012 and 2013, I tried to stop drinking alcohol on my own without success. During that first attempt at sobriety all that disappointment, anger, and impatience turned into depression, moodiness, fear, anxiety, and insomnia.

Right before mom had died I had gotten my Georgia real estate license, so after her death I was faced with the prospect of not just being dad's primary care giver but also his full-time business partner. Despite the progression of his cancer, dad still continued to work every day. I recognized that to do all of this I would need much better ways than alcohol to cope with disappointment and stress, control my anger, and, most practically, get enough sleep. Frightened and ashamed, I attended my first Alcoholics Anonymous meeting on June 13, 2014, a little less than a month after I said good-bye to my mom for the last time. When most people understandably turn to booze, I had to turn away – and that also hurt.

Admitting my obsession and dependence on alcohol and choosing the daily path of recovery has given me increased self-awareness about my relationship with myself, with others, and the world around me. But, perhaps even more importantly, admitting my addiction to alcohol and being in recovery has given me the strength to breathe, open the door to my true home, and with a more relaxed mind, body, and heart begin to clear away the cobwebs, scrub the floors, and shed light into the darkest corners where I was too afraid to look before. One of the darkest of the darkest corners has revealed the ways in which the racial and economic privilege I was born into, and the self-centered, ego-driven thought and behavior which our society rewards, was what had enabled me to satisfy my addiction to change (and to alcohol) and inflict pain on myself and others, with no severe consequences, for so long. In other words, my sobriety has given me the gift of critical consciousness, especially when it comes to the intersection of my personal life story and systemic oppression throughout our society. The systemic oppression that allowed for me to use and weaponize my privilege to satisfy my addictions, enabling me to harm myself, others, and even Nature.

For me, hitting bottom as a result of my obsessions and addictions has meant shining an enormous light onto the illusions that were lurking in that darkest corner. In that corner I found piles upon piles of accumulated debris and junk that had been carefully hidden under blankets by generations before me. The illusion I had been taught, and even reinforced within myself, made me see this pile of crap as either a scary monster in the corner or a monster protecting my home from dangerous intruders. But in fact, this supposed monster in the corner was nothing more than piles of greed, privilege, entitlement, paternalism, elitism, individualism, and violence under the dirty blankets of all the -isms and genocidal biases and stereotypes humans have devised throughout history.

This metaphor is the way I imagine systemic oppression to have existed within my own home for so long. As a white woman from the South, the trick my eyes have played on my mind in the dim light is that there is some kind of monster that I should fear, avoid, but also use when necessary for my own protection, like some vicious trained attack dog. This illusion was reinforced by my parents, other relatives, what I was taught in school, the social relationships I had (and did not have) growing up, and the segregated city I grew up in. As the illusion becomes more real, I have failed to see the reality of the different pieces of crap that lie under the blankets and the filth of the blankets covering it. This illusion makes it hard to even imagine why I might get rid of all the junk and dirt. It does not hurt me, and from what I've been told, it might even protect me from something. And, this is exactly what makes this illusion so powerful, dangerous, and seemingly indestructible. Systemic oppression is the corner pile of debris, junk, and crap underneath all the dirty blankets of fear and hate that I have been taught to see as something not worth thinking about and at the same time something not worth cleaning up. For me, the bright light of my sobriety and of critical consciousness, has shattered any illusions about what systemic oppression actually is and given me some important insights on how to get rid of that pile of crap, discard those filthy blankets, and sweep out the darkest corners of my own home.

Such an intentional house-cleaning requires us to first look at how we have arranged our own homes and be humble and honest about who we have allowed to dictate our use of space and where we have allowed the dirt to accumulate. What tricks of perception and illusions have we allowed ourselves to fall for that stop us from tidying up? In order to clean away the filth that has been allowed to accumulate we must commit to critical consciousness in our daily lives. This will require throwing out blankets, discarding broken furniture, maybe even replacing rotted floorboards underneath that corner pile. It may also require a trip to the basement to check on our foundation or an inspection of our roof. An on-going practice of deep cleaning and inspecting our home can be dirty, uncomfortable, and even hazardous, but it is absolutely necessary for establishing and maintaining our critical consciousness.

Re-Learning the World

My dad died on December 4, 2015. Writing and re-reading this sentence years later still feels unreal. I struggled badly with his death as I not only grieved losing him from my daily life but in all of his physical pain and my attempts to comfort him during his final days I had found it so difficult to pause, create a space of peace, and express to him in words my profound gratitude and love. Unlike with my mom and uncle, for whom there were nurses and hospice staff, I was dad's primary care-giver and it was just he and I in the ground-floor apartment of our home. So, in the midst of both caring for him physically and running the real estate business I found excuse after excuse for not putting my feelings for his life and what it meant to me into spoken words so that he could hear them. This still cuts to my heart, even though kind friends and family have told me over and over that my physical care and being there until the end was enough.

Another aspect of losing my dad was the sudden realization that my mom and my uncle were also missing from my life. I became aware in the day before dad's funeral that I had not had an opportunity to mourn their deaths fully since it had been three straight years of caring and loss. I learned this is what psychologists and grief counselors sometimes call "complicated grief" and I began attending group grief sessions. The group was a life-line to remind me that I was not alone, and that in fact I needed other people to help me; which, believe it or not, was something I had only fully come to realize for the first time in my life since beginning to attend A.A. meetings and working with a sponsor. Those grief sessions were also critical in helping me put one step in front of the other during the first month after dad's death, and very importantly, to stay sober.

Along with the grief group, a book by Thomas Attig, *How We Grieve: Relearning the World*, also had an enormous influence on how I found a way to handle and get through the emotional roller coaster during this time. The whole premise is in the title— grief completely changes our personal worldview and how we relate to the world. In grief, we must very literally re-learn the world. Grief affects us in ways that we cannot predict and that may not be comparable to others' experiences. Thomas Attig's book counsels that the best way to handle this is the recognition and acceptance that the loss is irreversible and is part of a personal growth process that has no rules or timelines. What is critical is not forgetting yourself in the grief process, and taking care of yourself and your life. It talks about the importance of taking time to remember the past and to feel the pain. And, most importantly, allowing yourself time and space to re-learn all of your relationships: with yourself, with others, with your daily routines, and with the world around you.

But, how do we re-learn the world when faced with such enormous personal loss to our entire ways of life, our livelihoods, our communities, our families, Nature? How do individuals in communities who have experienced rapid changes resulting in loss re-learn, which means in some capacity accepting, this fractured and broken world? It means courageously looking at ourselves in the mirror every morning with eyes wide open to truly see who we are. It is also listening to the ancestors who came before us and who made us who and what we are today. In other words, the personal work of re-learning the world also involves evaluating our personal identities, feelings, values, and beliefs about the past, present, and future. In the context of critical consciousness that we are most concerned about, it means looking more closely at our personal relationships with the systems and structures in our families, societies, and communities that lead to pain and loss; some of those root causes we discussed in the previous chapter. In this way, the practice of allowing ourselves the time and space to re-learn the world is another step on the journey of critical consciousness.

This idea of re-learning the world after loss sounds obvious on the surface. If we lose the most important elements of our world today, in order to continue on living, we must learn how to re-orient ourselves in a world without those elements. But, when it comes down to the unpredictable well of grief, this idea of re-learning and re-orienting is slow, exhausting, and down-right frightening work. One way I have found to ease my own impatience, fatigue, and fear is to remind myself on a regular basis that re-learning takes humility, self-forgiveness, and an awareness that I can make simple, uncomplicated choices throughout my day that can help me re-orient myself. Sometimes the choice is pausing what I am doing for thirty seconds and focus on my breathing. Sometimes the choice is to concentrate on running errands that need to be done or paying bills. And, sometimes the choice is to sleep-in when I do not have other obligations or responsibilities. The hard part for me is keeping it simple, and staying away from choices that are self-destructive in some way. This all takes some practice, thus the humility and self-forgiveness. Although we may not have control over the changes that have occurred or may occur, and certainly no control over how others around us will respond to those changes, we do not have to act as victims or martyrs.

The simple revelation here is that we do have choices about how we respond in the face of rapid change and loss. So, the question becomes, in such terrible circumstances why don't we make the choices that lead to less damage and suffering for ourselves and others more often? I think the answer lies in our broken relationships with our selves, with others, and Nature. Those of us taught to live in the Western world tend to think of suffering and grief as deep loneliness. This is why we need to both return home to ourselves, and why, just as important, we need others to help us re-learn the world.

Like I turned to a grief support group of a dozen other souls going through loss while grieving my own family, we created a "core group" in Bradford County that allowed participants to share with others their feelings and thoughts about the disruptions they were experiencing as a direct or indirect result of the changes brought about by the shale gas developments. It is clear we need togetherness and to share our experiences with others when faced with the impact of personal loss and sudden change. One very important effect of such group settings, beyond just a sense of not being alone and dying of heartbreak, is that when we participate in them as our authentic selves, our own way of thinking and internalizing and acting on change is frequently challenged by others, or we realize connections that we would not have realized by just relying on our own internal dialogue. In my personal experiences, sharing the experience of change and loss with others can speed up the re-learning process considerably.

For instance, we might learn about a book, movie, or song that has helped someone else get through a rough day or week. We might learn that someone else is experiencing the strange physical symptoms of grief that you have had and realize for the first time that you are not alone. Learning with and from others by listening to their grief experiences can also help build trust in others, which after a significant loss or change that may have felt not within our own control, can offer ways to mentally reset how we view ourselves in relationship with others, and thus give us a different perspective on ourselves and our lives during or after change and loss. In working with individuals in community as well as the whole community, these spaces to gather together and share in this way offer us new perspectives to see beyond our personal losses and fears. We need such togetherness to find and build hope and remind one another that no matter how dark it may seem everyone can make simple choices, whether it is to consciously focus on breathing, move our body, look out the window, or hug a friend. Most of the time we have some type of choice we can make, even in the most oppressive of circumstances. Once we start regularly making small, simple choices in our personal lives this can help us shift out of the emotionally-charged aspects of change and activate our physical and mental selves in order to be able to act and think on what change looks like now and into the future. This is essential work for the next steps in critical consciousness and cultural synthesis that will help us resurrect our communities and transform the world together.

Denial

Over the years, as a consultant, I have been invited to speak or meet with groups of people who are worried about future industrial and economic developments in their neighborhoods or communities. When we meet for the first time, in addition to sharing what we know about the environmental, social, economic, and public health risks of certain types of development projects, I also make sure to emphasize the urgency of the changes that communities in the cross-hairs of these developments face with examples from other places and people that I and my colleagues have worked with over the years. I think it is important to give these groups all the facts as well as some concrete steps they can take today to protect themselves in the future. My consultancy and the organizations I work with offer these groups free and do-it-yourself tools and resources, some found within their own communities and some from reputable experts and organizations, so that they can immediately start fortifying themselves, especially against negative psychological and social changes. However, rarely do these meetings end with people feeling hopeful or grateful. The most common attitudes communities express during and after such meetings revolve around two types of denial; denial that their experiences will be anything like what other communities have gone through, and denial that they can do anything at all to protect themselves.

In the first type of denial people express an attitude that their neighborhood or community has some unique or exceptional qualities that make them immune to the negative consequences of changes that have been experienced in other neighborhoods or communities. They let me know that the examples I give are not relevant to them and the tools and resources on offer are not appropriate for the unique and exceptional attributes of their community. It is like warning someone of an oncoming freight train, offering them steps they should take to either stop the train or get out of the way, and them responding, "Oh, we don't need to move, the train will stop before it gets to us. We are invincible against oncoming freight trains."

In my observations, this attitude is more often seen within groups that have relative advantages when it comes to wealth and social status and have not experienced being oppressed or marginalized from governance or decision-making systems in recent memory. The people who act out this type of denial point to things like their connections, access to politicians, news media, subject matter experts, and powerful organizations, extraordinary abilities to organize themselves, and their ownership of money, land, and a college education as some of the reasons why they are either safe from any changes that might negatively impact them.

The second type of denial manifests in an attitude of apathy, disinterest, and at times, fatalism. It is like warning someone of an oncoming freight train and them saying, "We have already been run over so many times why would we move now?" Perhaps not surprisingly this form of denial seems to be expressed more among groups that are less wealthy and that are currently marginalized or silenced from systems of decision-making or that have been marginalized or oppressed in the past. The people in this group also have their justifications for why they have this attitude. They tell stories about how it does not matter what they do because they have seen the disregard developers have for them before. Some point to the fact that they do not want to get up their hopes that this time will be any different or that they might be able to change the outcomes. And, that they do not need to hear from another outsider with promises it could be different this time. And so, as with the first type of denial, the tools and resources shared with these groups are many times dismissed as lacking the appropriate local context, not useful, or in the worst cases, an offer of false hope, potentially deceptive, and certainly not to be trusted.

Both groups who express these types of denial have one thing in common, they deny that the root causes, particularly the ill-logic of global capitalism, is already all around us, embedded within us, and that it has infected our society, culture, and psychology in fundamental ways. And, I bet most of us have experienced these denials at one time or another. We find ourselves so in awe of the receding waters, running out to the shoreline to see the spectacle of ships and fish on dry ground, that we fail to recognize that the tsunami wave is gaining momentum to crush and flatten us. In the first type of denial we have a sense of grandiosity and privilege that makes us believe we are too powerful to ever be crushed by the coming tsunami. And, in the second type we have a sense of victimhood and despair that makes us believe we are too weak to run, and most certainly ever get to higher ground, as the on-coming tsunami approaches. As we see in both types of denial I have described, the unwillingness to be critically conscious of root causes and systemic oppression and to recognize inherent and unconscious biases and self-deceptions, both act to deny the ultimate power and strength that inherently lies within our selves via connecting to our true home and within our communities via networks of mutuality and solidarity with other communities unlike our own and Nature herself. We either over-inflate (in the case of the first type of denial) or diminish (in the second type) the wholeness and holiness of ourselves, our communities, and Nature and the power they all offer us to face change.

Getting Over Ourselves

As frustrating as denial can be for someone like myself who works to co-create specific ways that people in themselves and in community can become more critically conscious, embrace difference and change, and lead their own communities to face change, I have learned over the years to expect this denial as an initial reaction to change. I have had to set aside my own expectations about what change should look like or how people should perceive it, and take these expressions of denial very seriously. Taking denial seriously means taking care to recognize and honor each individual's personal relationship and reaction to change — do they run away, hide, or fight?

After we have awakened critical consciousness within ourselves by simply remembering to breathe, returning home, and starting to clean up our emotional, mental, and behavioral patterns, we should begin to more clearly identify and diagnose those attitudes, beliefs, values, biases, and learned behaviors that have held us back from facing change with critical consciousness. In other words, we can begin to do the work on our own patterns of denial.

To do this self-evaluation requires taking an honest look at our past experiences with change and how we thought and behaved towards that change. Since this will be unique to every individual, I am going to use my own life experiences as an example of my past relationship with and reaction to change and the ways it has shaped my approach to critical consciousness and my commitments to cultural synthesis and liberation. I expect these personal experiences to be very different from some of your own. These examples are offered only as a prompt for recalling your own experiences with change. The lessons you should glean from remembering change in your own life will be different from mine and most likely from anybody else. So, the personal stories shared here are written to encourage you to frame your thinking about change in your own life as a personal, humbling step on the critical consciousness journey.

* * *

In 2000 I moved back to the East Coast from Seattle, Washington, where I had moved in my mid-20s. I had always wanted to live west of the Mississippi, and while my quality of life in Seattle was superb, I could not wait to be closer to my family and I was thrilled to be starting a new job that got me my first full-time position in federal government service. It was the start of what I thought would be a long career working in service to the American people and on behalf of conservation of our oceans and protection of marine wildlife. I was an idealist so I believed the job was my chance to save the world. I was also dangerously naïve. Armed with a graduate degree in marine policy and management that had included courses in government I thought I knew much more than I actually did. I had no idea how the U.S. government actually worked, nor how my position as a cog in the machine of government would mean compromising my own ideals of service to people and saving the world.

In my first months on the job I was on cloud nine; despite the fact that my specific position as an analyst of marine mammal scientific research permits was not exactly the policy job I had hoped for, I did realize it was a stepping stone to other roles and duties. Within a year I was working on the marine mammal small take program, which issues permits to private industry and public agencies whose activities might threaten, harm, or kill marine mammals in the course of development and research projects. This involved analyzing more complex issues related to the conservation of marine wildlife and human threats beyond just the scientific research permits to take photographs or tissue samples of whales and dolphins. I quickly learned that for most of the permits we issued to harass, harm, and kill marine mammals, the public comments and concerns were, beyond being a one or maybe two paragraph response to comments in the Code of Federal Register, disregarded. It seemed we served the permit applicant, not the American people nor the marine animals. And that is when I began feeling extremely uncomfortable about how U.S. conservation regulations, or at least the ones I had been hired to write and review, were being implemented.

We have laws that set the legal norms for what should and should not be done in the best interest of wildlife and the oceans, but when it comes to implementing those laws it means writing regulations (or codifying those legal norms), which is what each permit we issued constituted. And, those regulations and permits seemed more often than not to favor some private interest over public — whether oil and gas exploration and development, military contractors, satellite companies, or golf course developers. It was a rude and uncomfortable awakening for me about how government actually worked in practice, as opposed to classroom projects, theoretical scenarios, and textbooks.

One of my jobs in NOAA Fisheries' small take permit program was to work with oil and gas companies to develop endangered species and marine mammal monitoring and mitigation regulations and guidelines in the Gulf of Mexico and Arctic Ocean. At that time the program issued permits to oil and gas companies in the process of decommissioning old oil rigs, per U.S. Coast Guard and Department of Interior regulations. We also issued these permits to companies seeking to seismically survey the continental shelf in scouting out new oil and gas reserves and pipeline routes. At the time, NOAA and the Interior were in the process of completing a programmatic Environmental Impact Statement (EIS) that would assess the status of endangered, threatened, and marine mammal species in the Gulf of Mexico. Since issuing monitoring and mitigation regulations on these activities constituted a "non-exempt federal action," such an EIS had to be completed per the National Environmental Policy Act (NEPA) of 1969 prior to finalizing the regulations[79].

NEPA had been enshrined in federal law in 1969, seven years after Rachel Carson published *Silent Spring*, a galvanizing call for action to stop the human devastation of Nature. NEPA sought to ensure that federal activities were as protective of the environment and our human well-being as possible. It says in the Act that the law is designed "to encourage productive and enjoyable harmony between man and his environment, to promote efforts which will prevent or eliminate damage to the environment and biosphere and stimulate the health and welfare of man, and to enrich the understanding of the ecological systems and natural resources important to the Nation." NEPA, despite its paternal, masculine language which was common at the time as well as its many flaws in practice, still serves today as a reminder of the interconnected and life-giving relationship of humans and Nature and the possibility of organizing our lives and communities around that relationship. There is no other U.S. law that spells out the mutual interdependence between humans and Nature, and in many ways the law encapsulates the higher ideals I entered my federal job at NOAA imagining I would uphold.

But, immediately after the inauguration of George W. Bush, my office had begun receiving push-back on completion of the Gulf of Mexico EIS, and especially the requirement for completion of the EIS before issuing further regulations and permits on oil and gas activities. The Bush Administration told us that the EIS was unnecessary and that instead regulations and permits to allow rig removal and other oil and gas related activities on the coastal shelf in the Gulf should be expedited. I was confused, and then shocked and angered, that such behind-closed-doors political manipulation of the nation's environmental laws was taking place. Even more mortifying to me, as a relatively new federal employee, was that I was being asked to take actions that violated the very law I had just sworn to uphold. I truly identified as a "public servant," not a servant of private industry. I decided to bring up my deep concerns about this to my boss.

I will never forget walking into her office and telling her I was not going to issue a permit for oil and gas companies to remove old oil rigs in the Gulf of Mexico. My justification for this was that we had not followed proper procedures to fully assess the environmental risks. She practically laughed in my face and then dialed up a political appointee, who just several months before had worked for the American Petroleum Institute (API), and I was told in no uncertain terms that if I would not write the permit someone else would. At some point my boss told me- not sure if it was this time in her office, multiple times, or another time since we had such a tumultuous relationship - if I didn't like what I was doing I could just quit.

While the neglect of environmental laws and procedures I witnessed and participated in bothers me even more today as I witness the power private interests, most notably oil and gas developers, have over our laws and institutions, at the time I was ill equipped to understand, much less effectively confront the causes of this neglect and thus had no understanding of how to critically diagnose the systemic problems I witnessed and that gave me an uneasy feeling. I had no idea how or even if I could take action to officially challenge what I was being asked to do. So, instead of continuing to challenge the problem and acting to change it, I opted to make it about my own self-interest of keeping my job and issued the permits as I was told.

Analyzing this experience has been important to

understanding how I have coped with and denied change in the past. It is especially heartbreaking to see how my moral idealism about serving others and standing up for Nature quickly took second place when it came to my self-interested ambition and ego. While I knew what I was being asked to do was wrong, both legally and morally for me, I did not have the critical awareness or consciousness of the root causes that were operating. Nor did I have the first clue about how to confront those causes directly and completely refuse to be a part of it. When I took my job we weren't told anything about how we might report what we perceived as law-breaking going on within the government. All I knew at the time was that I was being asked to do something that was threatening the long-term conservation and protection of the oceans and marine wildlife I loved so dearly and it did involve violating the letter of the law specifically for oil and gas interests. I consulted trusted colleagues who had been in the government for 20 or more years and they all advised me to just do what I was told. My conscience was deeply troubled by all of this. So, when the right moment came, I left NOAA to pursue my own ambitions and idealized notions of how I thought I could save the world. I was still oblivious to the systemic corruption I had witnessed and the way it was handled by not only my bosses, but trusted co-workers, as just another day in the office. I still had no idea there were ways to actually report this to government watchdogs. My choice to do what I was told and then leave as soon as I had a way to pay my bills, left the looming threats to oceans and marine wildlife, law-breaking, and institutionalized corruption behind for others to confront, or suffer the consequences from. In 2003 I left

NOAA.

This personal story of my lack of critical consciousness to see or confront root causes and the corruption I witnessed and played a role in sadly does not end there. On April 20, 2010 tragedy struck the Gulf of Mexico. I was at Dickinson College when I heard the news that eleven oil workers had been killed as a result of an explosion and catastrophic failure of a blowout preventer on BP's Deepwater Horizon drilling rig in the Gulf of Mexico. As a result of the failure, the exploratory well that was being drilled into the subsea Macondo Prospect, started gushing oil out into the Gulf at an average rate of more than 1.5 million gallons of oil into the ocean a day[80]. My heart shattered.

A little less than ten years after my short-lived defiance and capitulation on those Gulf of Mexico permits, the oil and gas industry was still getting its way in the region and the ecosystems and marine wildlife were now in mortal danger. But, because there still had not been a comprehensive EIS done, that danger and any current or potential impacts from the oil spill to ecosystems, wildlife, or the humans whose livelihoods depended on them, would remain unknown. We will never know the full scope of the social, economic, or ecological impacts of the Deepwater Horizon spill. The devastation to the Gulf of Mexico ecosystem, and to the lives of those who depended on the Gulf for their livelihoods is still being felt eleven years after the disaster. Without such information we will never be able to atone or truly repair the harms to the biodiversity in the Gulf and to the well-being of local communities. If I had known more about what standing against law-breaking and corruption meant and I had fought to uphold the law and the common good rather than cave to my own self-interest, then maybe I would have voiced my resistance to issuing those permits more stridently. Maybe at least one EIS could have been done in the ten years prior to the Deepwater Horizon disaster. I often wonder if this would have at least helped us understand the impact of this devastating spill, if not altered the circumstances under which it was allowed to happen in the first place.

Knowing what I know now about the consequences of not being able to be critically conscious of and confront root causes, face change at the personal and community level, and take action in solidarity with my co-workers, will forever haunt me. I could have done more when I was confronted with a barrier to doing the right thing for the common good, but instead made the choice to leap over the barrier in pursuit of my own self-preservation and ambition was easier, and it was encouraged by those I looked up to. If I had only been more conscious of the world outside my bubble and had any sort of awareness beyond my privileged selfish notion of "saving the world." If I had had a concrete process and framework as part of a community of other people dedicated to ocean conservation focused not just on our careers or expertise but instead on facing change for the common good and the long-term conservation and protection of Nature, could we have made any difference?

The lesson to me in evaluating the way I lived my life and how I acted (or failed to act) in my life and career throughout my twenties, is that my relationship to change was led by some idealist notion of a world that existed only in my own mind and therefore was entirely self-serving as well as isolated from different ways that systemic oppression showed up in the world. I was somewhat conscious of systemic oppression after stumbling across and reading Freire. But things like injustice and inequality had not impacted me personally and somehow I still did not believe the level of corruption that I had seen with my own eyes was something that happened in the United States. At that time I did not make the connection between some of what I was reading in Freire and my own life or identity as a conservationist and advocate for the common good and community values. And, I did not imagine that the critical consciousness, cultural synthesis, and liberation that Freire wrote about had a direct connection to my life and personal experiences. I was, despite my stubbornness, privilege, and selfishness, unconsciously caught in, and being used by, the systems that had been built to maintain the ill-logic of global capitalism instead of valuing the common good and tapping into community values to topple those systems of oppression.

It turns out much of my family's history is deeply intertwined with creating and maintaining those systems. My ancestors were some of the original settler-colonizers of North America in the early 1600's. In the name of England's monarchs they committed horrendous atrocities against the indigenous peoples in what is today Nova Scotia, Virginia, North Carolina, South Carolina, and Georgia. And, after taking all the land and enslaving or killing any indigenous peoples who defied them, they stole and bought children, women, and men from their African villages and had them shipped across the North Atlantic as so many sacks of grain. Once reaching their destinations, the Africans were off-loaded and sold as chattel[81] to cotton, sugar cane, indigo, and rice operations throughout the Caribbean and southern colonies. In my in-depth genealogical research over the past seven years, I have discovered that most of my ancestors were involved in some way in every single aspect of North American indigenous removals, the enslavement and "breeding" of Africans for chattel, the control of Nature for profit, and the development of moral justifications and dissemination of such justifications in service to those genocidal acts and systems of oppression. Among my ancestors I have captains of ships, deer skin traders, slave owners, land owners, lumbermen, railroad and cotton clerks, preachers, and teachers. This family legacy taught me to expect access and opportunity and ownership to what is not my own. The rot of greed, privilege, manifest destiny, and entitlement infects my blood. And, this infection has led me to believe that getting ahead in life depends on doing all I can to maintain myself as host to the rot. Born into this way, was this what led me to not press too hard about the corruption I was asked to be a part of at NOAA? Is it also what made it fairly easy for me to quit without considering future consequences? It was not until I left my job in government and started learning about the interconnected relationships between what it means to be oppressed and to be oppressor and between humans and Nature that a consciousness of community, common good, and what individual versus community values meant started to emerge.

This lack of any sense of community values and any true recognition of the common good shaped my own experiences of change most strikingly in how I never considered other people who were not within "my" community. In fact, I was taught and am still surrounded by friends, family, and colleagues who believe, that this self-centered and very narrow sense of self in community is essential to maintaining not only their own privilege and power but also, somehow, the world's order. "This is just the way the world is," they say. Recognition of the realities in the wider communities within which we all live that are unlike "my" community, and any notion of solidarity for the common good with those that are not "mine" creates, especially among those in relatively privileged positions, a palpable fear that their comfort and safety could be threatened.

So, it follows that preserving privilege, power, comfort, and safety becomes an aversion to face change, and certainly to work for changes that benefit the common good. In this way, working to modify current systems and structures of societal oppression becomes a revolutionary act. Because, taken to their logical conclusion, such systemic changes would in fact threaten the world order from which those with privilege, power, comfort, and safety personally benefit.

And some, like myself, born with a bit more restlessness in our hearts, take it a step further. Being surrounded by this comfortable and entitled feeling that the systems were always on our side means we embrace and even promote constant change as long as we can use our privilege for ourselves to overcome any negative consequences. In my own life, the result of such learned and thoughtless behavior has led to selfish ambitions and feelings of entitlement, especially when I did not get what I thought I deserved. Because, you see, I could act as a petulant spoiled child if I felt wronged or shunned because I would just move on. Also, if I saw something more sparkly and exciting across the street I could cross over even if it meant leaving others who cared about me, communities that had embraced me, or projects I had started.

* * *

Whoa! Talk about how my relationship to change has been completely built around my privilege, entitlement, and disregard for others. And, as I have grown to be more critically conscious I recognize how easy the social pressures to behave with privilege, entitlement, and selfishness make it to fall back into a mindset that ignores community values and the common good instead of embracing community values and making the choice to stand up for the common good. This understanding of how everything from our ancestral lines to our mental patterns and learned behaviors shape our relationships to change is a critical part of our self-evaluation.

Evaluating our own past and current experiences and reactions to change will increase our critical consciousness in order to assist us in transforming those patterns and behaviors. We must analyze our relationship to change in such a way, and confess our "faults" so to speak, not because we have grown beyond them and can pat ourselves on the back, but because we live with them every day and must remain vigilantly conscious of them creeping back in. Our on-going self-evaluation of how we approach change, and the good dose of humility it can provide, is an essential component to the on-going practice of critical consciousness. In my experience and observations, it is also necessary to engage in this practice prior to engaging with others in order to enter the sacred space of community with open eyes, open hands, and an open heart.

To try this practice out for yourself, take an hour to think about an experience, or experiences, in your life where you have been confronted with some kind of event that involved change that made you feel strongly in some way. It doesn't matter the context -- friendships, family, work, social life -- and it doesn't matter exactly the feeling -- angry, hopeful, helpless. Some questions you might want to ask and answer about this experience in your re-telling might be: What was the experience like for you at the time? Did you recognize it as change as it was happening or later? How did you think or act once you realized that this was about change? What were the personal consequences of your thinking and behavior in response to the change? What does this reveal about your biases, learned behaviors, personal beliefs and values, emotional states? Does it reveal anything about the values you do or do not place on community values and the common good, including how you define these things? How does your family history and what you know about the lives of your ancestors shape your relationship with change, especially related to community values and the common good? And, in what ways can you use this self-evaluation to create a framework for consciously acting on change first for in yourself, and then in community with others? In other words, if confronted with change in the future how will you get over or get past yourself, if necessary, in order to consider others in the whole community? As you re-tell your personal story of change and do this bit of self-exploration with these questions, and others that might emerge, write it all out or speak it all out loud into an audio recorder or to a trusted friend or family member.

This individual self-evaluation and assessment of how we have faced change or circumstances in which change was possible is essential to understanding the foundations of critical consciousness within ourselves. To have this internal foundation will be very important as we construct a collective vision of the common good and community values, identify our building blocks for making that vision a reality, and select the adhesive that will glue those blocks together in support of transformation and liberation. In the next chapter we will continue the journey of critical consciousness towards cultural synthesis by stepping more outside ourselves and thinking about what community looks like and feels like for each of us, how we identify ourselves within community, and developing conscious and courageous spaces where we can share our community dreams with one another.

5. RESURRECTING OUR COMMUNITIES TOGETHER

P aying close attention to my own shadow, the parts of myself that are difficult, dark, and where fear resides, and confronting it has been important to how I am relearning the world. One of the driving factors behind my fascination with whole and beloved community, rather than just community or types of communities, and my proselytizing about community-centered research and community engaged participatory governance is that deep-down I am actually terribly frightened of this idea of whole community. It is one of my shadows. I admit to deep-down finding the whole, beloved community idea threatening to my self-hood, identity, ego, and certainly my racial and economic privileges. There are circumstances in my life and work within community that can feel like I am waging war with myself, and at times others. Through much soul-searching and contemplation I have discovered that the primary underlying reason: being in whole community cracks me wide open to others' judgments, exposing my shame and weaknesses, and my pride, privileges, and entitlements.

It is like those dreams I think we've all had from time to time when you arrive to work or a class without our pants or a shirt. I don't know about you, but most of the time no one seems to notice my nakedness in those dreams, but I am so preoccupied with covering myself that I feel terrified and incapacitated. In other words, I fear that being a part of whole community will open me up to judgment by others, which as someone hyper-attuned to other people's emotions makes me feel extremely vulnerable and raw.

Part of my reason for writing this book was to overcome this personal terror of others' judgment and the fear of being exposed and naked to others when in community. But, even more important I wanted to let others know, who may have similar fears about the idea of whole, beloved community, especially in the way we will learn about in this Chapter and Chapter 6, that there are ways to transform those fears into a desire to learn and grow instead of always feeling stuck, alienated, or hiding from others. For those who do not share this fear or who have grown beyond it, I felt it was also important that we remind ourselves from time to time when living, or seeking to live, in whole community, that both rejection and acceptance are challenge that we all will face if we participate in community with our whole selves.

A necessary prerequisite to facing rapid changes in ways that lead to transformation and liberation rather than further oppression and violence is insistence on placing individuals and communities that are presently, or have in the past, experienced the negative impacts of rapid changes brought about by industrial and economic developments at the center of any and all efforts to document, analyze, advocate, build, maintain, and protect their own selves and their communities. The phrase, "Nothing about us without us," first emerged in 16th Century Eastern European legislation as a linguistic effort to shift power from monarchs to nobility. In more recent times it has become an important statement of the

South African disability movement, and of social justice and racial equity movements in the U.S., that succinctly captures this demand to place individuals and communities who have most directly and negatively been impacted by change at the center of all organizing[82]. It is essentially a demand for local autonomy and self-determination. But, in order for this self-determination to be articulated from within communities in the first place, for the voices to come from inside the community and not only from outside experts and researchers, activists, or journalists who are merely witnessing or translating those voices, recognition of the root causes of systemic oppression today and in the past by communities themselves is critical. As we have learned, this is the critical consciousness that leads to conscientization and ideally to actions that liberate whole communities. In certain communities naming and recognizing oppression is so full of fear, anxiety, and violence from generations of forced silence and suppression that the act of finding and bringing back to life a community's vitality, autonomy, and self-determination takes an enormous individual commitment and engagement not just to structural liberation but to spiritual and soulful liberation as well.

It is in this recognition of the linkage between the political, psychological, cultural, and the spiritual that the process of critical consciousness in the whole community context is a process of not just awakening (as in "wokeness") but a process of Resurrection. Resurrection offers a deep spiritual and embodied path for communities who are faced with change. It also helps us remember that we must all dig deeper to uncover and raise up what in some instances are generations of hidden and silenced forms and structures of oppression in order to dismantle them and rebuild. The word Resurrection's association to the Christian tradition of the Holy Days of Lent and Easter and the crucifixion and rising from the dead of Jesus Christ provides direct spiritual teachings about confronting systems of violence and oppression and the commitments involved, as well as the ultimate freedom that awaits us all in that confrontation and commitment.

In order for the Resurrection to occur, Jesus had to first be crucified by the powerful Roman government at the behest of the Jewish leaders of the time. The crime was fomenting insurrection against the ruling Roman government and even worse actively defying and teaching against what were accepted, and expected, practices of the Jewish religious tradition. Jesus taught that these traditions and politics caused great suffering and violence to both the local people who were expected to pay tribute in coin to Rome, as well as the fowl, sheep, cattle, and goats who were brought to the temple for religious sacrifice. After his sentencing, crucifixion, and death, Jesus re-appeared in physical body to his family and disciples to demonstrate the miracle of Resurrection from the dead, and to speak with them about what he had taught them during his life that they had not yet understood. The responses of people immediately after the crucifixion and Resurrection of Jesus within the Christian Bible offer us profiles in denial, doubt, fear, loss, anger, humility, and eventual witness. These profiles parallel our own on the journey of critical consciousness. And, as with the experiences of Jesus' disciples and later followers, these initial individual profiles have the potential to not just shift one person's consciousness but that of an entire community.

Spiritual and religious stories and teachings like Jesus' Resurrection carry deep meaning to Christians as well as lessons for all of humanity in how we relate to one another and the world around us and how we choose to act in the face of change and injustice[83]. These lessons can provide our communities with an imaginative and immediately relevant road map on today's journey of critical consciousness and cultural synthesis in facing change and confronting systemic oppression. And, there are, as with all steps on the path of critical consciousness, personal lessons we must not ignore; about what individual attitudes and actions are necessary to confront those systems and the individual values and ethical commitments we must have and be willing to act from in order to rebuild, restore, transform, liberate, and participate in caring for our whole community and Nature. In our eagerness to work in community or with Nature we must never forget that the work must always be rooted, begin, and continually be fed from inside our hearts, minds, and bodies.

Finding Resurrection

Finding the personal lessons that are contained in the Resurrection story came recently for me. I'm not only a late bloomer in embracing and living my spiritual and religious convictions, but I also have trouble forgiving. As a child I had a difficult time imagining someone coming back "from the dead," and the Easter season and Jesus' Resurrection always seemed so fantastical that it took on a carnival atmosphere, made even more so with all the flowers, dyed eggs, bunnies, games, and loads of candy that have become synonymous with Easter in the U.S. However, I had no problem imagining the crucifixion. What inspired my imagination the most was the bloody almost life-sized and very human crucifixion that hung in the hallway of our Epsicopal church in Savannah during the Lenten holy days leading up to Easter. But, the whole notion of someone coming back to life after dying, even for my eight-year-old self, did not make sense. I didn't believe in the Resurrection, but I did believe in the Easter Bunny.

Some of my earliest and happiest memories from my childhood were from Easter week – going to church service, bible school, sharing community meals, flowers, and egg hunts. I especially remember how close I felt to my dad during those times. Now I see that closeness probably had to do with it being one of the only predictable times I saw my dad take time off from the office and work. And, it was also when his true emotions came a little closer to the surface. I only saw dad cry three times in my life, at an Easter week church service, at his mom's funeral, and after my mom's death.

But, then, when I was around nine or ten I found out the Easter Bunny wasn't real. This was more devastating to me than finding out Santa Claus wasn't real! I remember crying inconsolably for hours on the back stairs of our house on East Liberty Street where, when I was happy, I would sit and sing to the giant mulberry tree that lived there. I was very angry at my parents for lying to me about the Easter Bunny and in my young brain this deception became closely tied to an entire deception around the entire Easter week, the crucifixion, and the Resurrection. My inability to forgive my parents for their deception somehow later morphed into one more justification for my rejection of Christian beliefs; I saw the Resurrection as a useful, if delusional, myth passed down through the generations to soothe people's fears around dying and loss.

Then, after dad's death, my relationship with Christianity, and the story of Jesus' Resurrection in particular, changed dramatically. After being with my uncle, my mom, and then my dad as they all took their last breaths, I became acutely aware of the frightening physical and emotional realities, but also the mystery and beauty, surrounding the process of dying and death itself. It was during the periods before, during, and after their deaths that I began to see and feel people and Nature around me in a new way, as more interconnected and unified in both life and death. Daily activities like showering, getting dressed, running errands, eating lunch, going out to dinner, reading, and conversations with friends and family all became interconnected with my loss and grief, but also this immense feeling of unity with life, breath, and a sense of God and divine presence. This was a presence I could not shake, and I realized that those activities and moments of both loss and unity were in fact the moments when my uncle, mom, dad, and God were very much present and alive to me. It was deeper than a memory or nostalgia. It was a felt presence.

Somehow, this perceptual shift during my grief left me with a willingness to accept the idea of someone being able to rise from the dead in a very real and material sense. It opened me up to the mystery even if my rational mind did not completely accept it. Yes, it gave me comfort that my loved ones were still beside me and on a more profound and deep level it gave me a way to reconcile and psychologically process all the personal loss. But it was something much more profound as well. Something I still have not found the words to explain. The only way I know how to say it is that I have had my heart opened to the mystery of Christ's Resurrection and the many ways it serves not only as a story to comfort us at times of profound loss and grief, but also as a concrete and very real example of love in action in the world today.

Contemplating what the resurrection of Jesus teaches me in my own life and work has helped me recognize how to take actions that honor the love and unity of all life, as well as to embrace the practice of radical humility and forgiveness that such actions require[84]. Jesus took a stand for what he believed, whether in his teaching, his manner of living, and his actions, but it was not until after he was dead that his most devout followers even began to understand that his greatest lesson was Love[85]. But today, as Jesus' original lessons of "Love" have been reinterpreted into various religious and spiritual dogmas, as well as appropriated into greeting cards and romantic best-sellers, I worry that we have lost sight of the actual lessons and the immense power of this original Love to reconnect us with Spirit and God and to one another. A reconnection that, I believe, is necessary for dismantling corrupt and oppressive systems.

In order for Love to have revolutionary meaning in our lives today, it must be understood within the context of faith in a higher power *beyond* human will and action. For the followers of Jesus this is illustrated most profoundly in the events described in the Gospel leading up to Jesus' crucifixion in which he refused to demonstrate his claim that he was the Son of God through conducting some type of miracle on-demand, especially for the Pharisees and others in positions of power in society at the time[86]. Jesus was tortured and killed because he openly defied and taught of Love for God and for one another as the power that would undo the materially obsessed, corrupt, and violent religious, economic, and political society of his time. He was a threat to the status quo and dared to openly question how those in power were using the laws and traditions to enrich themselves further rather than loving God and one another.

Even for non-Christians, reading the Gospel teachings leading to Jesus' crucifixion and resurrection through this lens of Love provides direct insights into the short-sighted ways we organize ourselves and our communities today against corruption, greed, and all sorts of dangerous industrial and economic developments. For me, these insights provide lessons on *how not to* organize ourselves, as well as *how to* organize ourselves for liberation and transformation. In the *how not to* organize category, the events leading up to the resurrection teach us:

- *not to* solely focus on material (or technological) fixes to our oppression,
- *not to* think that our wealth and possessions will save us from oppression,
- *not to* attempt to confront and change corrupt practices and systems using the same thinking that produced those practices and systems of corruption,
- *not to* heap our grievances and resentments on our leaders while unconscious people and power-hungry religious and political leaders become the fuel for escalating violence, and

- *not to* think that our freedom and liberation from judgment and persecution is dependent on some public demonstration of our goodness and righteousness, whether in virtual (social media) or face-to-face interactions.

Instead, the Gospel read through the lens of Love teaches us:

- *to maintain* courage, hope, faith, and trust in a higher power,
- *to practice* peace and non-violence,
- *to defend* community values,
- *to act* on the common good, and, of course,
- *to love* the God of our understanding and one another.

In other words, the life, trial, crucifixion, and the resurrection of Jesus all contain profound teachings about how to act on behalf of liberation for all and to embody peace and Love. Jesus teaches us that death, and importantly death brought on by deep faith and surrender to a power greater than ourselves can lead us to act on behalf of Love for the greater whole, community values, and the common good. With the resurrection of Jesus we learn that death was not an end at all, but a beginning to spiritual understanding, insight, liberation, and a deeper connection to God and Spirit than we could have ever imagined.

None of these insights or teachings are confined to the way of Jesus or Christianity. Judaism also mandates this type of social justice work as a mitzvah for Jews and a commandment for Gentiles. Ditto with Islam. Social justice is in fact recognized as central to most teachings of organized religion. In fact, in our work toward critical consciousness and cultural synthesis this means being moved to both inaction and action by hope, faith, love, and surrender, as well as other convictions of the heart and soul that lead us to a truer sense of our fellow humans, a deeper spiritual life, and true liberation for all. Love in action leads to community, life, and liberation. Anything less is feeding into our human obsessions with material possessions, self-interests, and attachments to corrupt systems. So, our work is not just to transform, rebuild, or regenerate community, it is to breathe new life into and truly resurrect community in the full awareness (truth) of, and in grappling in public with (reconciliation) how we are each in our own ways part of oppressive and corrupt institutions and systems.

As we have learned, critical consciousness involves not just learning to perceive and critique social, political, and economic contradictions and the systems of oppression that keep these contradictions in place, it must also involve a willingness to grapple with our individual choices and emotions about our roles in these systems and allow certain parts of ourselves to die or fall away as we face change and become more critically conscious. By sharing my story of finding resurrection in my own life, I hope to offer a more soulful way to experience the losses that we may encounter along the journey toward critical consciousness. When we are paralyzed in the face of change and loss we must get beyond the denial, fear, anger, and all that freezes us and recognize that Love is the force that will allow us to break out of these patterns of oppression. It is the force that will help us to identify concrete actions that allow us to reclaim our own power to choose and act with self-determination in ways that liberate us all. But, to live into such a force, in a resurrected sense, we must be open to what this means in seeking whole community, and not just in our own personal lives or within the stories of other communities.

Seeking Whole Community

In a multi-racial, multi-cultural, multi-ethnic, multi-religious, and multi-lingual nation like the United States people hold so many different perspectives. Some are based on political or economic ideologies, racial, religious, ethnic, gender, economic, regional, or other identities that relate to certain values, beliefs, family and national mythologies, and attitudes. There is a natural tendency to keep ourselves divided and separated for safety rather than bringing ourselves together to find common ground, common goals, or values of community and wholeness. But to resurrect our communities across, and in spite of, these differences we need to: allow for parts of ourselves to die away and be prepared to grieve for that loss as well as expect new life; be aware of our own and others' pain, fear, and trauma at confronting differences and be able to respect and honor those feelings; and, be willing to let go of our need to control outcomes and be able instead to find and express love and forgiveness.

Attempting to be in such whole community dialogue requires a willingness to let go of both our individual identities, as well as our definitions of who we are, or think we are, in community. At the same time, it is essential that we not lose sight of how important our personal voice, as well as sense of safety is, and that we are able to fully express our fears, concerns, hopes, and dreams through sharing of opinions, values, and beliefs. It is a constant process of letting parts of ourselves die, remembering who we are, and then being reborn and resurrected. Of course, for this to be a life-affirming process and not something that leads to great suffering, trauma, and violence, we must all agree that the purpose of seeking out the meaning of whole community and developing a community change process is liberation for all of life based on love and non-violent action and not to promote a singular type of community, a certain type of identity, or a specific ideology.

As we saw in Bradford County, the occurrence and persistence of negative disruptions people experience with rapid changes can sometimes be explained by the very words people use to describe those changes and disruptions. But, despite my insistence that words matter and have consequences, you may have noticed that I have failed so far to define the word "community," which appears in the title and many times throughout this book. That is not an over sight, it is because I believe that there is not, nor should there be, one single definition of community. Rather, I think the concept of community is a holistic continuum that explains how we relate to one another and the world around us over time. Some of the motivation to write this book came from searching for a way to explain why I believe that singularly defining community is in itself one of the greatest problems we have in facing change and transforming our world, and yet something we either habitually do ourselves or are asked to do by others every single day. Trying to define community in this way also makes it very difficult to practice cultural synthesis and to act for the true liberation of all people, both oppressed and oppressor.

We commonly lump ourselves and people together as "community" based on a single characteristic or demographic or identity, whether race, income, education, sex, gender identity, place or home town, religion, you name it. Typically, we attempt to define communities by external and material markers that others can also identify, like the color of our skin, our countries of origin, neighborhoods we live in, schools we attend or that our children attend, places of birth, languages we speak, churches we attend, jobs we have, and on and on. But we all know that we are not one characteristic, one demographic, one identity, one circumstance, or one place. And, we also know that we each have complex and sometimes even contradictory identities that can mean when we try to fit neatly into one "community" we deny other parts of ourselves. Thinking of community in a more holy and holistic way, and as more of a continuum rather than rigid categories, gives us a more humane and integral way of identifying who we are in community, the relational aspects of what it means to be inside or outside of community, and who and what our communities mean to us. This recognizes and addresses the whole community and how we each intersect with that whole.

In all its permutations and meanings to denote a group of people, a place, or a shared interest, the word "community" is used by different people to denote very different things. There have been entire books, dissertations, scholarly papers, college courses, and public debates on the meaning of "community." But, if we just look at the history of the word, its etymology, and its everyday uses through time, we can see that the word "community" has changed from denoting feelings of fellowship and relationship in its original Latin to denoting the material and transactional qualities of physicality, place, land, ownership, possession, and individual identification in its current English use.

Following the linguistic history of the word community provides us with an interesting parallel to the ways we have related to one another in the past in contrast to how we relate to one another today. As human history has marched on, the word has become less relational and more transactional, from denoting being in full, integral relationship with self and others, to denoting today's focus on individual identification with some particular type of relationship denoting our race, class, ethnicity, age, gender, profession, hobby, or many other characteristics and factors. The history of the word community resonates with the systems of oppression we are trying to un-do today through the process of critical consciousness, and especially the work of cultural synthesis. For example, to someone like Peter Block, a facilitator and leader in dialogue practices, he describes community not as one *thing* but instead as a sense of belonging, more akin to the original Latin meaning of being in relationship with self and other. Block believes this sense of community as belonging has the most relevance to transforming our world for the greatest good of all[87]. Based on my work with communities undergoing rapid changes, I agree.

This idea of wholeness related to community is not a new concept, and importantly it is not an idea that Western Europeans can claim as theirs either. Being inter-connected, in mutuality, and acting out of or in reciprocity, are essential components of indigenous cosmologies around the world. In the U.S., this cosmology of whole community is perhaps best depicted within the 21st Century imagination through the ideas, beliefs, and values that arose and have been nurtured in the traditions of the black church and especially the teachings of Howard Thurman and Dr. Martin Luther King Jr. These traditions have been grounded in the belief that the struggle for the liberation of black people could only be realized through the prism of universal liberation of all peoples; as Walter Fluker said, "The universal themes of forgiveness, reconciliation, and hope which characterized King's and Thurman's vision of community have always been fundamental to the black community in general and the black church in particular."[88] These themes have been part of the spiritual quest towards what is known as the Beloved Community, and which should, in the end, I believe be our ultimate goal in seeking whole community.

Before we fully dive into shifting from our self in community to resurrecting our whole holy communities, and building a framework for transformative community change, let's learn about some practices that we can use to assist us in supporting each other to take a critical look at how our communities can approach change in less reactive and oppressive ways and in more generative and loving ways.

Dialogue Practices & Appreciative Inquiry

I learned first-hand about the positive power of dialogue practices in community change work and how these practices work to catalyze cultural consciousness through conducting ethnographic interviews and focus groups first in Boston and then, in a more participatory mode, during my work in

Bradford County.

From 2010 to 2011, a dozen farmers and landowners in Bradford County accepted my invitation to participate in focus groups for my Dickinson College post-doc research to explore their practical, emotional, and spiritual relationships to their land, water, and air, their attachments to places of memory, as well as their relationships with neighbors and family and how all those relationships and attachments were changing in the midst of shale gas developments rapidly taking place throughout the county. In the focus groups we employed the social science methods of photo-voice and participatory mapping.

These methods involve giving local residents a way to share their feelings, beliefs, and knowledge with someone else or other residents, and to collect qualitative sociological and anthropological data on their relationships to their local environment and their community during periods of change or in light of new developments. Photo-voice asks participants certain questions about how they relate to changes going on in their communities and then asks them to take photographs and write out their thoughts about these questions and then come back and share images and writings in conversation with the group[89]. In parallel with the photo-voice, the farmers and landowners were invited to participate in a group mapping process in which they were asked different questions about their land, special places throughout the County, water resources, relationships with neighbors, locations of new developments, and then asked to make notations on paper maps in response to those questions. Both photo-voice and participatory mapping allowed for visual and creative expressions of local relationships beyond just spoken communication.

What I began to realize after the first group meetings and reviewing our recordings was that the images, writings, and maps were only secondary to the intense emotions being shared during these meetings that seemed to alter how some, although not all, of the participants thought about their relationships to Nature, places, their neighbors, and the rapid changes taking place. Or, at least, it made them ask new questions. The new realizations they were coming to about what these developments might mean to their rural way of life and quality of life moved them, and me, to tears at certain points. And, the new questions about the developments in Bradford County and the changes taking place as a result, were not only asked during focus group meetings, they also began asking them to their neighbors, their local officials, and certainly the gas companies and developers.

I had learned how to sit with and comfort individuals expressing sometimes raw emotions and asking difficult questions when they had emerged from individual interviews in Boston, but the group setting was much more intense and complicated and I was concerned about the well-being of the participants and the ethical implications of my questions arousing such intense emotions, as well as my abilities to respond appropriately, and to comfort and assist groups through periods of emotional vulnerability. The two methods of photo-voice and participatory mapping, in asking participants to reflect deeply on what was important to them personally and then in a group setting, was asking them to engage in deeper dialogues about change within themselves and with others that dredged up unconscious worries, fears, and old memories that left many of them feeling emotionally vulnerable. It was a huge reminder that asking people to engage in dialogues about change should be done with great care and with an emphasis on personal safety.

In fact, one of the biggest lessons I learned during my work in Bradford County was the importance of creating spaces for dialogue that honor this vulnerability completely. I think of this as creating "brave space," since it is critical when we engage in generative dialogues about change, especially in whole community and not just with those we are most comfortable, that we stay open and honest with one another and not hide our true beliefs and values despite the fear and pain.

In the United States today we are more focused on our individual egos and judgments than with community needs and well-being. This leads to us to being woefully under-developed when it comes to having emotional tools to support one another, and even care for ourselves, when conflicts or arguments or difficult emotions arise in group settings. When entering into whole community dialogue it is essential to explicitly recognize that one of the reasons dialogues, especially for the purposes of critical consciousness and cultural synthesis, feel so difficult and painful and are sometimes perceived as unhelpful and even harmful, is because of previous experiences most of us have had in which someone did not respect the pain, fear, and vulnerabilities that surfaced in a group setting. And, in the worst of all cases, some of us have even experienced having our pain, fears, and vulnerabilities used as weapons against us.

Conscious of these previous negative experiences, we need to proceed with great caution to avoid causing any further harm or trauma to individuals or groups when inviting them into whole community dialogue. This means dialogue practice with the goal of developing a framework for whole community change takes enormous time, patience, and commitment on the part of participants and anyone organizing or facilitating. It is critical when organizing and hosting community dialogues in which there is the possibility that such fear and pain may arise that there is a clear process in place at the beginning to honor and speak about any vulnerabilities, safety concerns, or hurt feelings that may arise among participants at any point during the dialogue and well after the dialogue has officially ended.

To assist me in learning more about how to create these "brave spaces" and to just better understand what was happening for the participants in these focus groups, I sought out a social psychologist colleague at Dickinson College, Sharon Kingston, for guidance on how to both manage these groups and allow participants to get the most out of them. I had already realized that there might be something more profound going on than just a participatory research project, and she made me realize that what was occurring was in fact more of a type of social intervention; in using an open-ended participatory research process I had awakened within some of the participants a new consciousness of themselves as well as the world around them. This shook me when Sharon first said this, and not in a good way. Even though I had pretty much dismissed the idea of the objective observer in science, especially social science, during my doctoral research in Boston, I nonetheless had been taught to be the observer and not the manipulator, interventionist, or god forbid, experimenter. That was the domain of psychologists and therapists, not ethnographers or sociologists.

What Sharon was telling me was that I had in fact created an intervention that was changing people's thoughts and behaviors. And, honestly this scared me a little. It also made me feel deeply responsible for these peoples' well-being in ways I had not felt before. This realization, along with the phone call I had with Nancy about the non-disclosure agreements she and her husband had signed, turned my work in Bradford County upside down and changed my own perspective of my role within the community and what I was even doing there. I began to view my work less as "co-researcher" and more as facilitator, witness, teacher, and even friend or confidante. It also prompted me to search for a way to describe this way of working to my academic and professional colleagues. I looked into the social psychology literature on consciousness and found some incredible new ways to think about my work, especially in revisiting Paulo Freire's work on conscientization and cultural synthesis.

My conversations with Sharon and readings on method and approaches to studying consciousness made me realize for the first time that my approach to social science, with ethnographic group interviews and a focus on individual and group lived experiences and participatory methods, actually had a name in psychology and pedagogical disciplines – dialogue, or dialogic, practice – and that there were various methods and tools that had been developed to assist participants and facilitators in this practice, one of those being appreciative inquiry.

Dialogue practice is a form of conversation that when used in a community or group setting opens up a space for learning about ourselves in community beyond just what we identify as "our" community. Thus, it is an amazing practice for cultural synthesis. It can be frightening or intimidating because unconscious beliefs and biases and old memories may arise towards others in the group or within ourselves. We may have already pre-judged others in the group or our own expectations in certain ways either as a result of previous experiences or societal conditioning. But, experiences of being in dialogue with others who are not like us has the potential to open us up to the understanding that our personal values, beliefs, and biases are not representative of the broader, whole community. This openness to other ways of being in the world is a necessary first step to finding out what whole community means to us. It entails developing a common set of values that can resonate within and across different communities. It can also involve identifying common values by exposing our differences and our similarities when it comes to individual values and beliefs. When dialogue is practiced using an appreciate inquiry approach, the power to determine individual and collective actions that can lead to better outcomes for all with the ultimate objective of developing critical community consciousness and a practical framework for transformative community change is amplified.

Appreciative inquiry promotes positive change by focusing on key experiences and successes of the past. It relies on interviews and storytelling that draw out these positive memories, and on a collective analysis of the elements of success. This analysis becomes the reference point for further community action, and thus cultural synthesis. Appreciative inquiry is all about locating the generative force and energy for change. In my Bradford County experience, I learned that by asking a group of people open-ended and exploratory questions about their relationships with their own lives, their neighbors, their homes and environments, changes they were experiencing, asking them to take photographs and write about these things, and then just listening as they individually and collectively thought about those answers and shared their images and words, I was also giving them the space and time to develop deeper answers than they might normally, to truly listen to one another, and to develop their own questions. That is the heart of appreciative inquiry.

What the appreciative inquiry approach seeks to achieve is the transformation of people from those that see themselves in largely negative terms - and therefore are inclined to become locked in their own negative views of themselves - to people that see themselves as having within them the capacity to enrich and enhance the quality of life of all members of the community. As the late Ted Smeaton, in his *Inspiring Communities* Blog, once said: "Just as plants grow towards their energy source, so do communities and organisations move towards what gives them life and energy."[90] So, the most important lesson from appreciative inquiry is that people grow in the direction of the questions that they ask. The questions we ask and the way we construct them will focus us in a particular manner and will greatly affect the outcome of our inquiry. If we ask: "What is wrong and who is to blame?" We set up a certain dynamic of problem-solving and blame assigning. If we ask: "What is right and who is to thank?" We set up a dynamic of finding and imagining the good, celebration of that good, and gratitude for all the good.

I saw the power of dialogue practice and appreciative inquiry in action long after our Bradford County focus group meetings. In later private conversations with people who had participated in those meetings, they told me how the sharing of different perspectives and the questions asked during the focus groups not only opened windows into how they perceived events and circumstances in their own lives, but also in others' lives. Their self-consciousness and the consciousness of others and their shared experiences around change and the shale gas developments was exposed in a way that led them to ask their own and different questions. This radical self-awareness, and when done in groups awareness of others, is the true gift of appreciate inquiry.

Another consequence of appreciative inquiry is that it can raise conscious awareness of self and others' unconscious biases, those blind spots that either stop us from experiencing life to its fullest, finding practical solutions, or from seeing our neighbors as ourselves and separate us from whole community. While disorienting and uncomfortable at first, such revelations of our biases against others when approached with an open heart and mind, empathy, and care can be truly generative and transformative for individuals and entire groups[91].

Appreciative inquiry, as a method of open, learner's-mind, or beginner's-mind asks questions in a way that tends to leave more questions on the table than it does answers. This can be uncomfortable for a lot of us who have been taught that the role of questions is to find the "right" answers, or that asking questions when we don't understand something can be a sign of weakness. In order to be generative and transformative and positive, appreciative inquiry requires a level of humility and gratitude that some of us find difficult. But, in combination with individual and community gift, or asset, inventories described in this chapter as "Good Works," using dialogue practice and appreciative inquiry is a practical approach to raising individual consciousness, clarifying individual and collective values, and also has the possibility to transform personal and collective consciousness. Facilitated with care, people in dialogue using an appreciative inquiry approach become more aware of their inherent and unconscious bias and are more open to the potential of identifying and strengthening weak or missing social ties and building new social bonds and new social bridges with those we may not know or may have thought of as not a part of "our" community. Such social ties, bonds, and bridges can in turn support more robust civic engagement, long-term community well-being, and whole community transformation.

What I have learned from past and on-going participatory research in group settings is that getting people to share their personal values with one another is not an easy task. We all need a space where others will listen respectively and take us seriously, and there will be no judgment. In setting up the focus groups in Bradford County, that is, in essence what I had unknowingly provided – a space for personal sharing and serious listening where judgments of one another are kept in check. Once personal values are shared it can be the first step in raising self-awareness that then opens the doors to exploring and perhaps recovering an awareness of self and deeper consciousness, and in turn confidence, that eventually leads to deeper dialogues with others about the connections and disconnections between our individual and community values and the common good. But, as with any dialogue, where we have the possibility to feel vulnerable or judged, appreciative inquiry is not free of conflict and miscommunication and so ground rules, or what I like to refer to as "L.O.V.E. Rules," in which the acronym L.O.V.E. is both the thing that is ruling and the type of rules we follow, need to be established prior to meetings in order to ensure that the intention of our dialogues are clear and that harm is not done during dialogue. In this chapter I go into greater detail on what exactly this idea of "L.O.V.E. Rules" entails, and I encourage anyone who plans to use dialogue in community, whether to create a framework for transformative whole community change, for resilience planning, or any other type of conscientization and cultural synthesis work, develop and adopt their own set of L.O.V.E. Rules before any type of whole community dialogues begin.

Because of the care required in practicing dialogue this way, some communities working on developing frameworks for transformative whole community change may choose to call upon people with professional social psychology backgrounds or who have experience in counseling both groups and individuals in order to be available to assist when difficult emotions and feelings arise. However, it is important to recognize that for many rural and urban communities this type of professional help is not readily available, affordable, and it may not always be culturally appropriate. So, it is my hope that the combination of concrete examples, tools, and practices I outline in this book, approached with the utmost attention and care, can assist all of us in not only facing change, but in resurrecting community and transforming our little parts of the world and that that transformation will spread far beyond. At the very least, I hope it provides some breadcrumbs for others to follow.

L.O.V.E. Rules: Making Space for Dialogue

What is love in the context of facing change, resurrecting our communities, and transformative change? We began to answer this question by looking at the stories leading up to Jesus' crucifixion and resurrection as just one example of love in action through a particular faith or spiritual tradition. And, in his 1963 book, *The Fire Next Time*, James Baldwin expands on this idea of love in action in new and revolutionary ways: "Love takes off the masks that we fear we cannot live without and know we cannot live within. I use the word "love" here not merely in the personal sense but as a state of being, or a state of grace - not in the infantile American sense of being made happy but in the tough and universal sense of quest and daring and growth."

I have also found the acronym L.O.V.E., Listening, Observing, Validating, and Empathizing, a concrete way of creating, building, and maintaining generative and transformational dialogues that nurture whole communities. I use these four words as four concrete practices inspired by and centered in nonviolent, compassionate communication methods.[92] Alongside practicing critical consciousness and cultural synthesis L.O.V.E. can serve as our robust communication agreements for creating brave spaces that provide psychological and physical safety to address unmet needs and vulnerabilities that may come up, for building spaces that respect the humanity and dignity of every single participant, and for maintaining spaces that encourage everyone to express themselves with not just their minds and intellects, but also from lived, embodied experiences that have touched and perhaps changed their hearts. I invite you to think of love in action in this concrete way of being in community as well.

For many of us non-violent communication can be counter-intuitive when we find ourselves communicating with people who we vehemently disagree with or who have harmed or continue to harm us in some way. As much as well-known non-violent activists such as Martin Luther King Jr. and Mahatma Gandhi are revered as way-showers when it comes to peace and justice work, their embrace of non-violence and non-violent communication tactics when they were alive was, and still is today, deeply controversial. We cannot get past such controversy as long as we are flooded by neo-liberal commercialized, colonized, and watered-down messages of "Peace" and "Love" and find ourselves caught up in "Culture Wars" that replace human dignity, respect for all life, and moral imagination that non-violent teachers like Jesus, King, and Ghandi originally taught as foundational to finding moral and ethical grounding. These teachers' original calls were for revolutionary acts towards liberation for all, not the "Peace" and "Love" of some spiritual New Age with pretty art and entertainment and good feelings all around or just liberation for certain groups. But, of course, this is what the tsunami of capital does: weaponize theories of oppression and urgent acts of liberation and true people power to further oppress and suppress us all. If you doubt this, look up King's interview with Sander Vancour on NBC News in 1967, just eleven months before he was assassinated. King's words in this interview are critical to understanding the reason why acting from a non-violent philosophy in the United States at that time, and to this day, for black people and anyone who finds themselves the target of state-sanctioned violence, is the only moral, good, and practical choice when fighting for justice:

"Morally I was led to non-violence because I felt that it was the best moral way to deal with the problem. We were seeking to establish a just society. And it was my feeling then and it is my feeling now that violence creates many more socially destructive, and it creates many more social problems, than it solves. So I was led to nonviolence for deep moral reasons. Now there is no doubt about the fact that in our struggle in Montgomery and all over the United States for that matter nonviolence is also practically sound. It would just be impractical for the Negro to turn to violence. He has neither the instruments nor the techniques of violence. We are about 10 or 11% of the total population of the nation and I'd say are about 1/10ths of 1% of the fire power so it would just be totally impractical and unwise and unrealistic for the Negro to think of violence. And, well, I saw this in the beginning in Montgomery. But this wasn't the basic reason that I turned to nonviolence and I believed in it as a philosophy. I turned to it because I felt that it was the morally excellent way to deal with the problem of racial injustice in our country."[93]

The other misunderstanding that many of us have about non-violence as a mode of communication and action is that being non-violent means never feeling or acting in anger. To most of us, this is asking of us saintly behavior that we most certainly cannot live up to, so why would we set ourselves up for such failure? But all we have to do is go back to one of the original teachers of non-violence, Jesus of Nazareth, and we will find that he was at various times angry in both word and deed. Most notable was his anger at those who sold sacrificial animals and the money exchangers at the temple of Jerusalem during the Passover:

"The Passover of the Jews was at hand, and Jesus went up to Jerusalem. In the temple he found those who were selling oxen and sheep and pigeons, and the money-changers at their business. And making a whip of cords, he drove them all, with the sheep and oxen, out of the temple; and he poured out the coins of the money-changers and overturned their tables. And he told those who sold the pigeons, "Take these things away; you shall not make my Father's house a house of trade."[94]

Non-violence is, as King says, first of all the only moral way to confront injustice. It is not about strict policing of our emotions or even our behaviors as it is about the psychological and spiritual work of becoming more critically aware and conscious of our underlying motivations, intentions, and commitments to fighting for justice and peace in the world at times when we or those we care about feel powerless, angry, fearful, threatened, and harmed. And, non-violence is finding the courage to act from that moral sense, critical awareness, and non-violent consciousness rather than from unconscious emotional impulse alone.

Non-violent consciousness, motivations, intentions, and commitments are rooted in things such as faith in a higher power, human dignity and rights, the rights of Nature, the interconnectedness of all life, and the higher octaves of Love. As Howard Thurman, and many other contemporary religious and secular teachers have taught us, non-violence is deeply personal and spiritual work. It is also intensely alchemical and transformative in that it attempts to take the poison within ourselves— all that internalized oppression, anger, vengeance, and fear— and transform it into a healing tonic for liberation of the individual and community spirit and body, as well as a tonic of love for all life. Honoring our dialogues with L.O.V.E. allows for this alchemical transformation to take place. It is what each and every dialogue experience we enter into or develop with others should aspire to.

One of the potential gifts that can come out of the individual and community asset inventorying of "Good Works," described later in this chapter, is the gift of active and engaged Listening; the "L" in our L.O.V.E. Rules. Known as empathic listening, the practice of active and engaged listening is a core skill of non-violent communicators and can be used by anyone who finds themselves in dangerous, controversial, or uncomfortable situations. Many of us think of ourselves as good listeners but few of us actually are. It takes constant practice and a level of self-awareness that, at least in my own experience, is more learned than innate and is quite honestly, exhausting.

To align our dialogue sessions with this first L.O.V.E. Rule of Listening we should incorporate reminders into meetings about what active, engaged listening actually means and looks like. One constant reminder is to have a single physical object that must be held by anyone speaking. If you do not hold the object, you are to be listening with full attention and in silence. In Indigenous gatherings this object is sometimes referred to as a "talking stick," but any object that is large enough to pass meaningfully and that is respected by silence when one is not holding it can be used such as a brightly colored ribbon, a writing pen, or a small book.

The "O" in L.O.V.E. is Observing. This too, is something most people think of themselves as pretty good at, until that is we are asked to very specifically recall what we have observed. Some of this has to do with being aware of non-verbal communication clues people use and some of it has to do with being more aware of our physical surroundings. Once we become more attuned to non-verbal communication cues and how the arrangement of material objects in our surroundings impacts the way we communicate, we begin to realize we have super-powers that we never knew existed before! And, more importantly that these super-powers of Observation are immediately useful for creating and improving the types of brave spaces we need for whole community dialogue. Very simply, being consistently observant of one another and our surroundings helps us in deciding on the practical things of our meetings with one another: how to arrange our physical or virtual meeting spaces and how to watch for the non-verbal cues during meetings that could mean someone wants to speak or wants to withdraw. These observations also give us practical insights into other aspects of working in groups and producing meaningful dialogues, including when to look for outside or professional facilitation expertise, the timing of meeting breaks, or the optimum number of people in our meetings.

Validating each other and ourselves is the "V" in L.O.V.E.

Validating refers to our ability to comfort and celebrate ourselves and to reach out to someone else in their suffering as well as in their joy. In non-violent communication practice it is looking at someone in the eye when they are speaking to us, not engaging in personal attacks against people who we disagree with in terms of opinions, beliefs, and even values, and being willing to go beyond just listening and observing when people are being oppressed or feeling vulnerable and threatened to standing beside them and, if necessary, confronting the oppressors.

The emotional capacity to validate one another is closely associated with the final letter in L.O.V.E., "E" for Empathy. Empathy is probably the least understood word in our Love Rules. Importantly, empathy is not compassion and it is most certainly not sympathy. Those who feel compassion typically offer something of material or monetary value to someone who is suffering, those who feel sympathy may sometimes offer something of value but they many times only offer thoughts and prayers. In contrast, to empathize with someone who is suffering is to connect emotionally with that suffering, and to empathize with someone who is joyful is to emotionally connect with that joy. Others' suffering is our suffering, others' joy is our joy. Although I have never been a parent, it is how my mom and my friends with children describe how they feel as a parent. While empathy can be expressed as a denouncement of things of material or monetary value, it is much deeper than just tithing or material sacrifices. In this final L.O.V.E. Rule the most important thing to understand and remember is that we are all interconnected. To realize "whole community" and work towards generative and transformative community, to resurrect community, we must find and practice empathy and embody the principle that there is no liberation without liberation of all.

This broad description of the purpose of "L.O.V.E. Rules" is meant to be used by our communities to design our very own specific set of guidelines or ground rules for imagining, designing, facilitating, and creating a generative and transformative dialogue process that is meaningful and right for our particular communities. Unlike how we think of "Rules" as set in stone or some type of dogma handed to us from someone else, these rules are intended to be collaboratively generated, in other words, co-generated, and should evolve with the dialogue and with the community who practice them. That is why "Love" here is both a description of the type of "Rules" and a statement that "Love Rules!" The Love Rules for the specific community we are working in may be entirely different than those for another community or for another dialogue process. It is important to remind one another at each meeting and even to revisit the L.O.V.E. Rules as dialogue progresses. These reminders and revisions may be particularly important when new people or groups come in and out of the dialogue.

One very broad-reaching example of what I mean by "L.O.V.E. Rules" was developed in December 1996 by forty people of color and European-American representatives meeting in Jemez, New Mexico, for the "Working Group Meeting on Globalization and Trade." The intention of this meeting, hosted by the Southwest Network for Environmental and Economic Justice, was to develop common understandings between participants from different cultures, politics, and organizations on the implications of global trade on environmental and economic justice. Today, groups and communities working together towards environmental, climate, indigenous, and racial justice use these very broad principles. In summary, they are:

#1 Be Inclusive.

#2 Emphasis on Bottom-Up Organizing.

#3 Let People Speak for Themselves.

#4 Work Together In Solidarity and Mutuality.

#5 Build Just Relationships Among Ourselves.

#6 Commitment to Self-Transformation.

The full description of each of the six Jemez Principles can be found in their entirety in the Appendix. These Principles can be used as a starting canvas on which to sketch out our own community's "Rules," a more specific set of "Love Rules" for our own community dialogues on change and transformation. In developing our unique set of "Love Rules" or in adapting these Jemez Principles for our own communities, we may want to be more specific and localized than an "entire movement" for justice, but this is a very good place to start.

Good Works: Community Gifts & Relations

Beginning in the summer of 2011, after the formal conclusion of my post-doc research, I invited all of the Bradford County landowners I had met and worked with to participate in an on-going guided group process to foster open dialogue and create a space for continuing to share and learn from their experiences living amidst shale gas developments without fear of retribution from spouses, children, neighbors, elected officials, corporations, or government agencies. Over a year we held eight meetings of what they decided to call the "core group." This core group was composed of a diversity of local residents from a diversity of economic and social backgrounds and realities, some of whom had not participated in the interviews or focus groups I had conducted.

The core group's meetings allowed local residents to not only talk safely in a group setting of their experiences and expectations related to the developments and changes taking place, it also gave them a space to share their unique local history and culture, tell personal stories and share observations, create group stories, celebrate together, mourn together, identify places of special importance that they thought deserved protection from development, and very importantly learn together and make some decisions about taking meaningful actions for their whole community. In our first meetings, I introduced everyone in the core group to the Asset-Based Community Development framework, or ABCD. I relied on John P. Kretzmann and John McKnight's work and 1993 book, *Building Communities from the Inside Out: A Path Toward Finding and Mobilizing a Community's Assets* alongside Ted Smeaton's *Inspiring Communities* Blog to design the initial core group meetings. I particularly found Smeaton's practical and easy to understand descriptions of the assumptions of ABCD and what ABCD actually is, a good way to get the Bradford County core group comfortable with these new concepts.

We began our group exploration of asset-based approaches after I handed out index cards with one assumption about ABCD, borrowed from Smeaton, on each card. We took turns reading aloud these assumptions:

- All great change starts simply with a conversation.
- From little things big things grow; most sustainable, powerful change starts small.
- Successful community interventions start with a question not an answer.
- Communities themselves are the most successful architects of positive change.
- Exploring stories of what works in community is a powerful gateway to creating a vibrant creative community.
- Communities that grow strong first focus on what they have and build upon it.
- Every community boasts a unique combination of assets on which to build a future.
- Communities grow strongest when they actively build sharing, caring, inclusive relationships.
- Building a great community is too big a job to do alone; great communities utilize everybody's dreams, vision, resources, capacities and strengths.
- Communities are at their strongest and best when built on people's passions, aspirations, skills and abilities.
- Capture what people care about and you can change the world.

After our round-robin readings, we had a group dialogue about whether we agreed or disagreed with each statement, and why or why not. Because most of us tend to take a deficit-minded or needs-based approach to community change and developments, it can be important to remind ourselves and internalize the deeper meanings of what asset-based versus deficit and needs-based means in terms of community before diving into actually developing concrete actions based on the ABCD framework. The goal in having us read out loud these assumptions was to create a moment of shared voice and shared understanding as well as an opening to learning new information together. I wanted to convey some of the wisdom that Smeaton had taught about the inherent power that lies within people who are building and practicing community from an asset-based framework:

"Seeing the glass half-full as well as half empty is not to deny the real problems that a community faces, but to focus energy on how each and every member has contributed, and can continue to contribute, in meaningful ways to community development. People are seen as engines of community action, and as a source of power and leadership, these are considered assets of the community."[95]

In other words, asset-based approaches recognize that "people power" is inherent in all communities. An important way to awaken it is to focus on our individual and collective assets, or what I prefer to call gifts.

After this introduction to community assets, the core group launched into the "Good Works" of asset-based approaches — inventorying our individual and collective gifts and relationships that are at the heart of a community's people power. These "Good Works" are the building blocks for creating a community vision and framework for change.

One of the key assumptions to asset-based approaches is that communities grow strongest when they are internally focused and have built an inventory of their gifts and can articulate the value of those gifts, both internally and externally. Without a clearer focus and recognition on the positive attributes and resources in a community, they are typically ignored, unrealized, or dismissed. The gifts we are talking about include not only personal attributes and talents, types of specialized knowledge, life skills, but also relationships between people through social, kinship, or other networks. These are the building blocks that will be used to construct our framework for community change and help us realize our community's shared vision for the present and future.

The gifts of informal and formal networks of relations in our community can help us activate more formal institutional resources when necessary – such as local government, formal community-based organizations, and private businesses. In fact, much of the people power of asset-based approaches to community lies in the ability to mobilize these local networks of relations, and in some cases to leverage additional support from external networks. For nurturing the process ABCD and creating a transformative and generative framework for community change, these informal and formal networks and relationships are the essential adhesive or glue that can tie our building blocks together and help us realize our community's vision for the future by multiplying the power and effectiveness of each separate building block.

The first step in these "Good Works" is to create a comprehensive inventory or map of all gifts – the capacities, resources, relationships, knowledge, information, skills, and commitments of individuals, networks, and local institutions within the whole community. As an example, in the Bradford

County core group, we spent an entire meeting developing individual and community gift inventories by using the following questions as our guide:

- What are the gifts of the head that individuals in our community have to give? What types of knowledge does our community or group already possess? What relations (individual, informal groups, local institutions) are important to these types of knowledge? How might these gifts of the head contribute to the whole community?
- What are the gifts of the hand that individuals in our community have to give? What skills does our community or group already have? What relations (individual, informal groups, local institutions) are important to these skills? How might these gifts of the hand contribute to the whole community?
- What are the gifts of the heart that individuals in our community have to give? Where do our community or group spirit, values, and commitments lie? What relations (individual, informal groups, local institutions) are important to these spirits, values, and commitments? How might these gifts of the heart contribute to the whole community?

Whenever I've done this exercise with groups, whether the Bradford County core group, training people to participate in ethnographic fieldwork, students in a public art class, or as part of a non-violent communication workshop for activists, it gives people a more concrete appreciation for the fullness of their own and others' gifts as well as the positive attributes they bring to the group and that the group brings to the whole community. It also begins to get people to generate new ideas and think more creatively about how to mobilize local individual and community gifts towards a common purpose, whether it's protecting a tract of local forest, successfully completing an ethnographic field project, or organizing a targeted direct-action campaign.

What groups tend to find most challenging with Good Works, and this was especially true in our Bradford County group where those participating had already felt negative disruptions brought on by all of the rapid changes from shale gas developments, is thinking about how to mobilize informal networks or relations to activate more formal or external networks. The essential part for gluing our building blocks together. For the Bradford County group, such formal and external relationships consisted of local and state government, researchers, scientists, health professionals, oil and gas corporations, and environmental activists. But, by the time we were meeting in 2011 there had already been significant broken trust and betrayal between many of these external groups and individuals in the community. Getting beyond this distrust and betrayals was critical in looking at resurrecting the whole community of Bradford County. Actions based on people power and local gifts are required and essential for ABCD, but the more we can mobilize those actions arising from the community's informal and internal networks towards engagement with formal and external networks on the community's terms, the more solid our foundation for transformation will be. Recognizing, appreciating, accepting, and being able to strategize together about how to engage with formal and external networks requires working through the existing barriers to trust, reciprocity, and consensual relationships that are embedded within mainstream notions of community development. This is especially critical when internal-external network relationships are strained by on-going structural injustices and inequities around access to money, land, information, legal remedies, and policy decision-making.

One of the barriers to informal-formal and internal-external engagements has to do with our societal and psychological conditioning related to systems of oppression that have us believing that formal institutions have all the answers and that they will be our saviors. But, if community is in fact about belonging and our power is inherent within this community, then ABCD teaches us something different. Could it be that it is the informal networks, our own and our community's gifts that are the primary source of answers and most importantly the source for our own survival? Not formal institutions. This illusion that others will somehow step in and save us is what keeps us all in bondage[96]. And, in communities where there is a sense of distrust of these formal institutions, as there is in Bradford County and many frontline communities, these sentiments emerge not out of an inherent belief that they and their community have any power greater than the government, corporations, or outside elites, but instead out of a sense of betrayal and emerging anger and grievance that they have not been afforded the answers and outside assistance they deserved. It is also important to understand that while many are fighting back when confronted with such betrayal, anger, and distrust, others respond by complying and in some cases take up allegiances with those untrustworthy institutions. But whether fighting back or complying, these responses do not come from a place of community, people-centered power but rather from being backed into a corner, and from feelings that they have nothing else to lose or that they have everything to lose.

Under such circumstances of harm, fractured trust, and oppression, it can be extremely hard to imagine how those roles could be reversed. How can a community acknowledge its strengths and power and exercise that power to protect itself by developing relationships with those who they feel have been the ones who left them feeling powerless and who have harmed and betrayed them? Why would a community want to engage with formal institutions and networks that have been and continue to be so harmful? Through the eyeglasses of deficit and lack many of us have been taught to see the world through, and not the ABCD and gifts framework of internal community power, these questions are typically dismissed outright as complicity or betrayal or giving in. But it is critical we change these old, broken glasses to ones that see the internal gifts and true power that communities and people hold in order to have any chance of resurrecting our communities, dismantling oppression, and transforming our world. This is the reason why engaging in whole community dialogue and appreciative inquiry with nonviolent, compassionate communication is so critical. It shifts our mindsets towards listening, humility, deep questioning, and gratitude. The goal is to see another, more transformative and imaginative way to support and energize our communities from the inside first, before opening to the outside, so that the inside will always have enough consciousness and strength to act from both power and love[97]. Similar to the way we got in touch with our breathing in order to relax our body, mind, and soul in preparation for cleaning out the filthy, illusion-filled corners of our own home in Chapter Three, a contemplative, caring, and generative process of community dialogue and appreciative inquiry that focuses on Good Works allows us in group and community settings to sweep out the filth together and make space for renewed life.

However, it is essential not to rush or force the process of finding formal and external networks that could play a role in gluing our building blocks together. It could be that no such networks exist that support the community's vision. If our community is not ready to look at relationships that might exist between those inside and outside our community, we just set it aside as needing more work and return to it when the group is ready. All of this often takes time and patience. Even if there is resistance to informal networks and more formal networks working together, just by conducting Good Works and gift inventories we will start speaking from a place that recognizes our own strengths based on what we have identified as our internal people power.

By engaging in Good Works with patience and deliberation we may find that as a community we have new ways to articulate our gifts that can then open up surprising pathways to work with formal or external networks that we still distrust or feel a level of animosity towards. Some in the Bradford County group, for example, began speaking with scientists, health professionals, and environmental activists who began listening more to them and even more formally partnering with them to conduct data collection on water quality, air quality, and public health outcomes. As a result, they ended up filling certain gaps in their own knowledge, understanding, and language, as well as offering new types of relationships and networks that in turn helped the group strengthen their own sense of community in the face of the threats from shale gas developments.

In other words, using Good Works to shift towards a mindset of greater self-worth, community people power, inner knowledge, skills, and assets within informal internal networks will in turn allow communities to better communicate those qualities, and an overall sense of self-determination and confidence to formal external networks that can lead to consensual relationships and instill respect for long-term whole community change processes. Even more importantly, this work towards an asset mindset contributes to building greater cohesion among and between local networks, eventually leading to local and whole communities who are better able to face change and protect themselves from disruptions over the long-term.

Creating Transformative Whole Community Change

Now that we are ready to face change with critical consciousness and cultural synthesis and our feet are firmly planted in dialogue practices, appreciate inquiry, Good Works, and L.O.V.E. Rules, we are ready to get about the work of resurrecting our whole communities and transforming the world. Breathing, critical consciousness, cultural synthesis, and the various group practices we have learned about can be used in a variety of individual, group, and community settings, whether the main objective is to address a large controversial topic around different types of new or existing development projects or the objective is to resolve some specific conflict around a development project. For our purposes, though, we are specifically looking at how to utilize these practices in transformative ways. This section of the book uses real-world examples to demonstrate the potential these practices have to assist our whole communities in constructing a solid framework to consciously face change by confronting some of the root causes of systemic oppression today – the ill-logic of global capitalism and neoliberalism; commodification, privatization, and trivialization of human life and Nature; replacement of community values with individual or group identities and political ideologies; and willful ignorance and disregard of the mutual interdependence between humans and Nature.

In developing this framework for transformative whole community change, we are going to engage in some reverse engineering. In other words, we are going to begin at the end and imagine our framework complete without worrying about the details yet. This means having a clear vision of where we want to be on the other side of any sort of change, whether forced on us from the outside or emerging from inside. What is your vision of what exists on the other side of change? For example: "Our vision is one where every family in our community has a living wage, free health care, and access to healthy food."

The idea is to find a shared vision that we all agree we want our community to look or feel like. It should reflect a statement of shared values and beliefs, and it may include some type of high-minded ideals about well-being for all.

And, it should also be rooted in actions and lived experiences. For example, while doing this exercise in Bradford County in 2012, our group of farmers and landowners came up with this "vision statement" for their community: "Maintaining a rural, cohesive, multigenerational community in a healthy natural environment"

The important thing in imagining what our community envisions for the future is to remember that at this point we do not need any idea of "how" we are going to achieve that vision. In the first step, we simply imagine a vision together using appreciative inquiry dialogue practices, a Good Works mind-set, and our L.O.V.E. Rules. Only after we have settled on a current vision of what our community dreams on the other side of change may look like, will it be time to imagine how we are going to get there together. Only after we have a clear vision of what transformative whole community change looks like for us should we begin the process to construct our future. As the Major League Baseball coach Yogi Berra famously once said, "If you don't know where you're going you might wind up someplace else."

Based on what we learned in our Bradford County core group practicing appreciative inquiry, Good Works, and L.O.V.E. Rules while facing the on-going rapid changes from shale gas developments, the following six steps were crafted as an example recipe for cooking up whole community resurrection, transformation, and liberation. These ingredients and methods may or may not work in your community's kitchen depending on many different factors. So, these steps should only be used as a guide for developing your own community recipe. Experimentation and improvisation is not only welcome, it is wholeheartedly encouraged!

Step 1. Establish L.O.V.E. Rules

Before imagining our collective vision for the future, we need to establish together our L.O.V.E. rules. We may want to just keep it simple at Listen, Observe, Validate, and Empathize. Or, we may choose to adopt the Jemez Principles (see Appendix). Or, we may even do some research into other principles used in conducting respectful, conscious, and community-centered dialogues. The important element of the rules is that they are living and not set in stone. That means leaving open the possibility of modifying our L.O.V.E. rules based on our community's unique values and principles as the process continues and evolves.

Step 2. Conduct Initial Gift and Relations Inventory

To help us understand the what, who, and where of our whole community we should begin constructing our community change framework by conducting an inventory of the Good Works (the gifts and relationships) that already exist and that we know are already taking place in our local community. We need to ask the question: "What are the individual and collective gifts and informal and formal relationships that existed in the past and exist currently and that serve our whole community in generative and transformative ways?"

The goal of this second step is to identify people, organizations, structures, and places that require resurrecting or rebuilding and any new relationships that should be explored in order that our local community is both resilient and strong in the face of change. These people, organizations, structures, and places should offer protection and defense against negative disruptions to the well-being of all life within the community and within Nature.

Step 3. Host a Local Dialogue with the Whole Community to Imagine a Vision for the Future

Gathering together as many of the people and organizations who were identified in Step 2 as constituting the whole community, we can now initiate a dialogue on a future vision. This step is not to be rushed. It should take as long as necessary to ask questions of one another and ourselves. Remember to use your L.O.V.E. rules and the basics of appreciate inquiry and open-ended exploratory questions to ensure that all values and opinions and differences and similarities are part of the dialogue. The outcome of this dialogue about the future should be a vision statement crafted by and for our whole community that is broad and at the same time as specific as possible.

Once we have created a vision statement, it is important to remain engaged in dialogue about how the vision is understood by everyone participating in an open, honest, and respectful dialogue. At some point, there may be other people or organizations that should be invited to participate after the initial vision statement is developed. This makes it important to revisit the vision statement at the beginning of each new dialogue gathering to either re-affirm or, if necessary, modify the vision statement.

One way to facilitate this iterative process of visioning is to assess the relevance of the meaning of the initial vision statement at different times and at different meetings. This can be done by asking a diversity of people in the community to share their interpretations of each of the main words in the statement. In addition, this way of encouraging iterative dialogue on the vision statement reinforces the open and evolving nature of the process in developing a community change framework. This approach also allows for everyone to gain a deeper understanding of what is meant by the vision and how others in the community interpret that vision. It is always surprising to me how some words, like "safety" and "healthy," can have such different and even controversial meanings to different people.

Because many words can have multiple interpretations, it may be necessary to change some of the words to be more specific or more general, or add a bit more language to define them in the statement. As an example, when the Bradford County core group thought more critically and deeply about what each word (underlined here for emphasis) that made up their vision statement meant they came up with the following statement: "Maintaining a rural, cohesive, multi-generational community in a healthy natural environment." Then they developed general agreement on what each underlined word in the vision statement meant to the group: Maintaining - keeping things the same, implies taking a conservative and cautious approach to change; Rural – as distinct from urban life; describes a way of life, including certain beliefs and values rooted in Nature, family, land, simplicity, practicality; Cohesive - working together towards a common goal or not working against one another; defines community; Multigenerational - taking care of both the young and old and everyone in between as well as consideration of past generations and future generations; Community - defined as all residents of Bradford County; cohesive; Healthy - food, air, water unpolluted and clean; children and grandbabies health; Natural - not destroyed by humans, our rivers, forests, waterfalls, creeks are in their natural state as God intended; wild places for hunting, fishing, exploring Nature; Environment - natural heritage and what brings us life and joy, as opposed to human-built things like gas wells and compressor stations.

Such continuing and open dialogues on what our community's visions for the future mean in a practical way are essential to both avoid later misunderstandings within the community, and to ensure our vision is kept relevant, especially if new events emerge or new people are coming in and out of our gatherings and dialogues.

Step 4. Conduct Second Gift Inventory & Identify Community Building Blocks for Making the Vision a Reality

After we have created a vision statement that everyone present understands and agrees with, it is time to take a second inventory of all individual and community gifts and relationships. Remember that some new people and organizations may have come into the dialogue after Step 1 and 2, so we should ensure that they know the L.O.V.E. Rules and that all their gifts and relationships are accounted for before continuing to construct our framework. We should continue to ask ourselves and one another: "What are the gifts of the head, the heart, and the hands that everyone in the community has to offer to one another?" And, the overall question we should be thinking about in this step is: "What are our community's internal building blocks for achieving our vision of the future?"

Setting aside the relationships and ties that emerged during this second inventory for the time being, let us look at all of the gifts of the head, hand, and heart within the whole community that were revealed through the initial and this second inventory and select the ones (it could be all!) that are most relevant to our vision statement. In Step 4 we brainstorm together about ways these gifts and treasures need to be supported and mobilized in making our community vision a reality. These gifts are the community building blocks for constructing our future.

This is the step where we start to get the most energized and hopeful that in fact we do have the people power to make our vision for the future a reality. This is when I have seen even the most distrusting community or individuals break out of their dualistic and needs-based mindsets and biases when they realize, sometimes for the first time, that they do not require outside help at all, but that what they need is found right where they already are and with who they are already with. After a gift inventory dialogue, it is common to hear people say things like, "I never thought of that before," or tell each other, "I did not know you had a passion for baking bread." This process of discovery leads to greater appreciation and gratitude for our individual and collective gifts and the community potentials they hold.

After the second gift inventory, we may find that our whole community is still missing essential building blocks that we need to make our vision a reality. It is important, while keeping our gift mindset and spirit intact, to identify those missing building blocks as early as possible. Once identified, we need to take the time to determine where those building blocks or gifts are located and develop a process for how our community will access them.

Step 5. Identifying the Glue for Holding our Community Building Blocks Together

Now that we have identified community building blocks for our community's vision, it is time to turn to the relationships that were identified during the initial and second gift inventory. These relationships represent the social and organizational ties that should be strengthened and mobilized in making our community vision a reality. These relations are the adhesive elements, or glue, that ensure the building blocks of our vision can and will stick and stay together strongly. In this step it is important to ask ourselves and one another: "What are the internal relationships that we need to nurture? And, are there external relationships that we need to repair or build?"

Step 5, in essence, is about identifying those adhesive elements that are necessary to achieve our community's vision. Like in Step 4, when we look more closely at our community's gifts we may find that there are essential relationships related to our community's vision that are broken or missing from our internal inventory of gifts and relations. In those cases, it will be necessary to figure out how our community will reach out, repair, nurture, or acquire these new relationships or social ties required for making the community vision a reality. This can happen through social networking with other communities, inviting new people, groups, or informal organizations to participate in our dialogues, or building new relationships with more formal organizations and institutions with face-to-face meetings.

Step 6. Identify Specific Actions to Achieve the Whole Community Vision

Now that we have our building blocks and the glue to hold those blocks together, we need to pour our foundation by identifying concrete actions that need to be taken to make our community vision a reality. To do this, we will use Steps 2 thru 5, including the two gift inventories (Steps 2 and 4), dialogue on the overall intent and specific words that make up our whole community vision statement (Step 3), and identification of the relevant and specific building blocks and all the adhesive elements (Step 4 and 5) to develop from one to one-hundred different actions that our community can take towards realizing our vision. And voila, we have our whole community change framework! An example of how all the steps in this process fit together for the Bradford County core group during their 2012 dialogues is presented in the Appendix as Table 1.

Beyond "Resilience"

One of my hopes in providing these practical steps and an example recipe and framework for resurrecting our whole communities in order to face whole community change in transformative and generative ways, is changing how we talk and communicate about –the actual words, language, and channels we use— in order to more explicitly center the practices of critical consciousness, cultural synthesis, and liberation from systemic oppression that are essential to not just facing change, but for all life to be free and thrive in the face of change. As we have learned, the words we use matter and have real world consequences. So, as we identify and learn to appreciate our incredible community building blocks and the glue holding us all together, as well as the work it takes to construct and maintain a strong whole community vision, we must also identify and be critically aware of the vocabularies that most resonate within ourselves and communities for purposes of liberation, and guard against unconsciously accepting vocabularies that may keep us stuck within systems of oppression.

There are many books and articles written and many community organizations that I work with who focus on terms like "resilient" and "resilience," especially related to climate change and disaster response and recovery. And, it is my expectation that some could interpret this book and especially the idea of resurrecting our communities and transformative community change to be about "resilience." It is important that I have purposefully stayed away from using the word "resilience" throughout this book. What I have come to understand about the language of "resilience," when referring to transformative community change in the context of industrial and economic developments, is the ease with which it is both misinterpreted and appropriated for non-liberatory and even malicious purposes. So, "resilience" is in quotations here, not so much because it needs definition, but in order to keep it highlighted for readers to consider further. It is not the word I want to use when talking about the transformation of our whole communities and liberation for all, it does not resonate with everyone, it may be misinterpreted, and, most importantly, it is not a benign nor a neutral word. Before I detail the caution I and others have around use of the word "resilient," let's take a closer look at its current definition and use related to ecology and society.

"Resilient" as defined and used by psychologists, social scientists, and ecological scientists denotes the ways ecosystems, people, or organizations adapt to structural disruptions. It is often used to describe the ways that communities either suffer or thrive when faced with rapid or sudden change and various types of disasters. It is sometimes used in a short-hand way to describe an ecosystem, individual, organization, or community that is adaptive, sustainable, or thriving in the face of disruption or changes. But, in a critical context, the word gets distorted from its ecological origins when it is also used to mask an underlying mindset of how dangerous and destructive the world is and especially how destructive humans are to the world and each other. This way of defining "resilience," says that in this dangerous dog-eat-dog world, living organisms and systems need to be "resilient" in order to adapt and survive. It tosses aside any notion of re-imagining a less dangerous world or destructive society that is not bound to global capitalism or neoliberalism, and it most certainly tosses away any notion of autonomous self-determination or liberation that might allow for different ways of organizing society and politics around generative life, local knowledge and culture, reciprocity, non-violence, and sacred love. In this way, "resilience," like another word used by ecologists, "sustainability," has been conveniently modified to serve the sole interests of systems of oppression in the promotion of techno-bureaucratic organizations and solutions, Artificial Intelligence and surveillance networks, political ideologies based on identity and division, and exponential growth in global financial markets for carbon and other "green" commodities.

The most articulate critical analysis of the word "resilience" I have come across is found in Brad Evans and Julian Reid's 2014 book, *Resilient Life: The Art of Living Dangerously*. They explain that the use of the word "resilience" in the disaster response and recovery, "war on terrorism," and climate change contexts started from the assumption that because our world is so inherently dangerous and destructive, we need systems of "security" and "law and order" to protect ourselves. Unfortunately, building these systems without first dismantling and reimagining the current ill-logic of global capital and neoliberalism and other root causes of systemic failures only further oppresses individuals, communities, and Nature. In the terrorism context, the logical extension of this "resilience" approach have been actions by the U.S. government to create a new Department of Homeland Security and pass anti-terrorism legislation such as the USA PATRIOT Act. Both of these post-9/11 anti-terrorism moves have caused greater oppression and restriction of people's freedoms, particularly among immigrant communities and those who raise any questions about the dominance of global capitalism, the history of the American empire, the presence of American military and military operatives overseas, and anyone calling for greater government transparency and accountability to the people.

One of Evans and Reid's other lines of critique is that "resilience" focuses on individual and community "fitness" (i.e., survival of the fittest) and adaptiveness instead of addressing the actual underlying forces (i.e., root causes) that determine what "fitness" means and that make it impossible for most individuals and communities to successfully adapt and thrive. In the language of "resilience," the focus should be on evolutionary concepts like "survival of the fittest," or the even more alienating and unchanging "human nature." "Resilient" thinking of this kind would have us believe that this type of survival of the fittest and static human nature are the driving forces behind life, Nature, and society. There is no room for kindness, caring, reciprocity, transformation, and certainly not resurrection. In the United States, if we begin to question how a word like "resilience" may, rather than offering some type of new way to protect or buffer our communities against change, actually keep us in constant struggle, we are then questioning the very notion of American exceptionalism, which in turn is wedded to the underlying violence on which the United States was built – colonialism, capitalism, and militarism— and which is continuing to perpetuate our gradual slide into fascism. Therefore, uncritically and unconsciously accepting the language of "resilience" as a benign word for thinking about climate change, disaster policy, or development policy disregards choice and freedom, communal values, local assets, and networks of relations that are the necessary building blocks, glue, and foundation for community and societal well-being.

And, if we take a look at the history of the word "resilience" itself, it actually comes from the Latin for "leaping back." This entirely fails to capture the current and urgent need to imagine entirely new and original types of relationships with ourselves, one another, Nature, and the world. So, even in its original meaning it is inadequate to the task. You can see why I am skeptical of "resilience," both in the ways it has been adopted in various disciplines and the way it has become a part of language that signifies a particular regressive and repressive force in the United States. How can we use a word that has been used to discount the very things we are striving to appreciate and elevate in our practice of Good Works and L.O.V.E. Rules and that asks us to leap backward?

So, I encourage us all during the process of imagining a framework for community change to have conversations within our community about words such as "resilient" and "resilience." We should be asking ourselves and one another, what are the appropriate words to describe or encourage transformative whole community change? Such questions are important to our continuing work of critical consciousness. Using our collective consciousness and imaginations we can develop words and an entire language that truly matters and resonates with our whole community's unique experiences and values, including different perceptions of oppression, change, local places, critical consciousness, liberation, and visions for our collective future. Conscious use of language and words really does matter. Once our words match our visions and gifts, there is nothing we cannot do together. We can better communicate our visions and gifts to others inside and outside our own communities, and therefore realize and enact our full community power.

6. CARING FOR SELF, OUR COMMUNITIES, AND THE WORLD

G etting this far in the journey of critical consciousness, cultural synthesis, and liberation from our illusions, mental patterns, and behaviors around change and working within our whole community is equal parts emotionally uncomfortable, exhausting, and sometimes traumatizing. To honor this emotional strain, I want to remind you to breathe. Here's a simple and quick practice: Inhale deeply into your belly on a count of four. Hold your breath there for four more counts. Then let the breath out counting to six. Repeat breathing in this way until you feel both your body and mind start to relax.

It is important to not just mentally and emotionally recognize, but to also physically recognize through our bodies — and using the breath is a simple way to do this— the fear, confusion, and other feelings that have probably arisen on this journey. This slowing down with breath can also help us relax into feelings rather than run away or ignore them.

At the same time, we need to celebrate ourselves. It is a rare and amazing thing to find the courage to face change in ourselves, with others in community, to admit loss or the possibility of loss, relearn the world, and participate in the audacious task of resurrecting community in a world that many times seems dead-set on further killing ourselves or our neighbors and tearing us even further apart. It is important at certain points along our journey to pause, relax, and above all recognize, be grateful, and celebrate our inner strength in body, mind, and soul, because the trail ahead is a long and rocky one and we will need to remain fully conscious and also ready to act.

Central to remaining conscious is remembering that our resurrected communities require long-term care and maintenance and that transformation is always on-going. Caring for our whole communities means from time to time reassessing the foundations, building blocks, and glue that holds us together to ensure these elements are still appropriate and strong enough. If there are gaps or cracks, we may need to make repairs to avoid collapse or decay. Long-term care of our whole community means remaining aware of our own roles and responsibilities with others, remaining critically conscious of our internal oppression, biases and assumptions, and the actions we must take in both upholding our whole communities while dismantling systems of oppression that operate outside and inside. On both a collective and personal level critical consciousness and cultural synthesis is a never-ending journey, but we must remember that it should also be, as much as possible, a joyful one. We can continue to find that joy if we take care of our own minds, bodies, and spirits. Easier said than done sometimes, but this sort of long-term care and maintenance is essential if we are to truly transform ourselves and one another and liberate ourselves and each other.

The Realities of a Critically Conscious Life

There are visionaries and entrepreneurs in each of our communities who are constantly trying to move us collectively forward; individual souls who are entirely committed to re-imagining existing systems of oppression and building new systems of true liberation and autonomy for all. Maybe you even think of yourself or some people you know as visionaries or entrepreneurs. I consider my friend, colleague, and fellow native Savannahian, Dr. David Pleasant, to be one of these visionaries.

Dr. Pleasant is a Gullah Geechee man, an indigenous American (Seminole), and European. What I love about him is that he is constantly learning, growing, and synthesizing ideas, historical events, and current circumstances through his reading, writing, listening, speaking, singing, drumming, strumming, and practices of contemplation and prayer AND that he is always eager to share what he is learning with others and engaging them in dynamic dialogue. The goal of this engagement is not just to "talk" or "entertain" but rather, social-psychological transformation. As a visionary, he does not compromise on his values or beliefs in order to be accepted by others. He is a truth teller, and in African tradition he is what is known as a *griot*[98]. As a result of this no compromise position on social and personal transformation, particularly in a place like Savannah, Georgia, where "go along to get along" and "just is" "justice"[99] is etched on all our foreheads at birth, this is a difficult mission and can look and feel like a fool's errand, as Dr. Pleasant himself will tell you.

Fortunately for Savannah's future, this is a mission and vision that Dr. Pleasant continues to pursue from a place of love, critical consciousness, commitment to cultural synthesis, and rigorous scholarship. I am proud and humbled to be a small part of his transformative mission through the local collective he started, Which Way Savannah (WWS). The community dialogues he began through WWS on the deep historical antecedents for escape, rebellion, and freedom and their relevance to the present and future conditions facing Indigenous, African-descended, and European-descended residents of Savannah are nothing short of revolutionary. [100] But to witness the ways that organizations and individuals in the city attempt to silence, erase, and distort Dr. Pleasant, WWS, and our transformative work has been deeply disturbing and sickening. It has made me acutely aware of the way in which local minds, hearts, and bodies are addicted to and anesthetized by the "opportunities" dangled in front of them with promises of economic and industrial developments. It is not just metaphoric to compare the behavior of those who actively silence and disregard Dr. Pleasant and his work to drug addicts: denying, resisting, and even lashing out with anger and resentment at the ones who love them enough to use their own energy and resources to attempt an intervention. What is so remarkable about Dr. Pleasant is that despite this push-back he does not stop.

So, on the surface, the lessons I am learning working with WWS and Dr. Pleasant are harsh. Sometimes when you publicly ask too many questions and speak the truths that others have tried for generations to suppress and sweep into the corner and hide you will be ostracized and demonized not just by those who are in power, but most heartbreaking by those who have been the most silenced and oppressed by that power – those who are most in need of the medicine. I learned some of these lessons working with Carol and others in Bradford County for sure, but bringing it back home to the place where my own ancestors were such a violent force in the development and industrial development of this place and where so many of them are buried -- and even memorialized for the violence and atrocities they committed against others -- is distinctly different. In a place like Savannah, engaging in critical questions and truth-telling causes a tectonic shift in your social relations that can be isolating and confusing. There is also an emotional rawness and sense of urgency to the underhanded erasures, denials, and perverted appropriations that I have particularly observed Dr. Pleasant face. Through WWS we are asking others in our city to develop a set of community values, to honor the mutual interdependence of Nature, and work across political affiliations, class distinctions, religious beliefs, and ethnic and racial identities in ways that are not based on any specific affiliations, distinctions, beliefs, and identities. We are asking them to see the ill-logic of the single-minded focus on global capital and how it operates to obliterate local culture and Nature. We are challenging formal and informal organizations, as well as individuals, to actively work to become critically conscious of the unconscious neoliberal ideologies and techno-bureaucratic solutions that have taken over their bodies, minds, and souls. And, we are asking them to do this in the name of Love. As we have seen, this critical consciousness is necessary to dismantle the oppressive systems that continue to keep all of us, even the most "liberal" or "progressive" among us, in our segregated, addicted, and malnourished daily lives.

In our work together, Dr. Pleasant has taught me that this is what a commitment to emancipation and liberation looks, tastes, and feels like. It is not necessarily fun, quick, easy, or comfortable (although it can be). It is many times deeply depressing work. But it is also the most fulfilling, creative, soulful, meaningful, and loving work I have ever participated in. It is overflowing with transformative power. To get ourselves and others in our community into recovery and true wellness, awake from the stupor we are collectively in, and then to hold space with Love so that we can find the courage to imagine and create alternative systems in which we are critically conscious of our addictions and disconnections from each other and Nature, is the only path to true freedom and liberation for all.

Advocating for liberation for all in some parts of the United States today, most notably in the South and rural spaces, means experiencing social isolation and personal rejection. It means not having the support, and in fact being explicitly persecuted or ostracized for your ideas and thoughts. It may give comfort, as well as be quite shocking, to know that such treatment of those seeking liberation for all is nothing new. In fact, after the United States fought and "won" its bloody civil war against traitors from Southern states who believed that their rights to enslave other human beings and profit from their labor was a "God-given" right, this country has never fully embraced social integration, equality, justice for all, and fighting for the common good and community values. Instead, for at least the past eighty years, promoting policies and taking action for social integration, equality, justice for all, for the common good, community values, and even basic human rights has been treated as a threat to the United States government. And, so, as someone who engages in these activities to free ourselves and others you may be labeled as a traitor to the country. We must be prepared above all to face this criticism and worse with nonviolence and peace. As Thich Nhat Hanh says in his short essay, "The Roots of War" and nonviolence: "The roots of war are in the way we live our daily lives—the way we develop our industries, build up our society, and consume goods. We have to look deeply into the situation, and we will see the roots of war. We cannot just blame one side or the other. We have to transcend the tendency to take sides."[101]

Working in Savannah and both witnessing and experiencing the social stigma and criminality associated with the idea of working for freedom and liberation for all has made me curious about those who have done this work before us and how they were treated. I find this history helpful today in understanding both the legacies of visionary elders and ancestors, as well as understanding the tactics used by those in power to silence them. Beginning in 1938, the U.S. Congress created the House Un-American Activities Committee as one way to overturn President Franklin Delano Roosevelt's (FDR) New Deal policies and programs. Those New Deal programs had been designed to lift U.S. people out of the Great Depression and at the same time sent a clear message to Morgan, Vanderbilt, Rockefeller, Ford, and other tycoons of industry and financial markets that they had too much power and wealth and that the federal government would now be holding them accountable. Not surprisingly these power-hungry and extraordinarily wealthy men and the enterprises they owned and operated never quite forgot this threat posed by the federal government to their power and wealth. So, under the House Un-American Activities Committee, New Deal programs like the Works Progress Administration (WPA) employment and equality programs, were labeled as "communist" and "fascist"; two terms that have become synonymous, but that are in fact two distinct forms of political thought. For thirty years, those who continued to support or promote New Deal and related policies and programs for equality, justice, liberation, and human rights, were brought to trial and jailed or "blacklisted" for being "anti-American," "communist," "anarchist," "fascist," or "subversive." During and after World War II efforts to discredit and demonize social justice, human rights, and environmental advocates, especially within the federal government became much harsher and were amplified and publicized by U.S. Senator Joseph McCarthy. And, while the official public hearings and trials of those accused by the Committee ended in 1954, the labels and stereotypes stuck and are still with us to this day. The more "recent" murders of Medgar Evers (1963), Malcolm X (1965), Martin Luther King, Jr. (1968), Fred Hampton (1969), Bunchy Carter (1969), John Huggins (1969), Marcus Foster (1973), and Huey Newton (1989) provide stark evidence of how far the U.S. Government will go to suppress freedom, liberation, and peace to this day. It is also no coincidence that the majority of these murders were of black men speaking truth to power.

This 20th Century history of promoting disdain, criminality, and violence towards those who work for liberation, freedom, and justice for all is critically important to be aware of. To even begin to imagine how we raise critical consciousness on a community-wide level, dismantle systemic oppression, and perhaps most importantly, how we personally become more critically conscious in our own lives and recognize the importance of solidarity with others we must know where the roots of suppression and violent opposition to transforming oppressive systems are buried. By fully recognizing how deep, broad, and intertwined these violent roots go in our society, we can find the right tools to dig them out and plant love and freedom in their place.

The history and ongoing struggles of those who have found some of the right tools for this root removal work are worthwhile to learn about and study. However, in taking a critical stance on facing change, resurrecting our communities, and transforming our world, we must always guard against getting caught up in either the arc of the history of struggle or the individual personas involved in various struggles. When faced with change and uncertainty, we are too easily either frightened to act or lulled back to sleep by immersing ourselves too far in any sort of national mythology of exceptionalism or hero and heroine worship. Instead, the focus must be on how we each, within our own selves, creatively imagine our neighborhoods, our organizations, our whole communities as free and equal, how we separate lived reality from our collective myths, stories, and heroes and heroines, and how we yearn for and act to do more than "just go along to get along" and accept that when someone tells us, "Well, that just is the way it is. It has always been that way," that we do not accept that as justice.

The brutal reality of U.S. history is that people willing to stand up against oppression will be labeled with words such as communist, socialist, anarchist, anti-fascist, radical, and terrorist; words that in the past and today are triggers for political judgment, social isolation, criminal prosecution, and murder. Someone willing to take a long hard look at themselves in order to admit their own blindness, and challenge the oppression of others and themselves by taking the journey of critical consciousness to take action against systems of oppression are not celebrated in U.S. history books. They are at best deleted or sanitized, and at worst demonized. Our national history is strewn with the bodies of the martyrs of both physical and character assassinations who embraced critical community consciousness around systemic oppression, practiced cultural synthesis, and dedicated their very breath and life to liberation for all. We all owe a tremendous debt to our ancestors who had the courage to develop their own critical consciousness and act on it. They have undone certain aspects of oppression and made our work for community resurrection and transformation a wee bit easier by leaving us various teachings, tools, and practices that we must now adapt to our current and future world.

So, just like understanding the root causes of the consequences of economic and industrial developments, we must remain aware of the personal, social, and material consequences that come with developing critical consciousness within ourselves and within our communities. If we engage with tackling systems of oppression at their root, particularly from a critical consciousness approach and through non-violent means, it is likely that we will eventually find ourselves labeled and socially marginalized not just by the most obvious people—businesses, governments, mainstream media, politicians—but also by those who say they are there to help: our friends, neighbors, and sometimes family. My hypothesis for why this alienation happens relates to the aversion most of us have to honest and critical self-reflection and self-evaluation that we have touched on throughout this book. Our failure to return home and clean our own homes before working with others means we still operate with the illusions taught to us by previous generations who have learned to adapt within systems of oppression. Taking action against the oppression within our institutions and society and the root causes of harm to individuals and communities, means first courageously looking inside ourselves, in the darkest corners of our homes, and uncovering the illusions and deceptions we have been taught and that have been hiding us from our true selves all along. Once uncovered, those illusions and deceptions lose their power over us and the fear separating us from our whole communities, from Nature, and from the world falls away.

As difficult as it is, for the sake of our future humanity and our Mother Earth, it is imperative that we continue, with love, to ask those who do not want to or cannot see to open their eyes within their own homes first, find those dark corners, uncover and dispose of those illusions, and then use this new consciousness for the greater good of all. Fannie Lou Hamer said it better than anyone else ever has: "No one is free, until we are all free!!"

Perhaps none of this harsh reality is surprising to you. If you are living in a frontline community or are someone who studies, organizes, or works to assist those communities, you may have already been the target of industry or developer attacks yourself, or witnessed your family or neighbors as targets of such attacks, or found yourself being shut out of family and community conversations that promote the status quo when it comes to economic and industrial developments. Or, maybe you or someone you love has made a living promoting and benefiting from economic and industrial development projects that have used psychological, social, political, and legal tactics to silence, oppress, and even criminalize questions and opposition related to those projects and you are concerned about the violence and harm this causes. Regardless of what role or what side of a development project we find ourselves on, it is important that we incorporate practices of self-care, like breath work, meditation, prayer, journaling, and physical exercise, into our daily lives. This will keep us closer to our true homes, our selves, and help us prepare for authentic participation in the whole community practices of dialogue, appreciative inquiry, non-violent communication, and the sharing and honoring of individual and community gifts and treasures, which in the end will lead to community resurrection and transformation. These practices are how we care for our whole community.

Story Sharing as Community Care

"In a catastrophic age, trauma itself may provide the very link between cultures: not as a simple understanding of the pasts of others but rather, within the traumas of contemporary history, as our ability to listen through the departures we have all taken from ourselves."

I used this quote from Cathy Caruth's 1995 book, *Trauma: Explorations in Memory* (Johns Hopkins University Press), in a 2012 Research Note published in the journal *Culture, Agriculture, Food and Environment (CAFE)* about on-going work I was engaged with at the time with farmers and landowners in Bradford County[102].

At the time, I had thought that what I was documenting in the County could best be described as a type of community trauma, defined by Kai Erickson in his book on the devastating 1972 Buffalo Creek, West Virginia flood. As he defined it, community trauma was:

"a blow to the basic tissues of social life that damages the bonds attaching people together and impairs the prevailing sense of communality...works its way slowly and even insidiously into the awareness of those who suffer from it...it does not have the quality of suddenness normally associated with trauma, but it is a form of shock all the same."[103]

Later that same year I found myself as the subject of an attack by an oil and gas industry funded media and public relations campaign that called themselves "Energy In Depth." They attempted to discredit me on-line via a blog post that tried to tear apart my academic credentials and thereby discredit my findings in Bradford County related to how shale gas developments were an immediate threat to the health and well-being of local landowners and farmers. While this industry-led personal attack was devastating to me as a professional, and harmful to the trust and relationships I had built in the community with which I worked, it paled in comparison to how individuals and communities living in Bradford County (people who I had grown to know and love) were being treated every day. I had seen how the abuse local people are subject to every day by not only gas companies, but local and regional politicians and their own neighbors who support the gas developments, rips open old scabs and barely healed scars between families and friends, leaving festering wounds. At the time when I wrote the article for *CAFE*, Caruth's quote provided a conceptual path of departure from, or a way to move beyond, that initial analysis I had framed as "community trauma" and toward what I intended to be an expansion of my research in Bradford County that would not just document and assess the changes and community traumas local people were experiencing, but that might also reveal and act on the critical consciousness that was emerging out of these changes and traumas.

What led me to this were all the transformative and heart-felt stories that were being shared among the landowners I was listening to and the events I was witnessing. Many of these stories and events related to building alliances across economic and political differences to work together to protect their families and communities. I could see the outlines of how individuals and communities were becoming conscious of systemic oppression, especially with regards to the marginalization of rural communities and the mutual interdependence of humans and Nature, and were starting to articulate what their individual and community values were, first in private and then in public. Through these acts of private and public speech they were becoming conscious of what community meant to them in the past, present, and future. It was clear that this consciousness and thoughts about cross-class and cross-political alliances had occurred in response to the rapid changes being brought about by the shale gas developments in the County. I also realized I had played some role, through the focus groups and appreciative inquiry dialogue process, in this emergence of new stories. Or, at least I imagined that to be the case, and so the question I still had when writing that 2012 Research Note was: "Would this tentative first embrace of community values, critical consciousness, and newfound voice give local people the power to overcome the bullying by gas companies and their proponents, fight the suppression of local public participation in shale gas governance, stem the tide of the larger global forces of capitalism and neoliberalism, and determine their own future together?"

Sadly, for my friends and colleagues in Bradford County, eight years later the answer to that question has been "No." What was emerging never bloomed. Those community values, the critical consciousness, and the voices that had been shared and brought out during our work together have not lead to more meaningful or transparent public participation in shale gas governance in the County, has not stopped the bullying by gas companies across Pennsylvania that continues to this day, and has not stopped the tsunami of global capitalism and neoliberalism that continues to flatten, marginalize, and oppress rural landowners and small farmers throughout Pennsylvania and across the U.S. The realization that the hope I held and this path to critical consciousness did not lead to the growth of liberation among Bradford County landowners and the larger community has been not only sobering, but heartbreaking. Still, it is a reality that offers important lessons and new questions for how we care for ourselves, our communities, and Nature today and into the future. How does the process of critical consciousness and cultural synthesis get cut short, and why has it not reached its full potential in the case of Bradford County?

If we can take a closer look into what happened to cut this process off and set aside our disappointments, guilt, or sense of failing, we can see some of the deeper truths about the persistent and invasive roots of systemic oppression that keep us from realizing our own personal and community power in other settings as well. In the Bradford County case, it is evident to me more than eight years past my initial conclusions, that one of the reasons why this emergent consciousness and community action was stunted and did not reach its full transformational potential to resurrect community was that the brave space to authentically share personal and community stories, the space to actually care for themselves and one another, did not exist. Local people, busy in their daily lives, experiencing all sorts of personal, social, and familial stresses, and still experiencing disruptions from rapid change brought on by economic and industrial developments may not be able to authentically share their personal and community stories, not because there is not a strong desire to do so, but because there is simply not a space and time to do it.

Unfortunately, when I could not return to Bradford County in 2013 to lead the core group meetings no one replaced my role as convener of those regular meetings, and so the group met less and less frequently if at all. I tried to keep up with the different people in the group through phone calls and private visits when I could travel still, but the consistency was lacking. I had also realized that in lieu of being able to meet in person with all of them I would need to modify the type of work I was doing with them and so my relationships with some of them changed as a result and there were a couple of the original landowners who were no longer interested in working with me on the new direction I was going with this work, so they bowed out of future interviews and meetings. This was a big lesson: Outside facilitators and organizers who are not planning to be a long-term part of a community, such as the role I played in Bradford County, should not be the sole organizer or archivist of a dialogue or story sharing process where community resurrection and transformation is the goal. To just get out of the way and know that I am not the person who should be leading community work was the most sobering, humbling lesson I learned from my friends and colleagues in Bradford County, and a lesson I continue to learn every day.

In removing this brave space for dialogue that was created with the project via first the focus groups then the core group, it also removed the meaningful sharing of stories and the practices of appreciative inquiry, inventorying gifts, listening, observing, validating, and empathizing, or practicing L.O.V.E. Without the actual space to share the stories of personal and community change in the County that held the seed for resurrecting community and transforming a fractured world there was also no longer a space to practice Good Works or L.O.V.E. Rules.

Instead, as we stopped meeting regularly in Bradford County, Good Works were replaced by a renewed urgency to address all that was lacking (the deficits) in the community: getting basic needs around access to clean drinking water, the collapse of family farming in the region, and the palpable sense of fear related to change and dismissal of community values that has always lingered right below the surface. As a consequence, the practice of L.O.V.E. both inside and outside Bradford County was seen as counter-productive on all sides, with one side demanding justice and rights for landowners now, greater regulation, and legal fights against corruption, and the other side demanding less regulation and unfettered access to economic "opportunities" brought by the gas industry. The polarization in the County continues to destroy the space or time for dialogue that could nurture critical consciousness and whole community transformation. The lack of diverse news media outlets or diverse outside information and knowledge only increases this polarization further.

In 2015 and 2016, with horror, I watched as this polarization set the stage for further entrenchment and isolation when Donald Trump ran for president as an outsider in government with a platform that railed against big government and the urban "elite" and promoted xenophobia and cultural bias. Since Trump's presidency from 2016-2020, it seems the shadow of lack, deficit and depression, of internalized oppression and victimhood, and of retribution and anger, especially towards outsiders and urban communities, has fallen across Bradford County and has yet to lift in 2024. But, let me be entirely clear, this failure of community resurrection and transformation in Bradford County was not caused by the election and presidency of one man or my own inability to organize widely enough or to find someone to continue the core group meetings; outside forces and events simply provided a source of ignition poured on an already smoldering flame of fear, distrust, uncertainty, and bias that had been smoking just below the surface for decades. In the presence of such accelerants, and without a fire extinguisher, nothing has been spared.

So, how do we move past these sobering realities of what can go wrong when we attempt to work together to resurrect our communities and transform ourselves and our world? How do we use these bitter lessons to care for and maintain our communities over the long-term? The answer lies in continually and bravely reclaiming our Good Works and practicing L.O.V.E. despite the forces that continue to try and keep us busy doing other things, that polarize us, and that make all of our disagreements into personal attacks. We must insist on finding the time for and maintaining those brave spaces for dialogue, whether between two people or a dozen, that will allow us to share our stories with one another, to listen, to learn, and to always keep growing.

Some have referred to the practice of intentional, consciousness-raising storytelling as transformational, meaning that it allows individuals a chance to critically and deeply share their experiences, lessons, and insights, and at the same time allows for those listening to the story to engage as active listeners in a way that meaningfully impacts both the teller and listener. Such introspective, what I like to refer to as transformational story "sharing," not "telling," is especially powerful between individuals and communities who are currently feeling under threat or oppressed or who have a history of fear, distrust, or internalized oppression[104]. Story sharing has the potential to activate mental shifts, such as critical consciousness, both within individuals and collectively. This way of sharing our stories can in turn lead to systemic social-psychological changes and greater openness to building more diverse or stronger social ties and new bridges to other peoples' experiences. Such openness, if it can be kept alive, has the potential to help us relearn the world and reinvigorate our community values not just within our local communities, but across society. But, to do this, our story sharing and dialogue must be consistent over time and intentionally structured to honor self-determination and liberation.

This temporal consistency and intentional structure for transformational story sharing at a minimum should involve L.O.V.E. Rules and, if possible, be documented in such a way to ensure that any lessons learned or dialogues resulting from story sharing are completely owned by individuals in community or by the community as a whole. It is important to always keep in mind that the role of transformational story sharing for long-term community care needs to focus on reinforcing community relationships and strengthening individual and community values related to imagining, creating, and activating change processes in our communities that lead to liberation for all.

Solidarity, Mutual Aid, and Acts of Love

Another reason that the process of critical consciousness and community transformation was arrested in Bradford County was a lack of strong informal and formal networks to combat the oppressive forces that continue to polarize and tear apart the glue that should be holding the community's building blocks together. This polarization and breakdown in linkages across and between informal and formal relationships makes formulating or realizing nonviolent transformative change impossible. In this particular County, the glue that should be holding their community building blocks together, especially among local and state government and national and regional organizations, has been nearly impossible to properly reinforce and maintain against the corrosive lies and intentional community fragmentation from the shale gas industry and their economic and industrial development cheerleaders. These corrosive forces exist not just inside the County, but across Pennsylvania and the U.S. Such corrosion, if left unchecked prevents any long-term sticking together of personal and community networks. Against such corrosion, and without those brave spaces in which appreciate inquiry, gift inventories, and non-violent communication practices could consistently remind people of the importance of recognizing our whole communities, polarization and divisive speech and behaviors festers and grows.

The take away from this next heartbreaking lesson is that we must engage from the very beginning of our individual and community efforts to courageously face rapid change with the whole person and the whole community in order to build the proper defenses to combat whole systems and structures of oppression that have been built over decades and generations and that can emerge with a vengeance during periods of rapid change. It is so easy to slide into only addressing the single systems or structures of injustice and inequality and oppression or the individual person or single community that seems most harmed or abused in the present moment. This is the danger today in solely focusing organizing on race, ethnicity, or gender equality when the underlying root cause of all inequality and oppression in our society is the ill-logic of global capitalism, neoliberal politics, our abandonment of community values and the common good, and our denial of our mutual interdependence with Nature. So, to both resurrect our communities and work together to transform our fractured world we must resist this all too easy temptation for one-issue community organizing and one-size-fits-all solutions. Our world is just too interconnected, our lives too enmeshed with one another and Nature, that this single-mindedness only emboldens oppressive systems through keeping us polarized and vengeful.

An unforgettable dream I had one night in 2010 still serves as a warning of what one-issue organizing, disconnectedness, polarization and vengefulness can lead to:

I am looking across a simple stone bridge from behind a make-shift metal barricade. Standing by me are Carol, Carolyn, Laura, Ruth, Trudy, John, and other people who are unknown to me in my waking world. We are all filthy. Like we haven't taken a bath or shower in days, weeks maybe, and been in the same clothes for just as long. We all have different types of weapons. Mostly the variety you'd find in Claude's hunting cabinet- pistols, shotguns, rifles.

Across that bridge I see tanks, guns, no people. No human faces.

It is eerily quiet.

I hear a voice ask me, "Is it time?"

Anxiety wells up inside of me. I need to make a decision. Why do they think I am their leader? Who am I to make these decisions of life and death.

"I think so," I hear myself say. "You know this may not turn out

well," I add as a warning to all. I grab my weapon- a rifle- and look at the others' faces for the first time. They do not seem, or at least their faces do not convey anxiety or fear. Instead they look angry and eager and fear-less. That somehow increases my own worry even more.

"Okay," I state, motioning for them to follow me through an opening in the barricade across the bridge. I am out front, ready to lead, but Carol grabs me on top of my right shoulder.

"No," she says to me, "You stay here and cover us." "What?"
"Cover us," she repeats.

My anxiety triples, quadruples, and I can now hear the blood rushing from my heart to my ears. I know she is right. I need to stay and defend our side, but I also feel terrified for them. There is no way they can make it, even if I cover them as they charge that faceless, steel war machine across the bridge.

I nod and don't say a word, and step aside.

I take a position on the edge of the side of the road behind the barricade and look carefully across the bridge again at any sign of movement or hint of life. Nothing. A cold wall of metal and the hollow barrels of tank cannons and machine guns. Why can I not see faces or even bodies?

My friends, companions, fellow warriors, are preparing their weapons, and some are pulling bandanas over their mouths and nose.

"Ready?" I signal to them in a loud hushed whisper. My heart in my throat, my stomach churning with nausea.

"OKAY!" I say with resolve to them, my eyes trained on the opposite side of the bridge looking for any sign of movement. My finger lightly on the trigger of my rifle. I do not want them to be doing this. Not without me. It is sure suicide.

They proceed through the opening in the barricade slowly, with their guns raised. I can see no sign of movement on the other side.

Half way across the bridge I see a movement of something. I question myself. Should I shoot? Is this the time? And, in that millisecond of doubt a barrage of gunfire hits every single one of them- Carol, Carolyn, Laura, Ruth, Trudy, John. All dead. And, it is my fault. I did not shoot when I knew I should have.

When I awoke from that dream I felt such sadness, grief, and loss that I was sobbing, tears flowing down my face. This dream weighed heavy on my conscience for days and even fifteen years later it makes me feel a sense of terrible loss. And, it also emboldens me to fight even harder to reclaim that bridge in the name of life and not death, to disarm this endless war, to connect people and places and issues, to reimagine our organizing, and to love.

A whole person, a whole, beloved community, and a whole system approach means simultaneously recognizing the importance of our personal daily lives, our personal well-being, and our conscious awareness of how change impacts our own lives and well-being, while also remaining aware of the whole society and Nature within which our personal daily life, well-being, and consciousness exists. It is only in this wholeness that we can begin to resurrect our communities and provide the long-term care our communities require, which includes caring not only for our present selves in the present moment, but for our descendants' lives and their future selves. This time element is critical: Caring for our whole communities means simultaneously caring for our own lives as well as the lives of our ancestors and descendants, and the lives of our neighbors' in the past, present, and future. It is a multi-dimensional and quantum level of care that we all have access to in our bones and blood if we will only put down our weapons, breath, return home, and listen to ourselves and one another for long enough. This is what Howard Thurman and Dr. King called Beloved Community.

Returning to our L.O.V.E. rules, Jemez Principle #4 best captures this idea of wholeness. It says: "Work Together in Solidarity and Mutuality," and goes on to say "Groups working on similar issues with compatible visions should consciously act in solidarity, mutuality and support each others' work. In the long run, a more significant step is to incorporate the goals and values of other groups with your own work, in order to build strong relationships." This is the type of organizational empathy, reciprocity, and sharing that is essential to the resurrection and transformation of our communities and world today. And, such action based in solidarity and mutual aid are, in fact, the only lasting glue that will keep our community's together and prevent corrosive forces from further dividing us. Such actions of solidarity and mutual aid are what could be called love in action or power for the good. Martin Luther King Jr. wrote in *Where Do We Go from Here: Chaos or Community* that what is needed

"is a realization that power without love is reckless and abusive and that love without power is sentimental and anemic. Power at its best is love implementing the demands of justice."[105]

The word Solidarity, like Beloved Community and Love itself, is promoted in liberation theology and among certain groups and communities but it is mostly absent from and still new to U.S. scholarly or academic conversations, writings, and analyses around the dangers and destruction industrial and economic developments can bring to our local communities. These words and concepts have been used to describe activism and advocacy, which in our fractured world today leaves them subject to political ideologies, metaphors of war and terrorism, and deep divisions. Instead of Solidarity, words such as "resilience," and sometimes self-determination, are more acceptable for use in current social and environmental science research, especially when addressing issues of community change related to the climate emergency. But, in thinking about the words we use I feel like leaving out Solidarity means we lose the element of wholeness, and a sense of hope and imagination with regards to how we face change, resurrect our communities, and transform our increasingly fractured world. Because, when we relegate Solidarity, Beloved Community, and Love itself to the political and advocacy arena, when we only associate Solidarity and Love in Action with certain types of issues or groups of people, and even when we try to use them as tools of political analysis they become one more tool of systemic oppression. As we saw in Chapter 5 with the use of the word "resilience," relying on certain terms may allow us to fit ourselves into oppressive systems and get others to listen to our arguments about why this or that development project should be modified or stopped, but it will not necessarily be of any use in our work to dismantle those systems entirely. In caring for our whole communities over the long-term we need to demand that words and concepts like Solidarity and Love are just as important to the underlying theories of how we conduct social and environmental research and problem-solving programs as they are to political ideologies, advocacy strategies, and social services.

Incorporating the wholeness of our communities and the deeper beliefs in Thurman and King's Beloved Community into this work of facing change, resurrecting community, and transforming our world towards liberation for all is simplistic to say, but in practice, as we have seen, it is fraught with confusion, resistance, fear, and even danger. Such a holistic approach can be seen as complicity by the oppressed and weakness by the oppressor because it requires true solidarity in which oppressors may collaborate side by side with the oppressed to transform the systems and structures that have created and perpetuated those oppressive relationships in the first place. It requires fully and courageously adopting L.O.V.E. Rules in all our actions, and what Alexis Jemal, in his critique and analysis of critical consciousness literature refers to as "a radical posture of empathy." Such "radical empathy" requires, in Freire's words, "entering into the situation of those with whom one is in solidarity," as well as directly confronting those who are threatening that solidarity[106].

Now, an obvious question becomes: "Why the hell would I want to even give my time to, much less empathize, with someone who has harmed and abused me and my family and community, or continues to cause harm and abuse?" I and others who seek to live and teach the principles of non-violence have heard this question and understand the type of mindset this question arises from. But this line of questioning reflects a mindset still operating from a standpoint of lack, deficit, fear, shame, and revenge. I have also heard arguments that radical empathy extended to our oppressors is counter-intuitive to the professional advice given by victim advocates and trauma counselors to those caught in a cycle of abuse, where the solution is to cut off all ties to the abuser or abusive situation for the oppressed person's own safety and well-being. That argument fundamentally misunderstands the mindset required to adopt a posture of radical empathy and even what radical empathy looks like in practice. It does not mean recklessly keeping ones' self in a dangerous situation or putting ones' self in harm's way.

To shift our mindsets and overcome suspicions about radical empathy as complicity will require us to stop looking for an outside intervention or savior. It means we stop grasping for short-term, one-size-fits-all solutions to our anger, pain, or trauma that may stop short-term violence or abuse but does not address the systems and structures within which such violence and abuse is normalized and perpetuated. A major misunderstanding that must be corrected is that somehow radical empathy means to surrender or to forget the actions of our oppressors. It never, ever does. Radical empathy does not surrender or forget because the intention of radical empathy is liberation for all through solidarity, protection from harm, and non-violent action. To surrender and forget those who are harming us and causing us pain would allow that violence to continue and would be the opposite of liberation, solidarity, and non-violence.

What solidarity and radical empathy call for are interventions that rebuild or build individual and community social ties that allow us to center community wholeness, to creatively find multi-dimensional, quantum, and long-term solutions to oppression and trauma inside and outside ourselves and our communities, and to act together to enact those solutions. In solidarity and radical empathy, we reclaim, or claim for the first time, our individual and collective power over systemic violence, abuse, and oppression. Protection of our physical and emotional selves from the harm caused by abusers and oppressors means building and claiming this solidarity together in order to shift our mindsets and hearts away from deficit, lack, and retribution and towards individual and community assets and restorative and transformative forms of justice. It asks us to consider true liberation for all, even the liberation of our abuser and oppressor. And, it challenges us to recognize the interconnectedness and non-duality of life.

As long as there are oppressors there will be oppressed, so in order to topple systems of oppression it will be necessary to directly confront those systems in order to eradicate them entirely. But in order for these systems to be toppled, we need to somehow find ways for those who have been oppressors and those who are oppressed in different ways to work together. This will require some radical forgiveness as well as radical empathy. We urgently need the type of "fusion" movement and moral action for transformation and true liberation that Dr. King was speaking of after his 1965 march from Selma to Montgomery and just prior to his assassination, and that is being continued today under the leadership of Reverend Dr. William J. Barber II, Reverend Dr. Liz Theoharis, and many others from the streets of Detroit to the hollers of West Virginia with the Poor People's Campaign, in their call for a Moral Revival across all our political and social institutions[107].

Physically freeing ourselves from our abusers and oppressors in order to survive and be safe is what most of us think when we hear "liberation," and that is true. It is also true that if we stay trapped in revenge, fear, anger, guilt, or other emotions of oppression it means our oppressors, while physically no longer able to harm us, are still emotionally and spiritually enslaving us. We will never truly be liberated from oppression in any system or form as long as we are enslaved to others in any way—physical, emotional, mental, or spiritual. This is a difficult, but necessary, shift in mindset that we must make. Real world and past examples of what concepts like solidarity, mutual aid, beloved community, and other forms of love in action look like may help us to imagine a world in which the priority is on one thing only: true liberation and emancipation for all.

The most powerful examples of solidarity and mutual aid from modern times are programs designed to pool common resources in order to provide some free service to individuals and communities who have found it difficult to get those services on their own. Historically, soup kitchens and child care programs like the ones the Black Panther Party began in the 1960s are some excellent examples of mutual aid. But, types of mutual aid programs are only limited by people's moral imaginations. Beyond food and nutrition, they can cover laundry service, housing, heating and cooling, water, education, transportation, health, or really any of the basic requirements of human life. Some of the most life-affirming and effective mutual aid programs today are those being conducted among incarcerated individuals, homeless communities, and undocumented immigrants.

With their complete embrace of communal values and caring for the whole community regardless of the beliefs and identities of those seeking services or resources or the ability of those benefiting being able to pay in some way, these mutual aid programs are love in action and the manifestation of radical empathy. These collective actions for the common good create the space for individual and collective sharing and understanding that lead to mutual understanding, solidarity, and liberation for all. They require a sense of reciprocal relationality, caring, responsibility, and dignity extended to the least among us first, and an intention to make no moral judgments, especially regarding "othering" those who do not look, speak, believe, or have the same material resources or physical characteristics as ourselves. Isn't this the same as that most critical teaching of both Confucius and Jesus? The teaching that tells us to "Love our neighbor as our self"?

However, despite it being at the heart of almost all Western and Eastern spiritual traditions and teachings, in the U.S. and around the world, this idea of Solidarity has posed an existential threat to those who are in power and who profit off the oppression of others for over two thousand years. This threat to oppressive systems comes from the way solidarity and mutual aid defy those who benefit the most (or think they do) from those systems by bringing to life new forms of community wholeness that centers power within local communities, local places, and local community values and gifts. In our lexicon of the root causes of oppression, the ill-logic of global capitalism and all the political outgrowths from this economic system, the repressive and violent reactions to this existential threat by those who are most invested in oppression is what continues to feed our community divisions and keeps power further isolated in the hands of the few.

Just ask Jesus, John Brown, Malcom X, Huey Newton, Dr. King, Ghandi, and countless other ancestors whose names are lost to history about how their efforts at building solidarity, challenging systems of oppression, and liberation for all went for them. Each one of them was assassinated because they had fought for and begun to build "fusion" movements with cross-racial, cross-cultural, cross-spiritual, cross-gender, cross-class networks of individuals and communities that acted in solidarity to implement a certain theory of change with a vision of universal love and liberation for all. But, once we see and understand the web of oppression that we are all caught in, it is impossible not to see it and, I would argue, not to find a way to be in solidarity.

It is in this solidarity and through acts of radical empathy and love that we learn to see and share our whole selves and our whole communities. Once we see and understand the illusions we have been taught and the webs of oppression we are all caught in, it is impossible not to see it and begin to live our lives differently. Once we learn to see and feel the interconnectedness of all life and the networks of mutuality and shared destiny we are living within, we finally know that it is in caring for all these connections, networks, and our shared destiny where true transformation begins. We are now ready to take those final steps together to not just face change, resurrect our communities, and repair our fractured world together, but to imagine an entirely transformed way of life.

Join me? Let's walk across this bridge together!

ENDNOTES

---

[1] As my wise friend and teacher Trebbe Johnson states in <u>A Manifesto:</u> <u>The Gaia Enlightenment</u>: "When we cease to behave as if the natural world were mere background in our lives and begin to treat it as the magnificent, wise, and self-evolved force that it is, we are transformed." We modern humans so pervert the ego, self, and relations, seek self-satisfaction and self-soothing over self-realization and self-actualization (or confuse these things), attempt to control the natural world, rush to place blame on others for environmental devastation, and, in our disconnection and dismissal of the reality that all of life is mutually interdependent, perpetuate horrors not just in the course of industrial and economic developments but also in our daily life choices. Throughout my life an essential, integral, and hallowed connection to the natural world has been the one true source of hope, comfort, peace, and transformation. So, in this Introduction, and throughout the book, to honor this life force, when I refer to the whole natural world I have chosen one word, *Nature*. I have found that Nature, more than words like "natural resources," "environment," "ecosystem," or "ecology," captures the true essence embedded within and interconnecting all life on our shared planet, our Mother Earth, and the entire universe, whether we are talking about tree, squirrel, ocean, stream, salt marsh, rock, garden, bacteria, thunderstorm, mountain, or neutrino.

[2] To maintain focus on this frontline intimacy, honor our soul-affirming interrelationships with Nature, and to offer an alternative to the current identity politics dominating public and media discourse, I also pay close attention throughout the book to the use of pronouns and take heed of Adrienne Rich's words in her "Notes Toward a Politics of Locations": "...isn't there a difficulty of saying 'we'? *You cannot speak for me. I cannot speak for us.* Two thoughts: there is no liberation that only knows how to say 'I'; there is no collective movement that speaks for each of us all the way through. And so even ordinary pronouns become a political problem." My use of the pronouns "we" and "our" within these pages should not be taken as an assumption that I, Simona Perry, speak for the reader, think I have some all-seeing knowledge about the reader, or that the reader even shares, or should share, my opinions, experiences, or feelings. Instead, the decision to employ these collective pronouns is my attempt to incorporate relationality and co-generation of experience into the text. It is my hope that in some way, these collective pronouns will operate as a holistic counter-balance to the emphasis on individual differences in race, class, ethnicity, and genders, and the self-referential, self-obsessed behaviors and mentalities that have been encouraged and are such a dominant and toxic societal force today.

[3] This description of how truth and reconciliation and restorative justice processes work is from the now

archived website of the Greensboro Truth and Reconciliation Commission, that was formed in 2004 to
examination of the context, causes, sequence and consequence of the events of November 3, 1979 during
which five people were killed and ten wounded. Learning from Greensboro: Truth and Reconciliation in
the United States by Lisa Magarrell and Joya Wesley, Penn Press (2010) is a good overview of the
Commission's findings and process.

[4] Reconstructing the Gospel: Finding Freedom from Slaveholder Religion by Jonathan Wilson-Hartgrove, InterVarsity Press (2018).

[5] Sacred Instructions: Indigenous Wisdom for Living Spirit-Based Change by Weh'na Ha'mu' Kwasset (Sherri Mitchell), North Atlantic Books (2018)

[6] Pedagogy of the Oppressed by Paolo Freire, p. 35, 50th Anniversary Edition, Bloomsbury Academic (2018)

[7] SoulMaking: The Desert Way of Spirituality by Alan Jones, HarperSanFrancisco (1985)

[8] The research I began in 2009 in Bradford County, Pennsylvania was ethnographic. Ethnography is a method of qualitative inquiry that involves an inductive and grounded approach. Instead of setting out to "test" hypotheses, as an ethnographic researcher, I develop new hypotheses based on the systematic collection of observations, interviews, and artifacts. The interpretation of ethnographic data is an iterative process of coding interviews and observational notes for themes, then re-entering the site of research and asking new questions in order to refine those themes, and then developing a set of themes that can be used to convey a detailed cultural description of local culture to those outside that site. In general, ethnography has the ultimate goal of providing a detailed accounting of a particular culture or subculture, and it is also a useful research practice for monitoring local communities undergoing rapid change. See "Using Ethnography to Monitor the Community Health Implications of Onshore Unconventional Oil And Gas Developments: Examples from Pennsylvania's Marcellus Shale" by Simona L. Perry, *New Solutions* Vol. 23(1) 33-53, 2013 and "Development, Land Use, and Collective Trauma: The Marcellus Shale Gas Boom in Rural Pennsylvania" by Simona L. Perry, *Culture, Agriculture, Food, and Environment* Vol. 34 (1) 81–92, 2012.

[9] Otsego Lake is the headwater of the Susquehanna River and is the place called "Lake Glimmerglass" in his Leatherstocking Tales series of books by James Fenimore Cooper. See Library of America (July 1, 1985) ISBN-13 978-0940450202.

[10] Thomas Pownall's observations in 1754, A Topographical Description of the Dominions of the United States of America, UPitt Press, reprint 1949, p. 30.

[11] Albion's Seed: Four British Folkways in America by David Hackett Fischer, Oxford University Press (1989), p. 946.

[12] *"Seeing" Early Appalachian Communities through the Lenses of History, Geography, and Sociology* by David Colin Crass in The Southern Colonial Backcountry: Interdisciplinary Perspectives on Frontier Communities, University of Tennessee Press (1998), pp. 162-181

[13] *Native Americans in the Susquehanna River Valley, Past and Present* by David J. Minderhout in Stories of the Susquehanna Series, Bucknell University Press (2013), p. 244; Indians in Pennsylvania by Paul A.W. Wallace, Pennsylvania Historical and Museum Commission (2000), p. 200; *The Quest for the Susquehanna Valley: New York, Pennsylvania, and the Seventeenth Century Fur Trade* by Gary Nash in New York History (New York State Historical Association), Vol. 48(1967), pp. 3-27.

[14] Changes in Agriculture on the Six Nations Indian Reserve by Katherine Ann Sample, p. 131, Dissertation Thesis McMaster University (1968), Open Access Dissertations and Theses, Digital Commons@McMaster Thesis Number 3122.

[15] Nash, *The Quest for the Susquehanna Valley: New York, Pennsylvania, and the Seventeenth Century Fur Trade.*

[16] As Frederick W. Gnichtel described in an address delivered before the Trenton Historical Society on November 18, 1920, "The Trenton Decree of 1782 and the Pennamite War", 12 pp., Library of Congress. See History of Bradford County, Pennsylvania, 1770-1878 by The Rev. Dr. David Craft, L.H. Everts & Co. (1878).

[17] Craft, History of Bradford County, Pennsylvania, 1770-1878

[18] *Legislation Creating Bradford County* by John C. Ingham, The Settler: A Quarterly Magazine of History and Biograpy (The Bradford County Historical Society) Vol L:2(2012), pp. 59-74.

[19] Nash, *The Quest for the Susquehanna Valley: New York, Pennsylvania, and the Seventeenth Century Fur Trade.*

[20] Ibid.

[21] Heverly, Pioneer and Patriot Families of Bradford County, Pennsylvania 1770-1825, Volume 1 and Craft, History of Bradford County, Pennsylvania, 1770-1878

[22] A French Asylum on the Susquehanna River by Norman B. Wilkinson, Historic Pennsylvania Leaflet No. 11 (1991), Pennsylvania Historical and Museum Commission.

[23] Northern Tier Grasslands, 1830 – 1960, from Agricultural Resources of Pennsylvania, c 1700-1960, Pennsylvania Historical and Museum Commission's Pennsylvania Agricultural History Project archived website http://www.phmc.state.pa.us/portal/communities/agriculture/ Last updated August 26, 2015.

[24] Coddington Family Paper Farm Ledgers, 1830-1890 (private collection).

[25] The Anthracite Aristocracy: Leadership and Social Change in the Hard

Coal Regions of Northeastern Pennsylvania, 1800-1930 by Edward J. Davies, Northern Illinois University Press (1985); "The rural-urban economy of the Elmira-Corning Region" by Howard E. Conklin, *The Journal of Land and Public Utility Economics*, Vol. 20: 3-19.

[26] Similar to how ethnographer Kathleen Stewart describes the towns of Amigo, Odd, and Twilight, and other hollers in the Appalachian mountains of West Virginia in A Space on the Side of the Road: Cultural Poetics in an "Other" America, Princeton University Press (1996), p. 264.

[27] *Bradford County 2005: Chesapeake Bay, A Five-Year Strategy* by Bradford County Conservation District Board (2005), p. 80.

[28] See U.S. Environmental Protection Agency Corrective Action Hazardous Waste Report Site Descriptions of E.I. DuPont De Nemours and Company Incorporated in Towanda, Pennsylvania (https://www.epa.gov/hwcorrectiveactioncleanups/hazardous-waste-cleanup-ei-dupont-de-nemours-and-company-incorporated#Description) and Ingersoll Rand Company in Athens, Pennsylvania (https://www.epa.gov/hwcorrectiveactioncleanups/hazardous-waste-cleanup-ingersoll-rand-company-athens-pennsylvania#Description).

[29] Michael Woods, a social geographer, uses the term "global countryside" to describe the ways that global capitalism has affected the social, cultural, economic, and natural lives and landscapes of rural places in "Engaging the global countryside: Globalization, hybridity and the reconstitution of place," *Progress in Human Geography*, Vol. 31: 485-507.

[30] See U.S. Environmental Protection Agency Corrective Action Hazardous Waste Reports

[31] "U.S. Energy Future Hits Snag in Rural Pennsylvania" by Jon Hurdle, *Reuters* (March 12, 2009)

[32] See Collateral Damage by Tara Meixsell, self-published (2010); The End of Country by Seamus McGraw, Random House (2011); Under the Surface: Fracking, Fortunes, and the Fate of the Marcellus Shale by Tom Wilber, Cornell University Press (2012).

[33] More Than One River: Local, Place-Based Knowledge and the Political Ecology of Restoration and Remediation Along the Lower Neponset River, Massachusetts by Simona Lee Perry, Dissertation Thesis University of Massachusetts (2009), Open Access Dissertations, 117.

[34] See The Death of an American Jewish Community: A Tragedy of Good Intentions by Hillel Levine and Lawrence Harmon, Free Press (1992); The American City: What Works, What Doesn't by Alexander Garvin, McGraw-Hill (1996); Where We Want to Live by Ryan Gravel, St. Martin's Press (2016).

[35] These remarks were first heard during a live TV talk show filmed at the Keystone Theater in Towanda, Pennsylvania in 2012.

[36] Interview with Kathy Russell (2012).

[37] See Climate Investigation Center's report on America's Natural Gas Alliance, https://climateinvestigations.org/trade-association-pr-spending/americas-natural-gas-alliance/

[38] Tropical Storm Lee in 2011 caused the second highest flood on record in the county, cresting at 30.52 feet. The first highest flood record had been set in 1972 at 33 feet and that flood had washed away the old town center of Sheshequin, which had never been rebuilt.

[39] PA DEP reports on amount and value of Marcellus shale gas extracted can be found at https://www.dep.pa.gov/DataandTools/Reports/Oil%20and%20Gas%20Reports/Pages/default.aspx; U.S. gas prices were $4.84/Mcf in September 2011 according to the EIA price index-https://www.eia.gov/dnav/ng/hist/n3035us3m.htm; https://www.senatorgeneyaw.com/2021/06/14/sen-yaw-region-receives-more-than-27-8-million-in-marcellus-shale-impact-fees/

[40] US Census data- Bradford County profile- https://data.census.gov/cedsci/profile?g=0500000US42015

[41] Malin, Stephanie. 2014. There's no real choice but to sign: neoliberalization and normalization of hydraulic fracturing on Pennsylvania farmland, JESS 4(1):17-27

[42] The program was supposed to benefit farmers by basing their tax assessments on the use of their land rather than the fair market value of their land

[43] Unnameable Objects, Unspeakable Crimes by James Baldwin in The White Problem in America Johnson Publishing Company, Ebony Magazine Editors (1966).

[44] Sex, Economy, Freedom, and Community, 1992 by Wendell Berry in The Art of the Commonplace, Shoemaker & Hoard (2002).

[45] Jantz, Claire A., Hannah K. Kubach, Jacob R. Ward, Shawn Wiley, and Dana Heston. "Assessing Land Use Changes Due to Natural Gas Drilling Operations in the Marcellus Shale in Bradford County, PA." Geographical Bulletin 55, no. 1 (2014).

[46] Interview with Mike Lovegreen, director of B.C. Conservation District in 2009.

[47] Perry, Simona. Energy Consequences and Conflicts across the Global Countryside: North American Agricultural Perspectives, Forum on Public Policy, Vol. 2011, No. 2 (Environment), August 2011; Perry, Simona. Addressing the Societal Costs of Unconventional Oil and Gas Exploration and Production Environmental Practice Vol. 14, Issue 4, December 2012.

[48] Concerned Health Professionals of New York and Physicians for Social Responsibility, Compendium of Scientific, Medical, and Media Findings Demonstrating Risks and Harms of Fracking and Associated Gas and Oil Infrastructure (Ninth Edition), October 2023, http://concernedhealthny.org/

compendium/.

[49] The SRBC is an inter-state body given authority to issue permits for the withdrawal and consumption of water from the river

[50] Beauduy, Thomas W. *Accommodating a new straw in the water: Extracting natural gas from the Marcellus shale in the Susquehanna River basin.* Presentation at the 27th Annual Water Law Conference, American Bar Association, Section of Environment, Energy, and Resources (February 2009).

[51] Soeder, D.J. and W.M. Kappel. *Water resources and natural gas production from the Marcellus shale.* US Department of the Interior, US Geological Survey, Fact Shee 2009-3032. May 2009.

[52] Ground Water Protection Council and ALL Consulting, *Modern Shale Gas Development in the United States: A Primer.* U.S. Department of Energy, Office of Fossil Energy, National Energy Technology Laboratory (April 2009).

[53] 25 Pennsylvania Code Chapter 78, 54-66

[54] Yao, Yixin et al. "Malignant human cell transformation of Marcellus Shale gas drilling flow back water." *Toxicology and Applied Pharmacology* Vol. 288,1 (2015): 121-30. doi:10.1016/j.taap.2015.07.011

[55] Private conversation and direct observation with resident and Endless Mountains Outfitters owners in September 2010

[56] *DEP Investigating Source of Methane Bubbles In Susquehanna River,* September 13, 2010, http://www.paenvironmentdigest.com/newsletter/default.asp?NewsletterArticleID=16765&SubjectID=10

[57] Agency for Toxic Substances and Disease Registry (ATSDR). ATSDR Record of Activity/Technical Assist. UID IBD7. ATSDR, Washington, DC, 8 pp. (December 28, 2011); ATSDR. Health Consultation-Chesapeake ATGAS 2H Well Site 19–20. US Department of Health and Human Services, Washington, DC, 55 pp. (November 4, 2011); SAIC Energy, Environment & Infrastructure, LLC, and Groundwater & Environmental Services, Inc. 2011, August 30. Atgas Investigation Initial Site Characterization and Response, April 19, 2011 to May 2, 2011, Atgas 2H Well Pad Permit No. 37-015-21237 Leroy Township, Bradford County, PA. Chesapeake Appalachia LLC, Harrisburg, PA, 179 pp.

[58] Garth Llewellyn of Appalachia Hydrogeologic and Environmental Consulting, LLC, an independent investigator of water contamination problems throughout the northeast that worked with Carol, myself, and others in Bradford County, partnered with Dr. Frank Dorman at Pennsylvania State University to conduct broad spectrum forensic analysis of water samples taken from the three families on Paradise Road. This analysis was particularly interested in why the water was foaming and had other unusual characteristics beyond just methane in the water. In 2015 the results of their study were published in the Proceedings of the National Academy of Sciences (Garth T. Llewellyn, Frank Dorman, J. L. Westland, D. Yoxtheimer, Paul Grieve, Todd Sowers, E. Humston-

Fulmer, Susan L. Brantley,
Contamination attributed to Marcellus gas drilling. PNAS, May 2015, 112 (20) 6325-6330; DOI: 10.1073/pnas.1420279112). They positively identified at least one chemical 2-BE that is a common constituent of both high-volume hydraulic fracturing and drilling fluids. These impacts were likely caused by drilling or fracking fluids used in the gas wells, but as the authors note: "The data released here do not implicate upward flowing fluids along fractures from the target shale as the source of contaminants but rather implicate fluids flowing vertically along gas well boreholes and through intersecting shallow to intermediate flow paths via bedrock fractures. Flow along such pathways is likely when fluids are driven by high annular gas pressure or possibly by high pressures during HVHF (high-volume hydraulic fracture) injection. Such shallow- to intermediate-depth contaminant flow paths are not limited to HVHF but rather have been previously observed with conventional oil and gas wells. As shale gas development expands worldwide, problems such as those that occurred in northeastern PA will only be avoided by using conservative well construction practices, such as intermediate casing strings, proper cementation, and mitigating overpressured gas well annuli."

[59] "Century" farms in PA and Bradford County are lands that have been in continual agricultural operation for at least 100 years, and typically owned by the same family during that time.

[60] According to Sigmund Kvaløy, a Norwegian ecophilosopher, the Industrial Growth Society (IGS) is based on constant growth using industrial methods to create industrial products. He used the modern city as example, where it is based on specialization, quantification, and individual competition. According to Kvaløy, IGS is composed of "pseudo-diversity, and an impression of 'life and pipes' that cover over the standardization and simple trades." and "This society has a short-lived existence" (Sigmund Kvaløy (Setreng). Økokrise, Nature og Menneske: En Innføring i økofilosofi og økopolitikk (økofilosofisk fragment IV)/ Ecocrisis, Nature and Man: An Introduction to ecophilosophy and ecopolitics (ecophilosophical fragment IV) Oslo. 1973.)

[61] Wave: A Memoir by Sonali Deraniyagala. Knopf Doubleday Publishing Group (2013).

[62] Gerrit Knaap and Emily Talen, "New Urbanism and Smart Growth: A Few Words from the Academy." *International Regional Science Review* 28, 2: 107–118 (April 2005)

[63] See Henry Giroux's scholarship on neoliberalism and the cruelty of market fundamentalism, especially The Terror of Neoliberalism: Authoritarianism and the Eclipse of Democracy (Routledge, 2017), economic geographer David Harvey on how neoliberalism promotes an unbridled individualism that is harmful to social solidarity in A Brief History of Neoliberalism (Oxford University Press, 2005, online edn, Oxford Academic, 12 Nov. 2020), https://doi.org/10.1093/oso/9780199283262.001.0001.

[64] Simona Perry, <u>More Than One River: Local, Place-based Knowledge and the Political Ecology of Restoration and Remediation Along the Lower Neponset River, Massachusetts.</u> Open Access Dissertations, Paper 117, 2009.

[65] Garrett Hardin, <u>The Tragedy of the Commons</u>, American Association for the Advancement of Science, December 13, 1968, Science, Vol. 162, pp. 1243-1248; Richard, Auty, <u>Sustaining Development in Mineral Economies: The Resource Curse Thesis</u>, Routledge, 1993.

[66] Henrich, Joseph, Heine, Steven J. and Norenzayan, Ara, "The Weirdest People in the World?," *Behavioral and Brain Sciences*, Vol. 33, pp. 61-83, Cambridge University Press, June 15, 2010; Henrich, Joseph and Henrich, Natalie. <u>Why Humans Cooperate: A Cultural and Evolutionary Explanation</u> (Oxford University Press, 2007).

[67] The use of "opportunity" as a word to extinguish criticism about this or that development is not just used for energy and industrial developments. It is also the word most often used in my hometown of Savannah, Georgia to dismiss criticism about a certain art college that shares the city's name. Presenting evidence about the amount of revenue lost to the City from the college's ownership of tens of millions dollars worth of property in the City that it pays $0 in City or County property taxes on usually leads to someone, without evidence or facts referring to the "opportunities" the college has brought to the City.

[68] This relates to positive and constitutional economics, a branch of political economy distorted by politicians of libertarian and Republican Party orientation in the United States to justify programs such as school vouchers and reducing government financing for public services. This is what Nancy MacLean asserts leads to "democracy in chains" – when people cannot make choices democratically any longer. See Nancy MacLean <u>Democracy in Chains: The Deep History of the Radical Right's Stealth Plan for America</u> (Viking Press, 2017).

[69] Werner Erhard defines "possibility" as a declaration of what we create in the world each time we engage with the outside world. This opens up transformation and a way of implementing local community engagement that recognizes existing assets, ensures spaces and places for open community dialogue and dissent, and embraces change processes and even all the fear and anxiety that it conjures. See Werner Erhard's Lecture Series: "The Heart of the Matter" https://youtu.be/pRZC2DzWw-8?si=IuorOLSwzDGoLI78 and Peter Block's book <u>Community: The Structure of Belonging</u> (Berrett-Koehler Publishers, 2009)

[70] For more about the psychological consequences of such developments see Kai T. Erickson's <u>Everything in its Path: Destruction of Community in the Buffalo Creek Flood</u> (New York: Simon & Schuster, Inc. 1976) and Erickson's "Loss of community at Buffalo Creek" in *The American Journal of Psychiatry* 133(3):302-305.

[71] Simona Perry, More Than One River: Local, Place-Based Knowledge

and the Political Ecology of Restoration and Remediation Along the Lower Neponset River, Massachusetts, Open Access Dissertations, Paper 117, 2009.

[72] Davies, Thom. "Slow violence and toxic geographies: 'Out of sight' to whom?." *Environment and Planning C: Politics and Space* 40, no. 2 (2022): 409-427.

[73] Thich Nhat Hanh's *Dharma Talk* from December 13, 2012 "On Loneliness," https://youtu.be/FoYKHy78oiw?si=gRkQVOGXjLlfv63Y

[74] *The Gospel According to Luke 18* and *The Gospel According to John 3:16* from the New Revised Standard Version Bible, 1989. Division of Christian Education of the National Council of Churches of Christ in the U.S.A.

[75] Shiah, Yung-Jong. 2016. "From Self to Nonself: The Nonself Theory." *Frontiers in Psychology* https://doi.org/10.3389/fpsyg.2016.00124

[76] Richard Rohr's "A Necessary Negativity" in *Daily Meditations* June 18, 2021, Center for Action and Contemplation, https://cac.org/daily-meditations/a-necessary-negativity-2021-06-18/

[77] If we are someone who is seen by others as having any type of "power over" in certain circumstances, it is essential to have deep humility, to listen more fully and completely to others in community (especially when those communities are not our own), and to have the awareness to know when it is necessary to step aside and let others have more power.

[78] See Erich H. Witte and James H. Davis' edited volume, Understanding Group Behavior, especially Volume 1: Consensual Action by Small Groups and Volume 2: Small Group Processes and Interpersonal Relations. Psychology Press, 2013.

[79] Since 1969, NEPA has undergone various rulemaking by the White House Council on Environmental Quality. See the CEQ website page for a brief history of the Act and its evolution- https://ceq.doe.gov/laws-regulations/regulations.html

[80] See the 2016 National Oceanic and Atmospheric Administration and Deepwater Horizon Natural Resource Damage Assessment Trustees Final Report: *Deepwater Horizon oil spill: Final Programmatic Damage Assessment and Restoration Plan and Final Programmatic Environmental Impact Statement.* Retrieved from http://www.gulfspillrestoration.noaa.gov/restoration-planning/gulf-plan

[81] Chattel is defined by Merriam-Webster Dictionary as "an item of tangible movable or immovable property except real estate and things (such as buildings) connected with real property" and as "an enslaved person held as the legal property of another" or a "bondsman"

[82] Kumitz, Daniel. "Nothing about us without us: Self-representation in Social Protection in Southern Africa." Global Social Policy 16, no. 2 (2016): 215-217. "Nothing about us without us" is also a hallmark of Black and indigenous feminist theories and activisms, see especially Anastasia C. Curwood's book, Shirley Chisholm: Champion of Black Feminist Power

Politics. UNC Press Books, 2022.

[83] See Chapter 13 of Nicholas Thomas Wright's book Surprised by Hope: Rethinking Heaven, the Resurrection, and the Mission of the Church. Zondervan, 2008.

[84] Much of my thinking on borrowing the concept of Resurrection to denote "bringing back our sense of
and acts of community" is to capture not only the mystical, redemptive, and salvational qualities of the
Resurrection_but just as importantly the physical, embodied qualities of the Resurrection, what Wright calls "the life after life after death." I am indebted to the Right Rev. William Willoughby III, retired, and other members of the Episcopal Church of St. Paul the Apostle in Savannah, Georgia for leading and being part of a discussion group on N.T. Wright's book, Surprised by Hope, in which some of this chapter was further shaped and crafted.

[85] 1st Letter of Paul to the Corinthians 13 from New Revised Standard Version Bible: Anglicised Catholic Edition (Division of Christian Education of the National Council of the Churches of Christ in the United States of America, 1995).

[86] For examples see The Gospel According to Matthew 12:38-42 or The Gospel According to Mark 8:11-13 from the New Revised Standard Version Bible, 1989. Division of Christian Education of the National Council of Churches of Christ in the U.S.A.

[87] Peter Block, Community: The Structure of Belonging (Berrett-Koehler Publishers, 2009)

[88] Fluker, Walter Earl. "They Looked for a City: A Comparison of the Ideal of Community in Howard Thurman and Martin Luther King, Jr.," Journal of Religious Ethics (Spring 1990): 33-55, from p. 37

[89] Carlson ED, Engebretson J, Chamberlain RM. Photovoice as a social process of critical consciousness. Qualitative Health Research. 2006; 16:836.doi: 10.1177/1049732306287525 [PubMed: 16760539]

[90] From Ted Smeaton in his Inspiring Communities Blog (inactive since his untimely death in August of 2012) and as cited in Alison Mathie & Gord Cunningham's article "From clients to citizens: Asset-based Community Development as a strategy for community-driven development," Development in Practice, 13:5, 474-486 (2003), https://doi.org/10.1080/0961452032000125857

[91] Gergen, M.M., Gergen, K.J. and Barrett, F. (2004), "Appreciative inquiry as dialogue: generative and transformative", Cooperrider, D.L. and Avital, M. (Ed.) Constructive Discourse and Human Organization (Advances in Appreciative Inquiry, Vol. 1), Emerald Group Publishing Limited, Bingley, pp. 3-27.

[92] Adapted from conversations with nonviolent communication trainers, transformative change facilitators, and use of Marshall Rosenberg's

important book, <u>Nonviolent Communication: A Way of Life</u> now in its 3rd edition and available from the Center for Nonviolent Communication's online bookstore in English, Arabic, and Spanish - https://www.cnvc.org/store/nonviolent-communication-a-language-of-life

[93] Thanks to Dr. Pleasant for originally bringing this work to my attention. Interview by Sander Vancour on NBC News in 1967, available online: https://www.nbcnews.com/video/martin-luther-king-jr-speaks-with-nbc-news-11-months-before-assassination-1202163779741

[94] *The Gospel According to John 2:13-16* from the <u>New Revised Standard Version Bible</u>, 1989. Division of Christian Education of the National Council of Churches of Christ in the U.S.A.

[95] From Ted Smeaton in his *Inspiring Communities* Blog (inactive since his untimely death in August of 2012)

[96] The fight to free ourselves of this illusion is what keeps us all in bondage and at the same time is the on-going fight of abolitionists today, as Mariame Kaba so inspirationally captures in her book, *We Do This Til We Free Us* (Haymarket Books 2021).

[97] See Adam Kahane's book <u>Power and Love: A Theory and Practice of Social Change</u> (Berrett-Koehler Publishers 2010).

[98] The Cambridge Dictionary defines *griot*: noun [C] /ˈɡriː.oʊ/ uk. / ˈɡriː.əʊ/ in parts of West Africa, someone who passes on his or her society's history, especially through stories, poems, and music, and who takes part in ceremonies such as weddings and funerals.

[99] The most common responses to asking family members and local neighbors how we can fight for and get Justice in Savannah, Georgia are something like: "Well, honey, that **just is** the way it has been and always will be".

[100] David Pleasant, <u>Drumfolk: A MUSIC and Motion of LIBERATION!</u> RiddimAthon!, Inc. Publishing, 2024.

[101] Thich Nhat Hahn, <u>Peace Is Every Step: The Path of Mindfulness in Everyday Life</u> (Random House Publishing Group 1992).

[102] Simona Perry, "Development, Land Use, and Collective Trauma: The Marcellus Shale Gas Boom in Rural Pennsylvania" *Culture, Agriculture, Food and Environment* Vol. 34, Issue 1, 26 June 2012.

[103] See Erickson <u>Everything in its Path: Destruction of Community in the Buffalo Creek Flood</u> (New York: Simon & Schuster, Inc. 1976), p. 154

[104] The concept of "story telling" or "telling stories" is a one way "talking to" that places stories into the category of entertainment and commodity. I prefer "story sharing" because it captures the sense of reciprocity and back and forth that is central to transformation and community.

[105] Martin Luther King, Jr., *Where Do We Go from Here: Chaos or Community?* (Harper and Row: 1967), p. 37.

[106] Alexis Jemal, "Critical Consciousness: A Critique and Critical Analysis of the Literature," *Urban Rev.* 2017 November 49(4): 602–626, and Paolo Freire PoO 2000, p. 49

[107] See On Solidarity (Forum: "Solidarity Now") led by Mie Inouye from *Boston Review* September 2023, including Rev. William J. Barber II's "Moral Fusion", Rev. Liz Theoharis' "Poor Organizing" and many others. Available on-line and in print https://www.bostonreview.net/forum/solidarity-now/

APPENDIX

Jemez Principles For Democratic Organizing

On December 6-8, 1996, forty people of color and European-American representatives met in Jemez, New Mexico, for the "Working Group Meeting on Globalization and Trade." The Jemez meeting was hosted by the Southwest Network for Environmental and Economic Justice with the intention of hammering out common understandings between participants from different cultures, politics and organizations. The following "Jemez Principles" for democratic organizing were adopted by the participants. This and other environmental justice documents can be downloaded from: www.ejnet.org/ej

#1 Be Inclusive: If we hope to achieve just societies that include all people in decision-making and assure that all people have an equitable share of the wealth and the work of this world, then we must work to build that kind of inclusiveness into our own movement in order to develop alternative policies and institutions to the treaties policies under neoliberalism. This requires more than tokenism, it cannot be achieved without diversity at the planning table, in staffing, and in coordination. It may delay achievement of other important goals, it will require discussion, hard work, patience, and advance planning. It may involve conflict, but through this conflict, we can learn better ways of working together. It's about building alternative institutions, movement building, and not compromising out in order to be accepted into the anti-globalization club.

#2 Emphasis on Bottom-Up Organizing: To succeed, it is important to reach out into new constituencies, and to reach within all levels of leadership and membership base of the organizations that are already involved in our networks. We must be continually building and strengthening a base which provides our credibility, our strategies, mobilizations, leadership development, and the energy for the work we must do daily.

#3 Let People Speak for Themselves: We must be sure that relevant voices of people directly affected are heard. Ways must be provided for spokespersons to represent and be responsible to the affected constituencies. It is important for organizations to clarify their roles, and who they represent, and to assure accountability within our structures.

#4 Work Together In Solidarity and Mutuality: Groups working on similar issues with compatible visions should consciously act in solidarity, mutuality and support each other's work. In the long run, a more significant step is to incorporate the goals and values of other groups with your own work, in order to build strong relationships. For instance, in the long run, it is more important that labor unions and community economic development projects include the issue of environmental sustainability in their own strategies, rather than just lending support to the environmental organizations. So communications, strategies and resource sharing is critical, to help us see our connections and build on these.

#5 Build Just Relationships Among Ourselves: We need to treat each other with justice and respect, both on an individual and an organizational level, in this country and across borders. Defining and developing "just relationships" will be a process that won't happen overnight. It must include clarity about decision-making, sharing strategies, and resource distribution. There are clearly many skills necessary to succeed, and we need to determine the ways for those with different skills to coordinate and be accountable to one another.

#6 Commitment to Self-Transformation: As we change societies, we must change from operating on the mode of individualism to community-centeredness. We must "walk our talk." We must be the values that we say we're struggling for and we must be justice, be peace, be community.

Table 1. Creating Transformative Whole Community Change
Example from Bradford County Core Group 2012 Dialogue

COMMUNITY VISION STATEMENT: "Maintaining a Rural, Cohesive, Multigenerational Community in a Healthy Natural Environment"

BUILDING BLOCKS, Gifts & Assets:
canning, food preserving * gardening, food growing * raising animals for food and clothes * engineering * writing * natural history of native plants and animals * drawing and painting * child raising * caring for the elderly * local history * teaching * running a business * quilting

ADHESIVE ELEMENTS, Strength of Social Ties/Networks:
Household family is Strong
Extended family is both Weak and Strong
Neighbors is both Weak and Strong
Arts/Cultural alliance is Weak
Dairy farmers are both Weak and Strong
4-H is both Weak and Strong
Gas lease holders are Weak
Political party is Strong

FOUNDATION, Concrete Actions to Realize Community Vision Statement:
✾ Build local knowledge about growing and preserving food by teaching people of all ages these skills. Open a community kitchen to do this. ✾ Create a travelling art show based on photographs and poetry and writing from the 2010-2011 Dickinson College focus groups that conveys the rural, multigenerational community and natural environments in the County. ✾ Hold quilting workshops with people who have been negatively impacted by fracking to give them a way to creatively express themselves and share with others. ✾ Conduct more presentations to people in Bradford County about the impacts that have happened in Bradford County from fracking, including economic issues, and provide them with the knowledge and information to protect themselves. ✾ Explore reinitiating the local farmer's market. ✾ Support someone to run for elected office.

ACKNOWLEDGEMENTS

The stories of change from Bradford County, Pennsylvania, and the journey these stories take us on, would not have been possible without others placing their trust in me: Laura, Carol, Claude, Lynsey, Carolyn, Ruth, Margaret, Trudy, Mike, Sherry, John M., John H., Bruce, Rita, Dick, Sheila, Robin, Diane, Pat, Gina, Lily, David, Melody, Nancy, Kathy, Sally, Greg, Julie, and many more who spoke to me anonymously. The humility and responsibility I feel to uphold the trust they placed in me has made me a better human being. I am eternally grateful for their consent in using stories and words and welcoming me into their homes, sharing meals with me, introducing me to family and friends, opening up their daily lives, and infecting me with their deep love for the Endless Mountains region.

Just as important to these Bradford County stories were County officials and staff who accepted me as a trusted colleague, consented to interviews, and shared their expertise and knowledge: Ray Stolinas, Scott Molnar, Tony Liguori, Mike Lovegreen, and several County Commissioners. Their input provided the fuller context of local stories and changes experienced and observed.

For keeping me rooted in Nature, the deep past, and those who have come before, I am deeply grateful to the Susquehanna River and the humans who shared their experiences with me related to her, especially David Buck, the 2014 Susquehanna Sojourners, the late Ted Keir, Don Williams, and Neil Patterson. Nia:wen!

I am thankful for the scientists and environmental researchers who answered technical questions and offered their expertise and time to respond to community questions about groundwater and other environmental health concerns in Bradford County and Pennsylvania: Garth Llewellyn, Jim Llewellyn, Avner Vengosh, Robert Jackson, Robert Oswald, Michelle Bamberger, Tamara Gagnolet, and staff of the Center for Disease Control's Agency for Toxics and Disease Registry, and many more too numerous to list here.

I have been buoyed and am grateful to a vast network of artists, local farmers, environmental organizers, and community researchers in upstate New York including Sandra Steingraber, Nadia Steinzor, Abby Kinchy, Jeanne Simonelli, and many more.

Across the globe and within the United States I have learned so much from taking part in conversations and actions to tell the truth about how shale gas exploration and related developments are affecting local people, global human rights, and Nature. I am grateful to Tara Meixsell, Calvin Tillman, Tom Kerns, Seamus McGraw, Kenneth Klemow, Damian Short, and so many others who were critical to how I decided to present the evidence of harms and injustice in this book and elsewhere.

For inviting me to grow my restorative justice and advocacy wings and patiently letting me find my place in controversial public discourses on broader energy issues, I am forever grateful to my friend and sister from another mother, Lynda Farrell, founder of Pipeline Safety Coalition.

A huge thank you to Betsy Taylor at Livelihood Knowledge Exchange Network and Herbert Reid for their hospitality, enthusiasm, kindness, intellectual generosity, and mutual support-- especially in our shared dreams of a more just, inclusive, generative, and beloved community. And, to my other two Livelihood Knowledge Exchange Network sisters, Mary Hufford and Julie Maldonado, who have been central threads in my community research web of support over the years.

None of the field work in Bradford County would have been possible without financial support from a Mellon Post-Doctoral Geographic Information System (GIS) Scholar Position at Dickinson College. I am especially grateful to Susan Rose, for opening wide the doors of the College's Community Studies Center and making me feel like a part of the family. I am also grateful to Dickinson College alumni and students Manuel Saralegui, Giovanni Tiarachristie, Jordan Haferbeir, Nathan Toews, and all the students in my classes whose own interviews, observations, and thinking were critical to my learning and understanding of sense of place, identity, and energy justice. And, I am grateful to the administrative, logistical, and technical support of the Center for Sustainability's Neil Leary and Sarah Brylinsky, the School for Environmental Studies and Environmental Sciences' Candie Wilderman, ALLARM's Julie Vastine, GIS Specialist James Ciarrocca, and community psychology professor Sharon Kingston.

My intellectual and academic mentors and teachers from the University of Massachusetts and Eastern Mennonite University were also pivotal to maturation of my thinking about critical consciousness, cultural synthesis, community transformation, liberating structures, trauma and reconciliation, and participatory action research, especially: Katie Mansfield, Catherine Barnes, Bridget Mullins, Krista

Harper, the late Julie Graham, Enoch Page, Robert Muth, Jack Finn, Martha Mather and others in the UMASS School of Public Policy, Department of Anthropology, School of Natural Resources, and Department of Geography.

For accompanying me in the never-ending exploration towards my deepest taproots and grappling with generational and historical traumas, I am grateful to Trebbe Johnson, founder of Radical Joy for Hard Times, David Pleasant of The Pleasant Institute and Which Way Savannah, and my ever-widening circle of spiritual companions, mentors, and recovery sponsors in Savannah and elsewhere.

To Stephanie Gilmore, my friend, "book doula," and editor extraordinaire for her careful and loving review and editing of this book I will forever be thankful.

Heartfelt gratitude to my husband, Ernesto Brown, for his extraordinary patience, guidance, and willingness. He was by my side through every twist and turn of this book, including listening to my internal debates and reading many early drafts. I am blessed to have a partner who is so generous with his intuition, intellect, wisdom, sense of humor, and who believes in me even when he does not always agree.

Finally, no acknowledgment for this book would be complete without sending my deepest gratitude to those who may no longer be with me in this life, but who are always with me in my memory, creative imagination, and dreams: mom (Dianne), dad (Charlie), Uncle Lauvon, the old mulberry tree at 313 East Liberty Street, and canine companions Gus and Sam. You are my sunshine.

ABOUT THE AUTHOR

Simona Perry

Simona Perry, PhD, is an environmental social scientist with extensive training and experience in wildlife ecology, marine science, community-based participatory research, and trauma-informed facilitation. Perry holds a bachelor's degree in Wildlife Biology, a master's degree in Marine Policy, and a doctoral degree in the Human Dimensions of Natural Resource Conservation. Through her consulting company, c.a.s.e. (c.ommunity a.wareness s.olutions for e.mpowerment), she collaborates with rural and urban communities to raise awareness and build local and regional coalitions centering the interconnections between ecology, culture, politics, economics, and individual and community well-being. Before focusing her work on human communities, she was a marine mammal scientist, specializing in endangered large whale recovery and North American marine biodiversity planning. She serves on the Board of Directors of Environmental Health Project in Pittsburgh, Pennsylvania and with the Refugee Resettlement and Immigration Ministry at St. Paul Episcopal Church in Savannah, Georgia.